AND
HE WALKS
with Me

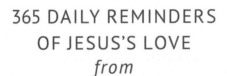

365 DAILY REMINDERS
OF JESUS'S LOVE
from
Our Daily Bread

Our Daily Bread
Publishing™

Requests for permission to quote from this book should be directed to
Permissions Department, Our Daily Bread Publishing, PO Box 3566, Grand
Rapids, MI 49501, or contact us by email at permissionsdept@odb.org.

ISBN: 978-1-62707-954-9
Printed in China
Second printing in 2020

And He walks with me, and He talks with me,
And He tells me I am His own,
And the joy we share as we tarry there,
None other has ever known.

From "In the Garden"
C. Austin Miles

INTRODUCTION

THIS TIME, IT'S PERSONAL.

Over the years Discovery House has published a number of *Our Daily Bread* collections of various kinds. But never before have we embarked on one that is solely about the most important relationship possible—our faith in Jesus Christ and what it means to walk closely with Him in moment-by-moment fellowship.

Just over one hundred years ago, a pharmacist-turned-songwriter named C. Austin Miles penned these words:

> *I come to the garden alone,*
> *While the dew is still on the roses;*
> *And the voice I hear, falling on my ear,*
> *The Son of God discloses.*

> *And He walks with me, and He talks with me,*
> *And He tells me I am His own,*
> *And the joy we share as we tarry there,*
> *None other has ever known.*

This beautiful song has warmed the hearts of Christians for more than a century, for it reminds us of the wonder of being a friend of the Savior. It helps us contemplate the marvelous reality that Jesus walks beside us through life, that He communicates personally with us through His Word and our prayers, and that He gently and lovingly reminds us that we belong to Him.

It is in the spirit of those lyrics that we have put together this latest compilation from the writers of *Our Daily Bread*—men and women who desire to encourage you to abide with Jesus. Each article presents a bit of a different perspective about what it means to enjoy your personal relationship with Jesus, which is the heart of the Christian faith.

Often we get bogged down with the peripheral things of Christianity—the things we have to say and do, the complications of church life, and the intrusion of outside forces that try to thwart our joy in Jesus. So it is important that we sometimes set ourselves apart from all that and bask in the presence of our Savior. It is our hope that this book allows you to do just that.

So, yes, this time it is personal. This selection of articles is about the personal, warm, and comforting fellowship we can have with Jesus Christ. May this book bring you closer to Him and allow yourself to be wrapped in His love in a fresh, new way. May it help you to walk with Him, talk with Him, and rest in the fact that you are His own. May the joy you share as you tarry with Jesus spark in your heart an increasing love for the One who gave everything on the cross for you.

—DAVE BRANON,
general editor and *Our Daily Bread* writer

LIVING CLOSE TO JESUS

READ: 1 John 1:1–4

Through him all things were made; without him nothing was made that has been made. JOHN 1:3

A LARGE BRITISH NEWSPAPER once asked its readers for the best answer to this question, "What is the shortest way to London?"

The winning entry said simply, "The shortest way to London is good company!" We know how true that answer is! Loving companionship shortens any journey, however long.

As believers in Jesus Christ, we enjoy the good company of our Savior. We "walk as children of light" (Ephesians 5:8 NKJV), daily enjoying fellowship and communion with the Savior. The closer we come to Him, the more He'll thrill us with His presence. While Jesus has no favorites, He does have intimates! They're the ones who, like the apostle John, share with Him their love and devotion (See John 13:23).

A seventeenth-century bishop named Francois Fénelon wrote these instructive words regarding our relationship to the Lord: "Tell Him all that is in your heart like one who unloads his pent-up feelings to a dear friend. Blessed are they who attain to such familiar, unreserved interaction with Him."

The journey to heaven, though often accompanied by trials, is shortened and made easier when Jesus Christ is our traveling companion.

Draw near to Him, for the joy of salvation comes only by living close to Jesus!　　　　　　　　　　　　　　　—HENRY BOSCH

The best way to enjoy your standing in Christ
is to begin walking with Christ!

HOLD MY HAND

READ: Deuteronomy 31:1–8

*"The LORD himself goes before you and will be with you;
he will never leave you nor forsake you. Do not be
afraid; do not be discouraged."* DEUTERONOMY 31:8

THE WAVES OF LAKE MICHIGAN were high and splashing onto the pier one day as I followed a young family out to a lighthouse. I overheard the young girl say to her father: "Daddy, please walk alongside me and hold my hand at this scary part."

Sometimes life can be scary for us too: Loss of loved ones. Financial woes. Health problems. As we carry these heavy burdens and cares, we long for a strong hand to hold ours to keep us steady and secure.

When Joshua took over the leadership of Israel, Moses reminded him of God's help in tough times. In the difficult days to come, Joshua would need to remember to trust God and His promises. Moses said, "The LORD himself goes before you and will be with you; he will never leave you nor forsake you. Do not be afraid; do not be discouraged" (Deuteronomy 31:8).

Isaiah 41:13 encourages us with these words from God: "For I am the LORD your God who takes hold of your right hand and says to you, Do not fear; I will help you." When life gets scary, God is with us; we can hold His strong hand.

Jesus will walk alongside us and hold our hand at the "scary" parts.
　　　　　　　　　　　　　　　　　　　　—ANNE CETAS

Fears flee in the light of God's presence.

JESUS AND ME

READ: Psalm 143:1–6

I remember the days of long ago; I meditate on all your works and consider what your hands have done. PSALM 143:5

SOMETIMES OUR MINDS run back through the years and yearn for that better time and place—the "good old days."

But for some, the past harbors only bitter memories. Deep in the night, they ponder their own failures, disillusionments, and fantasies, and think of the cruel hand life has dealt them.

It's better to remember the past as David did, by contemplating the good that God has done, to "meditate on all [His] works; . . . and consider what [His] hands have done" (Psalm 143:5). As we call to mind the lovingkindness of the Lord, we can see His blessings through the years. These are the memories that foster the highest good. They evoke a deep longing for more of God and more of His tender care. They transform the past into a place of familiarity and fellowship with our Lord.

I heard a story about an elderly woman who would sit in silence for hours in her rocking chair, hands folded in her lap, eyes gazing off into the far distance. One day her daughter asked, "Mother, what do you think about when you sit there so quietly?" Her mother replied softly with a twinkle in her eye, "That's just between Jesus and me."

I pray that our memories and meditations would draw us into His presence.   —DAVID ROPER

Fellowship with Christ is the secret of happiness now and forever.

HE'S WATCHING THE BOAT

READ: Mark 6:45–52

He saw the disciples straining at the oars, because the wind was against them. Shortly before dawn he went out to them, walking on the lake. MARK 6:48

JESUS WALKED ON WATER. That's astounding! It's a real miracle—an evidence of God's great power.

But something else happened in that story that should make us marvel even more. It has to do with Jesus's compassion and care for His friends.

After He put His disciples on a boat, Jesus went to the mountain to pray. But He didn't forget about them. He kept watching. When a strong wind kicked up waves and made their rowing a real struggle, He saw their plight. Soon He was by their side, calming their fears.

Tim, a friend of mine, read this passage and was impressed that Jesus watched the boat after He sent the disciples out into what He knew could quickly become stormy waters. As Tim reflected on the story, a truth came alive to him: Jesus watches us as we struggle and comes to our aid when we need it.

That insight took on new meaning for Tim a few days later when his doctor told him he had cancer. Tim knew there were some rough waters ahead, but he also knew that his Savior would be watching—ready to come to his assistance any time he struggled.

Are you facing tough times? Remember, Jesus is watching the boat.
—DAVE BRANON

Though you can see nothing but trouble,
God will surely see you through.

"HE LIVES DOWN THE STREET"

READ: John 15:1–5

"I am the vine; you are the branches. If you remain
in me and I in you, you will bear much fruit;
apart from me you can do nothing." JOHN 15:5

A SUNDAY SCHOOL TEACHER had been telling her class about the wonderful qualities of Jesus when He lived on earth. Then she asked, "Where does Jesus live now?" She fully expected one of the youngsters to say, "In heaven," but was surprised when a little girl from a poor section of town responded, "He lives down our street!" Apparently, someone lived in that child's block whose life truly radiated the Lord Jesus. The youngster told of that person's deeds of mercy and compassion. The spirit of Christlikeness was so obvious that the little girl thought it must be Jesus who lived on her street.

When we learn to abide in Christ, others will see Him reflected in what we do and say. Yet in our own strength we can't produce a Christlike life. We can have it only when we yield to the Holy Spirit within us. As we stay connected with Christ through obedience and confession of sin, His life will flow through us. In a vineyard, for example, the branch does not struggle to produce fruit. As it draws nourishment unhindered from the vine, clusters of luscious grapes will naturally appear.

Likewise, as we in faith abide in Christ, His strength will flow through us, producing the very character of the Lord Jesus. The abiding life is a fruit-bearing life.   —PAUL VAN GORDER

God plants grace in our hearts that He may
reap its fruit from our lives.

LIGHT IN THE DARKNESS

READ: John 12:42–50

"I have come into the world as a light, so that no one who believes in me should stay in darkness." JOHN 12:46

DURING A TRIP TO PERU, I visited one of the many caves found throughout that mountainous country. Our guide told us that this particular cave had already been explored to a depth of nine miles—and it went even deeper. We saw fascinating bats, nocturnal birds, and interesting rock formations. Before long, however, the darkness of the cave became unnerving—almost suffocating. I was greatly relieved when we returned to the surface and the light of day.

That experience was a stark reminder of how oppressive darkness can be and how much we need light. We live in a world made dark by sin—a world that has turned against its Creator. And we need the Light.

Jesus, who came to restore all of creation—including humanity—to its intended place referred to himself as that "light" (John 8:12). "I have come into the world as a light," He said, "so that no one who believes in me should stay in darkness" (12:46).

In Him, we not only have the light of salvation but we also have the only light by which we can find our way—His way—through our world's spiritual darkness.   —BILL CROWDER

When we walk in the Light,
we won't stumble in the darkness.

INTERNATIONAL FRIENDSHIP

READ: Colossians 1:1–12

We always thank God, the Father of our Lord Jesus Christ, when we pray for you. COLOSSIANS 1:3

IN 1947, NADIA FROM Bulgaria and Millicent from the United States became pen pals. For years they swapped photos, school experiences, and dreams. Then their letters stopped when Bulgaria's government policy banned personal contact with the West.

After many years of political upheaval and change, Millicent, on a whim, sent a letter to the last address she had for Nadia. To their delight, the letter got through. Before long, they discovered that both had married doctors and both collected seashells. Forty-eight years after their first letter, the two friends finally met at Miami International Airport, where Millicent exclaimed, "Nadia! I would know you anywhere!"

The letters of the apostle Paul overflow with affection and gratitude for his friends. In his letter to the Colossians, he wrote: "We always thank God, the Father of our Lord Jesus Christ, when we pray for you" (1:3). His letters also encouraged the Colossian people in their walk with Christ (v. 10).

Any friendship can be a gift from God. But nothing runs deeper than the relationships of those who share a bond in Christ. In fact, Jesus commanded His disciples: "Love each other as I have loved you" (John 15:12). In Him, friendships are treasures that will last forever. —MART DEHAAN

A true friend is a gift from God.

SWEET COMPANY

READ: John 14:15–26

*The Spirit of truth. The world cannot accept him, because
it neither sees him nor knows him. But you know him,
for he lives with you and will be in you.* JOHN 14:17

THE ELDERLY WOMAN in the nursing home didn't speak to anyone or request anything. It seemed she merely existed, rocking in her creaky old chair. She didn't have many visitors, so one young nurse would often go into her room on her breaks. Without asking the woman questions to try to get her to talk, she simply pulled up another chair and rocked with her. After several months, the elderly woman said to her, "Thank you for rocking with me." She was grateful for the companionship.

Before He went back to heaven, Jesus promised to send a constant companion to His disciples. He told them He would not leave them alone but would send the Holy Spirit to be in them (John 14:17). That promise is still true for believers in Jesus today. Jesus said that the triune God makes His "home" in us (v. 23).

The Lord is our close and faithful companion throughout our entire life. He will guide us in our deepest struggles, forgive our sin, hear each silent prayer, and shoulder the burdens we cannot bear.

We can enjoy His sweet company today.   —ANNE CETAS

The Christian's heart is the Holy Spirit's home.

YOUR NEVER-DYING FRIEND

READ: John 11:1–27

*Jesus said to her, "I am the resurrection and the life.
The one who believes in me will live, even though
they die; and whoever lives by believing in me will
never die. Do you believe this?"* JOHN 11:25–26

A MAN WHO WROTE to me frequently always signed his letters:
"Your never-dying friend." He believed that his strong faith in
Christ would keep him alive until Jesus returned. He based this
belief on his interpretation of Jesus's words, "Whoever lives by
believing in me will never die" (John 11:26). I haven't heard from
him for a long time, so I assume he has died. If so, he is in heaven
and now knows that his understanding of that verse was incorrect.

When Jesus spoke those words, He had in mind two kinds of
death: physical (separation of the soul-spirit from the body) and
spiritual (eternal separation from God). Before we receive Jesus as
our personal Savior, all of us are "dead in your transgressions and
sins" (Ephesians 2:1). But when we trust Him, we become spiritually
alive. Jesus said that everyone who believes in Him "has crossed
over from death to life" (John 5:24). When believers die, their
conscious relationship with God continues uninterrupted because
they are spiritually alive.

We who have trusted Christ as our Savior can rest assured that
we will never experience eternal separation from God. In that sense,
then, it would be appropriate to sign our letters with the words:
"Your never-dying friend." —HERB VANDER LUGT

Born once, die twice. Born twice, die once.

THE PERSON AND THE MUSIC

READ: Ephesians 2:1–13

*You He made alive, who were dead in trespasses
and sins.* EPHESIANS 2:1 (NKJV)

WHILE TRAVELING ON AN airplane, I noticed that one of the audio channels featured music from a CD titled *The Buena Vista Social Club*. Normally, that wouldn't have grabbed me, but this time I tuned in and enjoyed the selections. A few weeks earlier, I had seen a documentary film that told the story of the featured musicians. Famous in the 1960s, they were all but forgotten, but then they were rediscovered and brought together for this recording, as well as for a performance at Carnegie Hall. Because I had learned about them through the film, I became interested in hearing their music.

Have you had a similar experience with Jesus? Before you came to know Him personally, the Bible may have seemed remote and uninteresting. But now it's personal and alive because you know the author as your Savior and friend.

What a change Christ makes in our lives! In Ephesians 2, Paul celebrated this transformation. He began, "You He made alive, who were dead" (v. 1 NKJV). Now that Christ lives in our hearts, we want to hear His "music" in all of its expressions—through His Word, His creation, and His people.

Today, everywhere we look, we can see the work of Jesus Christ, the creator and conductor of life. Get to know Christ personally, and you will love to hear His music.   —DAVID MCCASLAND

*To appreciate the Master's music,
you must know the Master.*

OUR LORD'S COMMAND

READ: John 21:14–22

*"Come, follow me," Jesus said, "and I will send
you out to fish for people."* MARK 1:17

JESUS ASKED SIMON PETER a heart-searching question long ago on
the seashore in Galilee: "Do you love Me?" (John 21:15–17). Then
the risen Lord told His disciple Peter that his future would lead to
martyrdom. And Peter accepted that destiny without complaint.

But then Peter asked about the apostle John's future (v. 21).
We can only guess what motivated his question. Was it brotherly
concern? Was it fleshly curiosity? Was it resentment because he
thought John might be spared a martyr's death?

Whatever Peter's motive, Jesus responded with a counter-question
that applied not just to Peter but to every follower of His: "If I want
him to remain alive until I return, what is that to you? You must
follow me" (v. 22). In that question, Jesus was saying in essence,
"Don't worry about what happens in the life of anybody else. Your
task is to keep following Me steadfastly."

It is so easy to let our relationship with the Lord be overly influenced by the behavior and experiences of others. But we must not
be concerned with what God has planned for anyone else. Through
the conflicting voices that surround us, we must keep hearing the
Savior's clear command: "You follow Me."

—VERNON GROUNDS

To find your way through life, follow Jesus.

PAPA DIDN'T SAY "OH"

READ: Ephesians 5:1–10

*The LORD is gracious and compassionate, slow
to anger and rich in love.* PSALM 145:8

I HAVE A FRIEND who was working in his home office one evening, trying to get some necessary paperwork done. His little girl, who was about four years old at the time, was playing around his desk, puttering about, moving objects here and there, pulling out drawers, and making a good deal of noise.

My friend endured the distraction with stoic patience until the child slammed a drawer on one of her fingers and screamed in pain. Reacting in exasperation he shouted, "That's it!" as he escorted her out of the room and shut the door.

Later, her mother found her weeping in her bedroom and tried to comfort her. "Does your finger still hurt?" she asked. "No," the little girl sniffled. "Then why are you crying?" her mother asked. " 'Cause," she whimpered, "when I pinched my finger, Papa didn't say, 'Oh!' "

Sometimes that's all we need, isn't it? Someone who cares and who will respond with kindness and compassion, someone who will say, "Oh!" We have One named Jesus who does that for us.

Jesus loves us, understands our sorrows, and gave himself for us (Ephesians 5:2). Now we are to "walk in love" and imitate Him.

—DAVID ROPER

God's whisper of comfort quiets the noise of our trials.

OUR FEARLESS CHAMPION

READ: Matthew 8:23–34

He replied, "You of little faith, why are you so afraid?"
Then he got up and rebuked the winds and the waves,
and it was completely calm. MATTHEW 8:26

FALLING ASLEEP WAS A challenging event during my childhood. No sooner had my parents turned out the lights than the crumpled clothes I had thrown on the chair would take on the form of a fiery dragon and the thoughts of something living under my bed put me into a panic that made sleep impossible.

I've come to realize that the immobilizing power of fear is not just a childhood experience. Fear keeps us from forgiving, taking a stand at the office, giving our resources to God's kingdom, or saying no when all our friends are saying yes. Left to ourselves, we are up against a lot of fiery dragons in our lives.

In the story of the disciples in the storm-tossed boat, I'm struck by the fact that the only one who was not afraid was Jesus. He was not afraid of the storm. Neither was He afraid of crazy men in a graveyard or of the legion of demons that possessed that poor man (Matthew 8:23–34).

In the face of fear, we need to hear Jesus ask, "Why are you so afraid?" (v. 26) and be reminded that He will never leave us nor forsake us (Hebrews 13:5–6). There is nothing He can't overcome and therefore nothing for Him to fear. So, next the time you're haunted by your fears, remember that you can rely on Jesus, our fearless Champion! —JOE STOWELL

In times of fear, call out to Jesus, our fearless Champion.

THE EMPATHY FACTOR

READ: Hebrews 4:14–16

The Word became flesh and made his dwelling among us.
We have seen his glory, the glory of the one and only Son,
who came from the Father, full of grace and truth. JOHN 1:14

IN THE SUMMER OF 2005, I led a group of high school students on a ministry trip to Jamaica. Our goal was to build a playground at a school for deaf children in that beautiful island country.

Many of our students had previously visited the school and played with the kids. But one of our teenagers had a special connection to the Jamaican children. Chelsea too grew up in a world of quiet. Deaf since birth, she didn't hear a sound until she was eleven, when she received a cochlear implant. Now able to hear about thirty percent of the sounds around her, Chelsea understood the deaf in ways our other students could not. She had true empathy.

Empathy is a strong emotion. It can drive us to come alongside those who are in similar situations. It can cause us to care in a deeper way for those with whom we share a concern or a difficulty.

The most important example of empathy is the Lord himself. He became one of us (John 1:14). Because He did, He understands our struggles and weaknesses (Hebrews 4:15). Jesus knows what we are going through, for He endured this life himself. As we receive His grace in our time of need, we are better able to come alongside others. —DAVE BRANON

No one understands like Jesus.

THE QUIET ROAD

READ: Mark 6:30–46

Because so many people were coming and going that they did not even have a chance to eat, he said to them, "Come with me by yourselves to a quiet place and get some rest." MARK 6:31

FIFTY MILES WEST OF Asheville, North Carolina, I turned off the busy highway and drove the remaining distance to the city on the scenic Blue Ridge Parkway. On that late October afternoon I drove slowly, stopping often to savor the mountain vistas and the last of the brilliant autumn leaves. The journey was not efficient in terms of getting to my destination quickly, but it was effective in restoring my soul.

The experience caused me to ask, "How often do I travel the quiet road with Jesus? Do I exit the fast lane of my responsibilities and concerns to focus my attention on Him for a time each day?"

After Jesus's disciples completed a demanding period of ministry, He said to them, "Come with me to a quiet place and get some rest" (Mark 6:31). Instead of a long vacation, they had only a short boat ride together before being thronged by the crowd. The disciples witnessed the compassion of the Lord and participated with Him in meeting the needs of the multitudes (vv. 33–43). When the long day finally ended, Jesus sought renewal in prayer with His heavenly Father (v. 46).

Jesus our Lord is always with us whether life is hectic or calm, but there is great value in taking time each day to walk the quiet road with Him.   —DAVID MCCASLAND

Time spent with the Lord is always time well spent.

THE PERFECT PRAYER PARTNER

READ: Romans 8:31–34

Who then is the one who condemns? No one. Christ Jesus who died—more than that, who was raised to life—is at the right hand of God and is also interceding for us. ROMANS 8:34

FEW SOUNDS ARE AS beautiful as hearing someone who loves you praying for you. When you hear a friend pray for you with compassion and God-given insight, it's a little like heaven touching earth.

How good it is to know that because of God's kindness to us our prayers can also touch heaven. Sometimes when we pray we may struggle with words and feelings of inadequacy, but Jesus taught His followers that we "should always pray and not give up" (Luke 18:1). God's Word shows us that one of the reasons we can do this is that Jesus himself "is at the right hand of God and is also interceding for us" (Romans 8:34).

We never pray alone, because Jesus is praying for us. He hears us as we pray, and He speaks to the Father on our behalf. We don't have to worry about the eloquence of our words, because no one understands us like Jesus. He helps us in every way, presenting our needs before God. He also knows when the answers we ask for would not be good for us; He handles every request or concern with perfect wisdom and love.

Jesus is the perfect prayer partner—the friend who intercedes for us with immeasurable kindness. His prayers for us are beautiful beyond words, and they should encourage us to always pray with thankfulness.   —JAMES BANKS

There's no greater privilege than praying with Jesus.

THE SPIRIT OF FIKA

READ: Luke 24:28–35

When he was at the table with them, he took bread, gave thanks, broke it and began to give it to them. LUKE 24:30

THE COFFEEHOUSE IN THE town near my house is named Fika. It's a Swedish word meaning to take a break with coffee and a pastry, always with family, coworkers, or friends. I'm not Swedish, yet the spirit of *fika* describes one thing I love most about Jesus—His practice of taking a break to eat and relax with others.

Scholars say Jesus's meals weren't random. Theologian Mark Glanville calls them "the delightful 'second course'" of Israel's feasts and celebrations in the Old Testament. At the table, Jesus lived what God had intended Israel to be: "a center of joy, celebration and justice for the whole world."

From the feeding of 5,000 to the Last Supper—even to the meal with two believers after His resurrection (Luke 24:30)—the table ministry of Jesus invites us to stop our constant striving and abide in Him. Indeed, not until eating with Jesus did the two believers recognize Him as the risen Lord. "He took bread, gave thanks, broke it and began to give it to them. Then their eyes were opened" (vv. 30–31) to the living Christ.

Sitting with a friend recently at Fika, enjoying hot chocolate and rolls, we found ourselves also talking of Jesus. He is the Bread of Life. May we linger at His table and find more of Him.

—PATRICIA RAYBON

Make time to eat the Bread of Life.

BECOMING WHOLE

READ: John 5:1–9

*When Jesus saw him lying there, and knew that he already
had been in that condition a long time, He said to him,
"Do you want to be made well?"* JOHN 5:6 (NKJV)

JOHN STEINBECK'S PULITZER PRIZE-WINNING novel *The Grapes of
Wrath* begins with a scene in drought-ravaged Oklahoma during
the Great Depression. With the crops dying and the land choked
by dust, the women watched the men to see if they would break
under the strain. When they saw the men's will to carry on, they
took heart. Steinbeck writes, "Women and children knew deep in
themselves that no misfortune was too great to bear if their men
were whole." The issue was not happiness, prosperity, or satisfaction,
but wholeness. This is the great need of us all.

In the King James Version of the Bible, the word *whole* is often
used to describe Jesus's work of physical healing. When the Lord
encountered a man who had been disabled for thirty-eight years,
He asked, "Wilt thou be made whole?" (John 5:5–6 KJV). After
Jesus healed the man, He challenged him to also embrace spiritual
wholeness: "See, you are well again. Stop sinning or something
worse may happen to you" (v. 14).

If we only want something Jesus can do for us, our relationship
with Him will be limited. When we want Jesus himself, He brings
completeness to our lives. Christ wants, first and foremost, to make
us whole. —DAVID MCCASLAND

Only Jesus can give wholeness to a broken life.

WHAT KIND OF SAVIOR IS HE?

READ: John 6:47–51, 60–66

*From this time many of his disciples turned back
and no longer followed him.* JOHN 6:66

LAST YEAR, FRIENDS AND I prayed for healing for three women battling cancer. We knew God had the power to do this, so every day we asked Him to do so. We had seen Him work in the past and believed He could do it again. There were days in each woman's battle where healing looked like it was a reality, and we rejoiced. But the three women all died that fall. Some said that was "the ultimate healing," and in a way it was. Still, the loss hurt us deeply. We wanted Him to heal them all—here and now—but for reasons we couldn't understand, no miracle came.

Some people followed Jesus for the miracles He performed and to get their needs met (John 6:2, 26). Some simply saw Him as the carpenter's son (Matthew 13:55–58), and others expected Him to be their political leader (Luke 19:37–38). Some thought of Him as a great teacher (Matthew 7:28–29), while others quit following Him because His teaching was hard to understand (John 6:66).

Jesus still doesn't always meet our expectations. Yet He is so much more than we can imagine. He's the provider of eternal life (vv. 47–48). He is good and wise; and He loves, forgives, stays close, and brings us comfort. May we find rest in Jesus as He is and keep following Him. —ANNE CETAS

I trust in you, LORD; I say, "You are my God."
—Psalm 31:14

KILLER PLANTS

Read: Luke 14:16–26

"If anyone comes to me and does not hate father and mother, wife and children, brothers and sisters—yes, even their own life—such a person cannot be my disciple." Luke 14:26

SOME FOREST WORKERS FIGHT fires. Others battle fast-growing plants. A *Mercury News* article reported that teams of volunteers are working hard to remove invasive plants from the redwood forests of the Santa Cruz Mountains. Workers point out that many of the non-native species they are fighting are sold in garden stores. The German ivy plant, for example, has become a serious problem in California. This fast-growing exotic houseplant competes with the native species, smothering and shading everything in its path. It can completely cover and destroy a tree.

Thinking about these homegrown invaders can help us understand something even more crucial than saving trees. Jesus warned us that anything that competes with Him for our hearts can choke our spiritual lives. He said that even the natural love of family can be dangerous and keep us from following Him (Luke 14:16–26). Our Lord demands our undivided love and loyalty.

Once we value Christ above everything else, we will learn to love our family with a deeper and healthier love. But until our ultimate loyalty is determined, homegrown affection will do in our hearts what fire or German ivy will do in a forest.

We shouldn't let anything compete with Christ.

—MART DEHAAN

The more we love Christ, the more we'll love others.

A BLANKET FOR EVERYONE

READ: John 18:15–28

*Above all, love each other deeply, because love
covers over a multitude of sins.* 1 PETER 4:8

LINUS VAN PELT, BETTER known as simply "Linus," was a mainstay in the *Peanuts* comic strip. Witty and wise, yet insecure, Linus constantly carried a security blanket. We can identify. We have our fears and insecurities too.

The disciple Peter knew something about fear. When Jesus was arrested, Peter displayed courage by following the Lord into the courtyard of the high priest. But then he began to show his fear by lying to protect his identity (John 18:15–26). He spoke disgraceful words that denied his Lord. But Jesus never stopped loving Peter, and He ultimately restored him (See John 21:15–19).

Peter's emphasis on love in 1 Peter 4:8 came from one who had experienced the deep love of Jesus. And he, in turn, stressed the importance of love in our relationships with the words "above all." The intensity of the verse continues with the encouragement to "love each other deeply, because love covers over a multitude of sins."

Have you ever needed that kind of "blanket"? I have! I have needed to be "covered" in the manner that Jesus covered disgraced, shame-filled people in the Gospels.

To followers of Jesus, love is a blanket to be graciously and courageously given away for the comfort and reclamation of others. As recipients of such great love, let us be givers of the same.

—ARTHUR JACKSON

God loves you and me—let's love each other.

THE JESUS WAY

READ: Mark 1:21–39

*Very early in the morning, while it was still
dark, Jesus got up, left the house and went off to a
solitary place, where he prayed.* MARK 1:35

EVER HAVE ONE OF those hectic days when you need more time than the clock offers? When everyone is after you for help and your tasks seem endless? You might wonder: Did Jesus ever struggle like this? And if so, how did He handle it?

Consider the day in Jesus's life recorded in Mark 1:21–34. It began with a visit to the synagogue to teach, which He did with authority. Then things got rough. A demon-possessed man started shouting at Jesus. Calmly but sternly the Teacher cast out the demon.

When Jesus left the synagogue, He and His friends went to Peter's house. But He couldn't rest; Peter's mother-in-law was sick and needed His healing touch. Later, the entire town gathered outside so Jesus could heal more sick people and cast out more demons. It must have been a tiring day.

How did Jesus respond? Did He take the next day off? Head for the cool mountain streams of Caesarea Philippi? No, the next day He got up before sunrise, found a solitary place, and prayed (v. 35). He sought the rejuvenating power of His Father's presence.

How do you handle a tough day? Get alone with the Savior and seek His help. Start your day the Jesus way.   —DAVE BRANON

If you're too busy to pray, you're too busy.

THE HUMANITY OF JESUS

READ: Hebrews 2:9–18

*For we do not have a high priest who is unable
to empathize with our weaknesses, but we have
one who has been tempted in every way, just as
we are—yet he did not sin.* HEBREWS 4:15

I ONCE OVERHEARD THIS comment about a person who was always critical: "The trouble with him is that he's forgotten what it's like to be human!" How easily we forget our past struggles and become unsympathetic toward those who are struggling today. But there's one who hasn't forgotten what it's like to be human—Jesus.

In Hebrews 2:9–18, we "see" Jesus's humanity more fully. As a man, He was able by God's grace to experience death in our place. And during His earthly life Jesus was made perfect through His sufferings (v. 10). But there's more. "Both [Jesus] who sanctifies and [we] who are being sanctified are all of one" (v. 11 NKJV). Because of this oneness, Jesus is not ashamed to call us brothers and sisters (See v. 11).

In a body like ours, Jesus lived, worked, and overcame every obstacle, so He knows what it's like to be one of us. Having passed through all these experiences without sinning, He then went to heaven and is now our approachable High Priest at the throne of grace (vv. 17–18; 4:14–16).

We all need someone who knows what it's like to be human yet has limitless power to help us overcome our human weaknesses. Jesus is that one. He longs to hear us speak His name and ask for His help. —JOANIE YODER

No one understands like Jesus.

JESUS IS NEAR

READ: Genesis 28:10–22

When Jacob awoke from his sleep, he thought, "Surely the LORD is in this place, and I was not aware of it." GENESIS 28:16

SAMUEL, WHO WAS FOUR, had finished eating his dinner and asked if he could be dismissed from the table. He wanted to go outside to play. But he was too young to be out alone, so his mother said, "No. You can't go outside by yourself. You need to wait for me to finish and go with you." His quick reply: "But, Mommy, Jesus is with me!"

Samuel had learned well from his parents that the Lord is always by his side. We see in our Bible reading today that Jacob had learned that lesson too. His father Isaac had blessed him and told him to find a wife from among his mother's family (Genesis 28:1–4). He followed that directive and traveled toward Haran.

As Jacob slept, the Lord came to him in a dream and said, "I am with you and will watch over you wherever you go . . . . I will not leave you" (v. 15). When Jacob awoke, he knew that he had heard from God, and said, "Surely the LORD is in this place" (v. 16). Confident of God's presence, he committed himself to following Him with his life (vv. 20–21).

If we have received Jesus as our Savior (John 1:12), we can be confident and take comfort in the truth that He is always present with us (Hebrews 13:5). Like Jacob, may we respond to His love with wholehearted devotion. —ANNE CETAS

Our loving God is always near—forever by our side.

JESUS LOVES ME

READ: Romans 8:31–39

*Keep yourselves in God's love as you wait for the mercy of our
Lord Jesus Christ to bring you to eternal life.* JUDE 1:21

ON COLD DAYS, our old dog moves around the yard, finding a sunny
spot to stretch out on the grass to keep herself in the warmth of
the sun.

This reminds me that we must "keep" ourselves in the love of
God (Jude 1:21). That doesn't mean we have to act in some special
way to make God love us (although our desire is to please Him).
Because we are His children we're loved no matter what we do or
fail to do. It means instead that we should think about His love
and bask in its radiance and warmth all day long.

"[Nothing] will be able to separate us from the love of God"
(Romans 8:39). He loved us before we were born, and He loves us
now. This is our identity in Christ; it is who we are—God's beloved
children. That's something to think about throughout the day.

Five times in John's gospel he described himself as the disciple
Jesus loved (13:23; 19:26; 20:2; 21:7, 20). Jesus loved His other disciples too, but John reveled in the fact that Jesus loved him! We can
adopt John's theme—"I am the disciple Jesus loves!"—and repeat
it to ourselves all day long. Or we can sing that familiar children's
song in our hearts, "Jesus loves me, this I know." As we carry that
truth with us throughout the day, we'll bask in the warmth of His
love!   —DAVID ROPER

*God loves us not because of who we are,
but because of who He is.*

IN JESUS'S NAME

READ: John 14:12–21

*"Until now you have not asked for anything
in my name. Ask and you will receive, and
your joy will be complete."* JOHN 16:24

ONE OF MY FAVORITE collections of photos is of a family dinner. Preserved in an album are images of Dad, his sons and their wives, and his grandchildren in a time of thanksgiving and intercession.

Dad had suffered a series of strokes and was not as verbal as usual. But during that time of prayer, I heard him say with heartfelt conviction: "We pray in Jesus's name!" About a year later, Dad passed from this world into the presence of the One in whose name he placed such trust.

Jesus taught us to pray in His name. The night before He was crucified, He gave a promise to His disciples: "Until now you have not asked for anything in my name. Ask and you will receive, and your joy will be complete" (John 16:24). But the promise of asking in Jesus's name is not a blank check that we might get anything to fulfill our personal whims.

Earlier that evening, Jesus taught that He answers requests made in His name so that He will bring glory to the Father (John 14:13). And later that night, Jesus himself prayed in anguish, "My Father, if it is possible, may this cup be taken from me. Yet not as I will, but as you will" (Matthew 26:39).

As we pray, we yield to God's wisdom, love, and sovereignty, and we confidently ask "in Jesus's name."   —DENNIS FISHER

---

*Nothing lies beyond the reach of prayer except
that which lies outside the will of God.*

RHYTHMS OF GRACE

READ: Matthew 11:25–30

*"Take my yoke upon you and learn from me, for
I am gentle and humble in heart, and you will
find rest for your souls."* MATTHEW 11:29

A FRIEND AND HIS wife, who were in their early nineties and married for sixty-six years, wrote their family history for their children, grandchildren, and generations to come. The final chapter, "A Letter from Mom and Dad," contains important life lessons they've learned. One caused me to pause and take inventory of my own life: "If you find that Christianity exhausts you, draining you of your energy, then you are practicing religion rather than enjoying a relationship with Jesus Christ. Your walk with the Lord will not make you weary; it will invigorate you, restore your strength, and energize your life" (See Matthew 11:28–29).

Eugene Peterson's paraphrase of Jesus's invitation in this passage begins, "Are you tired? Worn out? Burned out on religion? . . . Walk with me and work with me. . . . Learn the unforced rhythms of grace" (MSG).

When I think that serving God is all up to me, I've begun working for Him instead of walking with Him. There is a vital difference. If I'm not walking with Christ, my spirit becomes dry and brittle. People are annoyances, not fellow humans created in God's image. Nothing seems right.

When I sense that I'm practicing religion instead of enjoying a relationship with Jesus, it's time to lay the burden down and walk with Him in His "unforced rhythms of grace."

—DAVID MCCASLAND

Jesus wants us to walk with Him.

JESUS IN DISGUISE

READ: Matthew 25:31–40

"The King will reply, 'Truly I tell you, whatever you did for one of the least of these brothers and sisters of mine, you did for me.'" MATTHEW 25:40

WHEN A FRIEND CARED for her housebound mother-in-law, she asked her what she longed for the most. Her mother-in-law said, "For my feet to be washed." My friend admitted, "How I hated that job! Each time she asked me to do it I was resentful, and would ask God to hide my feelings from her."

But one day her grumbling attitude changed in a flash. As she got out the bowl and towel and knelt at her mother-in-law's feet, she said, "I looked up, and for a moment I felt like I was washing the feet of Jesus himself. She was Jesus in disguise!" After that, she felt honored to wash her mother-in-law's feet.

When I heard this moving account, I thought of Jesus's story about the end of time that He taught on the slopes of the Mount of Olives. The King welcomes into His kingdom His sons and daughters, saying that when they visited the sick or fed the hungry, "Whatever you did for one of the least of these brothers and sisters of mine, you did for me" (Matthew 25:40). We too serve Jesus himself when we visit those in prison or give clothes to the needy.

Today, might you echo my friend, who now wonders when she meets someone new, "Are you Jesus in disguise?"

—AMY BOUCHER PYE

When we serve others, we serve Jesus.

NAME ABOVE ALL NAMES

READ: Philippians 2:5–11

*"She will give birth to a son, and you are
to give him the name Jesus, because he will save
his people from their sins."* MATTHEW 1:21

IF YOU KNEW FOR certain that you were going to lose your voice
and that you would never be able to speak again, what would you
want your final words to be?

A man with throat cancer faced an operation that would save
his life but not his voice. Just before surgery, he spent time with
his wife telling her of his love. He did the same with his daughter.

Then he asked his doctor to let him know precisely when the
anesthetic would make him unconscious. As the man was slipping
off to sleep, he said distinctly, "Jesus! Jesus!" That was the last word
he chose to utter in this life—"Jesus!"

How meaningful is the name of Jesus to us? Other names,
like the names of those we love, are inexpressibly precious. But for
those of us who are redeemed by God's grace, the name of Jesus
is the most meaningful. And it is to our heavenly Father as well.
He "exalted him to the highest place and gave him the name that
is above every name, that at the name of Jesus every knee should
bow, . . . and every tongue acknowledge that Jesus Christ is Lord,
to the glory of God the Father" (Philippians 2:9–11).

Throughout the rest of our lives and into eternity, let's magnify
that wonderful name—Jesus.   —VERNON GROUNDS

The name of Jesus is precious to those who know Him.

CONNECTING WITH JESUS

READ: Psalm 63:1–8

Because your love is better than life,
my lips will glorify you. PSALM 63:3

IN HIS BOOK *Objects of His Affection*, Scotty Smith shares his journey of learning to personally experience the passionate love of God. As a young boy, he lost his mother suddenly in a car accident. Because of this, he closed off his wounded heart to others—including God. Several years later he received Jesus as his Savior and began to learn the truths of Christianity. Yet his relationship with the Lord in those days was, as he described, "side by side rather than face-to-face. Important, but not intimate."

Do you ever feel that way? You talk to the Lord a little bit, read His words in the Bible, but don't sense a passionate connection with Him like that expressed by the psalmist David in Psalm 63. Scotty suggests ways to overcome the obstacles to intimacy, from which we may glean these two ideas.

Live honestly. Open up to the Lord about the pain of your losses and admit your failures. "Come near to God and he will come near to you" (James 4:8; see also 1 John 1:9). *Ponder and believe the Scriptures about God's character and His longing for you.* "Your love is better than life" (Psalm 63:3; see also Psalm 139 and Ephesians 1:3–6).

Being close in a relationship takes time and effort—even when it's with the Lord. —ANNE CETAS

God pursues us in our restlessness, receives us
in our sinfulness, holds us in our brokenness.
—Scotty Smith

RISKY BUSINESS

READ: Matthew 8:23–27

"Lord, save us! We're going to drown." MATTHEW 8:25

DENIS BOYLES KNEW IT would be challenging to interview a man on a roller coaster—especially when the interview took place during an attempt to set a world's record for continuous riding. After several times around the track, Denis was so overcome with fear he could hardly talk.

Then the man showed him how to use his body and feet to lean into the loops, twists, and turns. Writing in *AARP Magazine*, Boyles explained how that took away the terror. It also taught him a lesson about risk and fear. The roller coaster felt risky though it was quite safe. But driving his car to the amusement park posed a far greater risk of injury. Risk and fear are easily confused. As Jesus and His disciples crossed the Sea of Galilee, a storm came up and waves swept over their boat. Incredibly, Jesus was asleep. The disciples woke Him and said, "Lord, save us! We're going to drown!" (Matthew 8:25). In a gentle rebuke, Jesus asked, "'You of little faith, why are you so afraid?' Then he got up and rebuked the winds and the waves, and it was completely calm" (v. 26).

Like the disciples, the more we learn about Jesus, the more we trust Him. Our greatest risk is failing to depend on Him when life seems out of control.   —DAVID MCCASLAND

*Keep your eyes on Jesus, and you'll
soon lose sight of your fears.*

THE SOURCE OF IMPACT

READ: Acts 4:1–13

When they saw the courage of Peter and John and realized that they were unschooled, ordinary men, they were astonished and they took note that these men had been with Jesus. ACTS 4:13

THE NOBEL PRIZE IS awarded annually to people in a variety of fields who have made an extraordinary impact. Leaders in economics, physics, literature, medicine, and peace are recognized for their contributions. When a person is acknowledged with a Nobel Prize, it is the ultimate affirmation of years of training, effort, education, and sacrifice in pursuit of excellence—investments that are the source of their impact.

We might wish to make a significant impact spiritually in our world, but we wonder, *What is the source of spiritual and ministry influence? If we want to make an extraordinary impact for Jesus Christ, what must we invest in?*

Christ's first followers were impacted from spending time with Jesus. Israel's religious leaders recognized this. Acts 4:13 tells us, "When [the leaders] saw the courage of Peter and John and realized that they were unschooled, ordinary men, they were astonished and they took note that these men had been with Jesus."

Training and education are valuable in the service of the Savior, but nothing can replace time spent in His presence. He is the source of whatever spiritual impact we might have on our world. How much time have you been spending with Jesus—your source of impact? —BILL CROWDER

To master this life, spend time with the Master.

BLUNDERS TO WONDERS

READ: John 21:15–19

Restore us to yourself, LORD, that we may return;
renew our days as of old. LAMENTATIONS 5:21

ARTIST JAMES HUBBELL SAYS, "Mistakes are gifts." Whenever he's working on a project and something goes wrong, he doesn't start over. He looks for a way to use the mistake to make something better. None of us can avoid making blunders, and all of us have favorite ways of dealing with them. We may try to hide them or to correct them or to apologize for them.

We do that with our sin sometimes too. But God doesn't throw us away and start over. He redeems us and makes us better.

The apostle Peter tended to do and say whatever seemed best at the moment. He has been referred to as an "impetuous blunderer." In his fear after Jesus was arrested, Peter claimed three times that he didn't know Jesus! Yet later, on the basis of Peter's three declarations of love, Jesus turned Peter's humiliating denial into a wonderful occasion of restoration (John 21). Despite Peter's flawed past, Jesus restored him to ministry with these words: "Feed my sheep" (v. 17).

If you have made a blunder so big that it seems irreversible, the most important matter is whether you have put your faith in Jesus. When we love Him, Jesus can turn our most serious blunders into awesome wonders. —JULIE ACKERMAN LINK

God can change our blunders into wonders.

ALL THAT IS PRECIOUS

READ: 1 Peter 2:1–10

As you come to him, the living Stone—rejected by humans but chosen by God and precious to him. 1 PETER 2:4

THROUGHOUT MY LIFE, I'VE accumulated a lot of stuff. I have boxes of things that at one time were important but over time have lost their intrigue. And, as an unrepentant collector, I've also realized that the thrill is in searching for and acquiring a new piece to add to the collection. Then my attention turns toward the hunt for the next item.

While we pile up many things that are important to us, very little of it is really precious. In fact, over time I have learned that the most precious things in life are not material items at all. Rather, it's the people who have loved me and built into my life who are precious. When I find my heart saying, "I don't know what I'd do without them," I know that they are indeed precious to me.

So when Peter refers to Jesus as "a chosen and precious cornerstone" (1 Peter 2:6), it should resonate in our hearts that He is truly precious—our prized possession above everything and everyone else. Where would we be today without the constant unfailing companionship of His faithful presence, wise and perfect guidance, merciful patience, comfort, and transforming reproof? What would we do without Him? I can't even imagine! —JOE STOWELL

Of all that is precious, Jesus tops the list.

COSTUME OR UNIFORM?

READ: Romans 13:11–14

Clothe yourselves with the Lord Jesus Christ, and do not think about how to gratify the desires of the flesh. ROMANS 13:14

EUNICE MCGARRAHAN GAVE AN inspiring talk on Christian discipleship in which she said, "A costume is something you put on and pretend that you are what you are wearing. A uniform, on the other hand, reminds you that you are, in fact, what you wear."

Her comment sparked memories of my first day in US Army basic training when we were each given a box and ordered to put all our civilian clothes in it. The box was mailed to our home address. Every day after that, the uniform we put on reminded us that we had entered a period of disciplined training designed to change our attitudes and actions.

"Put aside the deeds of darkness," the apostle Paul told the followers of Jesus living in Rome, "and put on the armor of light" (Romans 13:12). He followed this with the command to "clothe yourselves with the Lord Jesus Christ, and do not think about how to gratify the desires of the flesh" (v. 14). The goal of this "putting aside" and "putting on" was a new identity and transformed living (v. 12).

When we choose to follow Christ as our Lord, He begins the process of making us more like Him each day. It is not a matter of pretending to be what we aren't but of becoming more and more what we are in Christ. —DAVID MCCASLAND

Salvation is free, but discipleship will cost you your life. —Dietrich Bonhoeffer

ENJOYING HIS MEAL

READ: 1 Corinthians 11:23–34

*When he had given thanks, he broke it and said,
"This is my body, which is for you; do this in
remembrance of me."* 1 CORINTHIANS 11:24

IT'S NOT ABOUT THE table, whether it's square or round. It's not about the chairs—plastic or wooden. It's not about the food, although it helps if it has been cooked with love. A good meal is enjoyed when we turn off the TV and our cell phones and concentrate on those we're with.

I love gathering around the table, enjoying a good chat with friends and family and talking about a multitude of topics. However, instant technology has made it difficult. Sometimes we are more concerned about what others—sometimes miles away—have to say than what the person just across the table is saying.

We have been invited to another meal at the table when we come together in one place to celebrate the Lord's Supper. It's not about the church, if it's big or small. It's not about the type of bread. It's about turning off our thoughts from our worries and concerns and focusing on Jesus.

When was the last time we enjoyed being at the Lord's Table? Do we enjoy His presence, or are we more concerned with what's going on somewhere else? This is important, "for whenever you eat this bread and drink this cup, you proclaim the Lord's death until he comes" (1 Corinthians 11:26).   —KEILA OCHOA

*Remembering Christ's death gives us courage
for today and hope for tomorrow.*

WALKING IN THE LIGHT

READ: Hebrews 12:18–24

*In him was life, and that life was the
light of all mankind.* JOHN 1:4

DARKNESS DESCENDED ON OUR forest village when the moon disappeared. Lightning slashed the skies, followed by a rainstorm and crackling thunder. Awake and afraid, as a child I imagined all kinds of grisly monsters about to pounce on me! By daybreak, however, the sounds vanished, the sun rose, and calm returned as birds jubilated in the sunshine. The contrast between the frightening darkness of the night and the joy of the daylight was remarkably sharp.

The author of Hebrews recalls the time when the Israelites had an experience at Mount Sinai so dark and stormy they hid in fear (Exodus 20:18–19). For them, God's presence, even in His loving gift of the law, felt dark and terrifying. This was because, as sinful people, the Israelites couldn't live up to God's standards. Their sin caused them to walk in darkness and fear (Hebrews 12:18–21).

But God is light; in Him there's no darkness at all (1 John 1:5). In Hebrews 12, Mount Sinai represents God's holiness and our old life of disobedience, while the beauty of Mount Zion represents God's grace and believers' new life in Jesus, "the mediator of a new covenant" (vv. 22–24).

Whoever follows Jesus will "never walk in darkness, but will have the light of life" (John 8:12). Through Him, we can let go of the darkness of our old life and celebrate the joy of walking in the light and beauty of His kingdom.   —LAWRENCE DARMANI

*If you're a believer in Jesus, how has your life
changed since He came into it? What are some
ways you'd like to grow in your faith?*

THE FRAGRANCE OF CHRIST

READ: 2 Corinthians 2:14–17

*For we are to God the pleasing aroma of Christ
among those who are being saved and those
who are perishing.* 2 CORINTHIANS 2:15

WHICH OF THE FIVE senses brings back your memories most sharply? For me it is definitely the sense of smell. A certain kind of sun oil takes me instantly to a French beach. The smell of chicken mash brings back childhood visits to my grandmother. A hint of pine says "Christmas," and a certain kind of aftershave reminds me of my son's teenage years.

Paul reminded the Corinthians that they were the aroma of Christ: "For we are to God the pleasing aroma of Christ" (2 Corinthians 2:15). He may have been referring to Roman victory parades. The Romans made sure everyone knew they had been victorious by burning incense on altars throughout the city. For the victors, the aroma was pleasing; for the prisoners, it meant certain slavery or death. So as believers, we are victorious soldiers. And when the gospel of Christ is preached, it is a pleasing fragrance to God.

As the aroma of Christ, what perfumes do Christians bring with them as they walk into a room? It's not something that can be bought in a bottle or a jar. When we spend a lot of time with someone, we begin to think and act like that person. Spending time with Jesus will help us spread a pleasing fragrance to those around us.

—MARION STROUD

When we walk with God, people will notice.

JESUS REACHED OUT

READ: Matthew 14:22–33

*Immediately Jesus reached out his hand
and caught him. "You of little faith," he said,
"why did you doubt?"* MATTHEW 14:31

SOMETIMES LIFE GETS BUSY—CLASSES are hard, work is exhausting, the bathroom needs to be cleaned, and a coffee date is on the day's schedule. It gets to the point where I force myself to read the Bible for a few minutes a day and tell myself I'll spend more time with God next week. But it doesn't take long before I'm distracted, drowning in the day's tasks, and forget to ask God for help of any kind.

When Peter was walking on water toward Jesus, he quickly became distracted by the wind and waves. Like me, he began to sink (Matthew 14:29–30). But as soon as Peter cried out, "immediately Jesus reached out his hand and caught him" (vv. 30–31).

I often feel as if I have to make it up to God after being so busy and distracted that I lose sight of Him. But that's not how God works. As soon as we turn to Him for help, Jesus reaches out without hesitation.

When we're unsettled by the chaos of life, it's easy to forget that God is standing in the middle of the storm with us. Jesus asked Peter, "Why did you doubt?" (v. 31). No matter what we're going through, He is there. He is here. Next to us at that moment, in this moment, ready to reach out and rescue us.   —JULIE SCHWAB

*God is waiting for us to turn to Him so
He can reach out and help.*

JUST LIVING?

READ: Ecclesiastes 1:1–11

I consider everything a loss because of the surpassing worth of knowing Christ Jesus my Lord, for whose sake I have lost all things. I consider them garbage, that I may gain Christ. PHILIPPIANS 3:8

THERE'S A GULF OF difference—far wider than the Grand Canyon—between living for something and merely living. But what is a worthy purpose for our existence?

Ty Cobb, one of baseball's all-time greats, made a revealing admission: "For years I ate baseball, I slept baseball, I talked baseball, I thought baseball, I lived baseball." But then he added, "When you get beyond those years of playing professional baseball, you can't live on baseball."

Certainly there is a vast multitude of purposes to which we can devote our energies. But in the end none of them will prove sufficient. One purpose alone gives enduring motivation to life. The apostle Paul stated that lasting purpose this way: "For to me, to live is Christ" (Philippians 1:21).

Knowing Christ, trusting Him, abiding in fellowship with Him, and serving Him—this is the one driving purpose that saves life from being little more than a monotonous march of meaningless days (Ecclesiastes 1:1–11). Even when we are old and infirm, we can serve Him through a ministry of example and intercession. This makes life a joyful journey with our Savior and Friend, the Lord Jesus, whose face we will see when we reach our eternal home.

—VERNON GROUNDS

Life's purpose is found in a person—the Lord Jesus Christ.

HEAVEN REJOICES

READ: Luke 15:1–10

*"In the same way, I tell you, there is rejoicing
in the presence of the angels of God over one
sinner who repents."* LUKE 15:10

JOANN HAD BEEN RAISED in a Christian home. But when she went to college, she began to question her beliefs and walked away from God. After graduation, she traveled to a number of countries, always looking for happiness but never feeling satisfied. While experiencing some difficulties, she recognized that God was pursuing her and that she needed Him.

From Germany, Joann called her parents in the US and said, "I have given my life to Christ, and He's changing me! I'm sorry for the worry I have caused you." Her parents were so excited that they called her brothers and sisters-in-law to come over immediately. They wanted to tell them the exciting news in person. "Your sister has received Christ!" they said, rejoicing through tears.

The woman in Luke 15 who found her lost coin called her friends and neighbors together to rejoice with her (v. 9). Jesus told this story, and others about a lost sheep and a lost son, to the religious people of His day to show how He came to earth to pursue lost sinners. When we accept God's gift of salvation, there is rejoicing both on earth and in heaven. Jesus said, "There is rejoicing in the presence of the angels of God over one sinner who repents" (v. 10). How wonderful that Jesus has reached down to us, and heaven rejoices when we respond!　　　　　　　　　　—ANNE CETAS

Angels rejoice when we repent.

CROOKED HOUSE

READ: Revelation 3:14–20

I counsel you to buy from me gold refined in the fire, so you can become rich; and white clothes to wear, so you can cover your shameful nakedness; and salve to put on your eyes, so you can see. REVELATION 3:18

WHEN ROBERT KLOSE FIRST moved into his one-hundred-year-old house, its strange sounds were disconcerting. A carpenter told him the house was crooked. Klose admitted, "I could see it in the floors, the ceilings, the roofline, the door jambs, even the window frames. Drop a ball on the floor and it will roll away into oblivion." Seventeen years later, the house is still holding together. He has gotten used to it and has even grown to love it.

In Revelation, Jesus confronted a church that had become accustomed to its crooked spirituality and had even grown to love its inconsistencies. Laodicea was a well-to-do city. Yet that very wealth led to its delusion of self-sufficiency. This had bled into the culture of the church and produced a crooked, "we don't need Jesus" type of spirituality. Therefore, Jesus rebuked these believers, calling them "lukewarm, . . . wretched, pitiful, poor, blind and naked" (3:16–17). He rebuked them because He loved them and still wanted an ever-deepening communion with them. So He gave them opportunity to repent (v. 19).

If self-sufficiency has skewed your fellowship with Jesus, you can straighten it through repentance and a renewal of intimate fellowship with Him. —MARVIN WILLIAMS

Repentance is God's way of making the crooked straight.

ARE YOU DISTRACTED?

READ: Luke 10:38–42

*But Martha was distracted by all the preparations that
had to be made. She came to him and asked, "Lord,
don't you care that my sister has left me to do the work
by myself? Tell her to help me!"* LUKE 10:40

WE CAN BE SO occupied in doing something good that we miss out
on doing something better.

In the story in Luke 10, Martha was preparing an elaborate meal
for Jesus and His disciples. That's good. We all appreciate a well-
prepared dinner. But she became distracted (the Greek word means
"not knowing which way to turn"). That wasn't good, although it
was not at all unnatural. Martha also became irritated. She didn't
like it that Mary was listening to Jesus instead of helping. That
too was an understandable reaction. Perhaps we can remember a
time when we were perturbed because a brother or sister got out of
helping around the house.

We can't blame Martha for being irritated. Yet Jesus did. I think
He did so because she was preparing a more elaborate meal than
necessary. This may be implied in the first part of verse 42, which is
translated either something like this: "But a few things are necessary,"
or like this: "Only one thing is needed." A small variety of food would
have been adequate! If she had done this, she could have fed the group
a nourishing meal and still found time to join Mary at the feet of Jesus.

We all enjoy getting together for a meal. And that's good. But
let's be careful that we don't become so preoccupied with food that
we are distracted and overlook the better part—fellowship with one
another and with the Lord Jesus Christ.   —HERB VANDER LUGT

For God's people, worship must come before work.

A SHARED BOND

READ: Ephesians 2:12–18

*There is neither Jew nor Gentile, neither slave
nor free, nor is there male and female, for you are
all one in Christ Jesus.* GALATIANS 3:28

WHEN I NEEDED A locksmith to get into my car, I had a pleasant surprise. After he arrived and began opening my little Ford's door, we began chatting and I recognized his warm, familiar accent.

It turned out that my rescuer was originally from Jamaica—a land I've visited often and have grown to love. This changed a negative event into a positive one. We were in a small way kindred spirits because of our shared love for that beautiful island nation.

This struck me as a reminder of an even greater camaraderie—the joy of meeting someone new and discovering that he or she is also a believer in Christ.

In some places, this is not unusual because there are many believers. But in those lands where there are few believers, the joy of meeting someone else who loves Jesus must be even greater. It's thrilling to share together the amazing reality of the freedom from sin we have through Christ!

For all who know Jesus, there is a shared bond, a oneness in Christ (Galatians 3:28), a joy of fellowship that can brighten even the darkest day. Praise God that He brings a bond of unity to all who know Him as Savior. —DAVE BRANON

Christian fellowship builds us up and binds us together.

JESUS WEPT

READ: John 11:1–4, 38–44

*The sting of death is sin, and the power of sin is the law.
But thanks be to God! He gives us the victory through
our Lord Jesus Christ.* 1 CORINTHIANS 15:56–57

I WAS ENGROSSED IN a book when a friend checked to see what I was reading. Immediately, she recoiled and said, "What a gloomy title!" I was reading "The Glass Coffin" in *Grimm's Fairy Tales*, and the word *coffin* disturbed her. Most of us don't like to be reminded of our mortality. But the reality is that out of 1,000 people, 1,000 people will die.

Death always elicits a deep emotional response. Even Jesus displayed strong emotions at His dear friend's funeral. When He saw Mary, whose brother had recently died, "he was deeply moved in spirit and troubled" (John 11:33). Another translation says, "a deep anger welled up within him" (NLT).

Jesus was troubled—even angry—but at what? Possibly, at sin and its consequences. God didn't make a world filled with sickness, suffering, and death. But sin entered the world and marred God's beautiful plan.

The Lord comes alongside us in our grief, weeping with us in our sorrow (v. 35). But more than that, Christ defeated sin and death by dying in our place and rising from the dead (1 Corinthians 15:56–57).

Jesus promises, "He who believes in Me, though he may die, he shall live" (John 11:25 NKJV). As believers, we enjoy fellowship with our Savior now, and we look forward to an eternity with Him where there will be no more tears, pain, sickness, or death.

—POH FANG CHIA

Christ's empty tomb guarantees our victory over death.

EYEWITNESS

READ: 1 John 1:1–7

*We proclaim to you what we have
seen and heard.* 1 JOHN 1:3

"YOU DON'T WANT TO interview me for your television program," the man told me. "You need someone who is young and photogenic, and I'm neither." I replied that we indeed wanted him because he had known C. S. Lewis, the noted author and the subject of our documentary. "Sir," I said, "when it comes to telling the story of a person's life, there is no substitute for an eyewitness."

As Christians, we often refer to sharing our faith in Christ as "witnessing" or "giving our testimony." It's an accurate concept taken directly from the Bible. John, a companion and disciple of Jesus, wrote: "We have seen, and bear witness, and declare to you that eternal life which was with the Father and was manifested to us—that which we have seen and heard we declare to you" (1 John 1:2–3 NKJV).

If you know Jesus as your Savior and have experienced His love, grace, and forgiveness, you can tell someone else about Him. Youth, beauty, and theological training are not required. Reality and enthusiasm are more valuable than a training course in how to share your faith.

When it comes to telling someone the wonderful story of how Jesus Christ can transform a person's life, there is no substitute for a firsthand witness like you. —DAVID MCCASLAND

Jesus doesn't need lawyers; He needs witnesses.

HOW TO TREAT A FRIEND

READ: John 15:9–15

*"I no longer call you servants, because a servant does
not know his master's business. Instead, I have called
you friends, for everything that I learned from my
Father I have made known to you."* JOHN 15:15

SUPPOSE AN OLD ACQUAINTANCE stops by unexpectedly at your
home during breakfast. You offer to take the day off, but he insists
that you keep your regular schedule. So you invite him to go with
you to work, and he accepts. How would he feel if you then ignored
him completely—didn't converse with him, failed to acknowledge
his presence at coffee breaks and lunch, and neglected to introduce
him to anyone? We would all agree—that's no way to treat a friend!

Jesus told His disciples that they were His friends (John 15:15).
And we who know Christ as our personal Savior have the assurance that we too are His friends. Do we, however, treat Him as
our Friend?

Evaluate your friendship with the Lord by asking yourself these
questions: Do I talk with Jesus in prayer throughout the day? Do I
take time to read and meditate on His Word? Do I enjoy fellowship
with Him? Am I concerned about what He thinks of my activities?
Do I introduce Him to others? Do I ignore Him or respect Him?
Can others tell that I have a close relationship with Christ?

Let's make certain that each day we give Jesus Christ the consideration He deserves as our Savior, our Master, and our Friend!

—RICHARD DEHAAN

Christ's friendship calls for our faithfulness.

THE ART OF COMMON PEOPLE

READ: Matthew 4:18–25

"I have not come to call the righteous,
but sinners to repentance." LUKE 5:32

THE ITALIAN PAINTER CARAVAGGIO (1571–1610) received scathing criticism in his day for depicting people of the Bible as common. His critics reflected a time when only members of royalty and aristocracy were considered appropriate subjects for the "immortality" of art. His commissioned canvas of *Saint Matthew and the Angel* so offended church leaders that it had to be redone. They could not accept seeing Matthew with the physical features of an everyday laborer.

According to one biographer, what the church fathers did not understand was that "Caravaggio, in elevating this humble figure, was copying Christ, who had Himself raised Matthew from the street."

Caravaggio was right about the people of the Bible. Jesus himself grew up in the home of a laborer. When His time came to go public, He was announced by a weather-worn man of the wilderness we know as John the Baptist. His disciples were fishermen and common people.

Jesus lived, loved, and died for wealthy people too. But by befriending those who had been demon-possessed, lepers, fishermen, and even despised tax collectors, the teacher from Nazareth showed that no one is too poor, too sinful, or too insignificant to be His friend.   —MART DEHAAN

Jesus wants you for a friend.

SHOWING REAL LOVE

READ: John 13:1–5, 33–35

"By this everyone will know that you are my
disciples, if you love one another." JOHN 13:35

IN SOME YEARS, the Chinese New Year happens to fall on the same day as Valentine's Day—February 14—in nearly forty countries worldwide. While these two festivals have very different origins, there are some similarities in how they are celebrated. In both cases, loved ones give gifts to express love for one another. Whether it is giving roses to your beloved on Valentine's Day or *hong bao* (red packets with money) to family and friends on Chinese New Year, they represent tokens of love.

Our Lord Jesus Christ commanded His disciples to "love one another," because "by this everyone will know that you are my disciples, if you love one another" (John 13:34–35).

The love that our Lord wants His disciples to have for one another is different from the romantic kind displayed between loving couples and the brotherly kind shown between friends or family. It's an unselfish love. The Greek word John used in Jesus's command is *agape*—God's kind of love that expects nothing in return. That was what Jesus showed to His disciples when He "poured water into a basin and began to wash his disciples' feet" (v. 5). That is the kind of love He displayed when He went to the cross for us.

Today, look for someone to whom you can show such unselfish love.   —C. P. HIA

———

Bear one another's burdens, and so fulfill
the law of Christ. —Galatians 6:2 NKJV

REFRESHING CANDOR

READ: John 4:7–26

*But whoever looks intently into the perfect
law that gives freedom, and continues in it—not
forgetting what they have heard, but doing it—
they will be blessed in what they do.* JAMES 1:25

OF THE MANY THINGS I love about my mom, chief among them
may be her candor. Many times I have called to ask her opinion on
a matter and she has consistently responded, "Don't ask my opinion
unless you want to hear it. I'm not going to try to figure out what
you want to hear. I'll tell you what I really think."

In a world where words are carefully parsed, her straightfor-
wardness is refreshing. It is also one of the characteristics of a true
friend. Real friends speak the truth to us in love—even if it isn't
what we want to hear. As the proverb says, "Wounds from a friend
can be trusted" (Proverbs 27:6).

This is one of the reasons Jesus is the greatest of friends. When
He encountered the woman at the well (John 4:7–26), He refused
to be pulled into a tug-of-war over secondary issues. Instead He
drove to the deepest issues and needs of her heart. He challenged
her about the character of the Father and lovingly spoke to her of
her broken dreams and deep disappointments.

As we walk with our Lord, may we allow Him to speak candidly
to the true condition of our hearts through the Scriptures—that
we might turn to Him and find His grace to help us in our times
of need.   —BILL CROWDER

Jesus always tells us truth.

A GENUINE FRIEND

READ: 1 Samuel 20:32–42

*Two are better than one, because they have a good
return for their labor.* ECCLESIASTES 4:9

IN THE NOVEL *SHANE*, a friendship forms between Joe Starrett, a
farmer on the American frontier, and Shane, a mysterious man
who stops to rest at the Starrett home. The men first bond as they
work together to remove a giant tree stump from Joe's land. The
relationship deepens as Joe rescues Shane from a fight and Shane
helps Joe improve and guard his farmland. The men share a sense of
mutual respect and loyalty that reflects what Scripture says: "Two
are better than one . . . . If either of them falls down, one can help
the other up" (Ecclesiastes 4:9–10).

Jonathan and David modeled this principle as well. Circumstances tested their friendship when David suspected that King
Saul wanted him dead. Jonathan doubted this, but David believed
it to be true (1 Samuel 20:2–3). Eventually, they decided David
would hide in a field while Jonathan questioned his father about the
matter. When Saul's deadly intent became clear, the friends wept
together and Jonathan blessed David as he fled (v. 42).

You have a genuine friend in Jesus if you have accepted His
offer of salvation—a friend who is always loyal; one who lifts you
when you stumble. He has shown you the greatest love one friend
can have for another—love that led Him to sacrifice His life for
you (John 15:13).   —JENNIFER BENSON SCHULDT

Jesus is your most trusted Friend.

FEARFUL TEARS

READ: Revelation 5:1–12

*I wept and wept because no one was found who was worthy
to open the scroll or look inside.* REVELATION 5:4

JOHN, THE GREAT APOSTLE and the one Jesus loved, was reduced
to tears.

In a vision he received while imprisoned (Revelation 5:1–12), he
found himself in God's throne room as future events unfolded. In
heaven, John saw God hold up a sealed scroll. He wept because as
he observed the glories of God's presence, he saw no one who could
open the scroll—no one with the power to reveal God's final revelation and to complete the concluding chapter of history's drama.

As an apostle, John had observed the power of sin in the world.
He had witnessed Jesus's life and death on earth to conquer sin. He
had seen Him ascend into heaven. But now he was fearful when
he saw that no one was worthy to open the scroll and vanquish sin
forever (v. 4).

Imagine the drama of what happened next. An elder approached
John and said, "Do not weep!" And he pointed him toward Someone he knew: "See, the Lion of the tribe of Judah" (v. 5). John
looked, and he saw Jesus—the only One with the power to take
the scroll, open the seals, and complete the story. Soon John's tears
were dry, and millions of angels were proclaiming, "Worthy is the
Lamb!" (v. 12)

Are you crying? Behold, John's friend—Jesus. He is worthy.
Turn things over to Him.   —DAVE BRANON

*The Lamb who died to save us is the
Shepherd who lives to lead us.*

IT'S BEAUTIFUL

READ: Mark 14:3–9

"Leave her alone," said Jesus. "Why are you bothering her?
She has done a beautiful thing to me." MARK 14:6

AFTER BEING AWAY ON business, Terry wanted to pick up some small gifts for his children. The clerk at the airport gift shop recommended a number of costly items. "I don't have that much money with me," he said. "I need something less expensive." The clerk tried to make him feel that he was being cheap. But Terry knew his children would be happy with whatever he would give them, because it would come from a heart of love. And he was right—they loved the gifts he bought.

During Jesus's last visit to the town of Bethany, Mary wanted to show her love for Him (Mark 14:3–9). So she brought "an alabaster flask of very expensive perfume, made of pure nard" and anointed Him (v. 3). The disciples asked angrily, "Why this waste?" (Matthew 26:8). Jesus told them to stop troubling her, for "she has done a beautiful thing to me" (Mark 14:6). Jesus delighted in her gift, for it came from a heart of love. Even anointing Him for burial was beautiful!

What would you like to give to Jesus to show your love? Your time, talent, treasure? It doesn't matter if it's costly or inexpensive, whether others understand or criticize. Whatever is given from a heart of love is beautiful to Him.   —ANNE CETAS

A healthy heart beats with love for Jesus.

ONE OF US

READ: Hebrews 2:9–18

Because he himself suffered when he was tempted, he is able to help those who are being tempted. HEBREWS 2:18

AT THE MEMORIAL SERVICE for Charles Schulz (1922–2000), creator of the beloved *Peanuts* comic strip, his friend and fellow cartoonist Cathy Guisewite spoke of his humanity and compassion. "He gave everyone in the world characters who knew exactly how all of us felt, who made us feel we were never alone. And then he gave the cartoonist himself, and he made us feel that we were never alone. . . . He encouraged us. He commiserated with us. He made us feel he was exactly like us."

When we feel that no one understands or can help us, we are reminded that Jesus gave us himself, and He knows exactly who we are and what we are facing today.

Hebrews 2:9–18 presents the remarkable truth that Jesus fully shared our humanity during His life on earth (v. 14). He "taste[d] death for everyone" (v. 9), broke the power of Satan (v. 14), and freed "those who all their lives were held in slavery by their fear of death" (v. 15). Jesus was made like us, "fully human in every way, in order that he might become a merciful and faithful high priest in service to God" (v. 17).

Thank you, Lord, for sharing our humanity so that we might know your help today and live in your presence forever.

—DAVID McCASLAND

No one understands like Jesus.

FORSAKEN FOR OUR SAKE

READ: Matthew 26:36–46

*Keep your lives free from the love of money and be content
with what you have, because God has said, "Never will I
leave you; never will I forsake you."* HEBREWS 13:5

DOES HAVING A FRIEND nearby make pain more bearable? Researchers at the University of Virginia conducted a fascinating study to answer that question. They wanted to see how the brain reacted to the prospect of pain and whether it behaved differently if a person faced the threat of pain alone, holding a stranger's hand, or holding the hand of a close friend.

Researchers ran the test on dozens of pairs and found consistent results. When a person was alone or holding a stranger's hand while anticipating a shock, the regions of the brain that process danger lit up. But when holding the hand of a trusted person, the brain relaxed. The comfort of a friend's presence made the pain seem more bearable.

Jesus needed comfort as He prayed in the garden of Gethsemane. He knew what He was about to face: betrayal, arrest, and death. He asked His closest friends to stay and pray with Him, telling them that His soul was "overwhelmed with sorrow" (Matthew 26:38). But Peter, James, and John kept falling asleep.

Jesus faced the agony of the garden without the comfort of a hand to hold. But because He bore that pain, we can be confident that God will never leave or forsake us (Hebrews 13:5). Jesus suffered so that we will never have to experience separation from the love of God (Romans 8:39). His companionship makes anything we endure more bearable.   —AMY PETERSON

Because of God's love, we are never truly alone.

AT HOME WITH JESUS

READ: John 14:1–4

*"If I go and prepare a place for you, I will
come back and take you to be with me that
you also may be where I am."* JOHN 14:3

"THERE'S NO PLACE LIKE HOME." This phrase reflects a deeply rooted yearning within us to have a place to rest and to belong. Jesus addressed this desire for rootedness when, after He and His friends had their last supper together, He spoke about His impending death and resurrection. He promised that although He would go away, He would come back for them. And He would prepare a room for them—a dwelling place. A home.

He made this place for them—and us—through fulfilling the requirements of God's law when He died on the cross as the sinless man. He assured His disciples that if He went to the trouble of creating this home, that of course He would come back for them and not leave them alone. They didn't need to fear or be worried about their lives, whether on earth or in heaven.

We can take comfort and assurance from Jesus's words, for we believe and trust that He makes a home for us; that He makes His home within us (see John 14:23); and that He has gone ahead of us to prepare our heavenly home. Whatever sort of physical place we live in, we belong with Jesus, upheld by His love and surrounded in His peace. With Him, there's no place like home.

—AMY BOUCHER PYE

Jesus prepares a place for us to live forever.

EXPECT AND EXTEND MERCY

READ: Luke 18:9–14

*"But the tax collector stood at a distance. He would not
even look up to heaven, but beat his breast and said,
'God, have mercy on me, a sinner.'"* LUKE 18:13

WHEN I COMPLAINED THAT a friend's choices were leading her deeper into sin and how her actions affected me, the woman I was telling this to—a woman I prayed with weekly—placed her hand over mine. "Let's pray for all of us."

I frowned. "All of us?"

"Yes," she said. "Aren't you the one who always says Jesus sets our standard of holiness, so we shouldn't compare our sins to the sins of others?"

"That truth hurts a little," I said, "but you're right. My judgmental attitude and spiritual pride are no better or worse than her sins."

"And by talking about your friend, we're gossiping. So—"

"We're sinning." I lowered my head. "Please, pray for us."

In Luke 18, Jesus shared a parable about two men approaching the temple to pray in very different ways (vv. 9–14). Like the Pharisee, we can become trapped in a circle of comparing ourselves to other people. We can boast about ourselves (vv. 11–12) and live as though we have the right to judge others.

But when we look to Jesus as our example of holy living, our desperate need for God's grace is magnified (v. 13). As we experience the Lord's loving compassion and forgiveness personally, we'll be forever changed and empowered to expect and extend mercy, not condemnation, to others. —XOCHITL DIXON

*When we realize the depth of our need for mercy,
we can more readily offer mercy to others.*

TAKE A NUMBER

READ: John 14:15–27

*"Peace I leave with you; my peace I give you. I do not
give to you as the world gives. Do not let your hearts
be troubled and do not be afraid."* JOHN 14:27

WE HAVE AN ANCIENT cherry tree in our backyard that looked like it
was dying, so I called in an arborist. He declared that it was "unduly
stressed" and needed immediate attention. "Take a number," my
wife, Carolyn, muttered to the tree as she walked away. It had been
one of those weeks.

Indeed, we all have anxious weeks—filled with worries over the
direction our culture is drifting or concerns for our children, our
marriages, our businesses, our finances, our personal health. Jesus
has assured us that despite disturbing circumstances we can be at
peace. He said, "My peace I give you" (John 14:27).

Jesus's days were filled with distress and disorder: He was belea-
guered by His enemies and misunderstood by family and friends.
He often had no place to lay His head. Yet there was no trace of
anxiety or fretfulness in His manner. He possessed an inner calm,
a quiet tranquility. This is the peace He has given us—freedom
from anxiety concerning the past, present, and future. The peace
He exhibited: His peace.

In any circumstance, we can turn to Jesus in prayer. There in His
presence we can make our worries and fears known to Him. Then,
Paul assures us, the peace of God will come to "guard [our] hearts
and [our] minds in Christ Jesus" (Philippians 4:7). Even if we've had
"one of those weeks," we can have His peace.   —DAVID ROPER

In the midst of troubles, peace can be found in Jesus.

THE HONOR OF FOLLOWING

Read: Mark 1:14–20

"Come, follow me," Jesus said, "and I will send
you out to fish for people." Mark 1:17

WHILE VISITING JERUSALEM, A friend of mine saw an old rabbi walking past the Wailing Wall. The interesting thing about the aged rabbi was the five young men walking behind him. They too were walking bent over, limping—just like their rabbi. An Orthodox Jew watching them would know exactly why they were imitating their teacher. They were "followers."

Throughout the history of Judaism, one of the most honored positions for a Jewish man was the privilege of becoming a "follower" of the local rabbi. Followers sat at the rabbi's feet as he taught. They would study his words and watch how he acted and reacted to life and others. A follower would count it the highest honor to serve his rabbi in even the most menial tasks. And because they admired their rabbi, they were determined to become like him.

When Jesus called His disciples to follow Him (Mark 1:17), it was an invitation to be changed by Him, to become like Him, and to share His passion for those who need a Savior. The high honor of being His follower should show in our lives as well. We too have been called to catch the attention of the watching world as we talk, think, and act just like Jesus—the rabbi, the teacher of our souls.

—JOE STOWELL

Follow Jesus and let the world know He is your rabbi.

THE SLOW WALK

READ: Job 16:1–5

"I will ask the Father, and he will give you another advocate to help you and be with you forever." JOHN 14:16

CALEB WAS SICK. Really sick! Diagnosed with a nervous system disease, the five-year-old suffered from temporary paralysis. His anxious parents prayed. And waited. Slowly, Caleb began to recover. Months later, when doctors cleared him to attend school, all Caleb could manage was a slow, unsteady walk.

One day his dad visited him at school. He watched his son haltingly descend the steps to the playground. And then he saw Caleb's young friend Tyler come alongside him. For the entire recess, as the other kids raced and romped and played, Tyler slowly walked the playground with his frail friend.

Job must have ached for a friend like Tyler. Instead, he had three friends who were certain he was guilty. "Who, being innocent, has ever perished?" asked Eliphaz (Job 4:7). Such accusations prompted Job to bitterly declare, "Miserable comforters, all of you!" (16:2).

How unlike Jesus. On the eve of His crucifixion, He took time to comfort His disciples. He promised them the Holy Spirit, who would be with them forever (John 14:16), and assured them, "I will not leave you as orphans; I will come to you" (v. 18). Then, just before He returned to His Father, He said, "I am with you always, to the very end of the age" (Matthew 28:20).

The One who died for us also walks with us, step by painstaking step. —TIM GUSTAFSON

Sometimes the best way to be like Jesus is to sit quietly with a hurting friend.

WALKING ON WATER

READ: Mark 6:45–56

Immediately, he spoke to them and said: "Take courage! It is I. Don't be afraid." MARK 6:50

DURING AN ESPECIALLY COLD winter, I ventured out to Lake Michigan, the fifth largest lake in the world, to see it frozen over. Bundled up on the beach where I usually enjoy soaking up the sun, the view was breathtaking. The water was actually frozen in waves creating an icy masterpiece.

Because the water was frozen solid next to the shore, I had the opportunity to "walk on water." Even with the knowledge that the ice was thick enough to support me, I took the first few steps tentatively. I was fearful the ice wouldn't continue to hold me. As I cautiously explored this unfamiliar terrain, I couldn't help but think of Jesus calling Peter out of the boat onto the Sea of Galilee.

When the disciples saw Jesus walking on the water, their response was also fear. But Jesus responded, "Take courage! It is I. Don't be afraid" (Mark 6:50). Peter was able to overcome his fear and step out onto the water because he knew Jesus was present. When his courageous steps faltered because of the wind and waves, Peter cried out to Jesus. Jesus was still there, near enough to simply reach out His hand to rescue him.

If you are facing a situation today where Jesus is calling you to do something that may seem as impossible as walking on water, take courage. The one who calls you will be present with you.

—LISA SAMRA

When we call out to God, He hears.

A FIRM FOUNDATION

READ: Deuteronomy 6:1–9

These commandments that I give you today are to be on your hearts. Impress them on your children. Talk about them when you sit at home and when you walk along the road, when you lie down and when you get up. DEUTERONOMY 6:6–7

BEFORE SHE WAS TWO years old, my granddaughter Katie did something that would make any grandpa proud: She began to recognize cars by make and year. This all started when she and her daddy began spending time together playing with his old collection of toy cars. Daddy would say, "Katie, get the 1957 Chevy," and she would pick it out of the hundreds of tiny cars. And once, while he was reading a Curious George book to her, she climbed down from his lap and ran to get a miniature Rolls Royce—an exact replica of the car pictured in the book.

If a two-year-old child can make such connections, doesn't that show the importance of teaching children the right things early on? We can do this by using what I call the FIRM principle: Familiarity, Interest, Recognition, and Modeling. This follows Moses's pattern in Deuteronomy 6 of taking every opportunity to teach biblical truths so children become familiar with them and make them a part of their lives. Using their interests as teaching opportunities, we repeat Bible stories so they become recognizable, while modeling a godly life before them.

Let's give the children in our lives a FIRM foundation by teaching them about God's love, Christ's salvation, and the importance of godly living. —DAVE BRANON

Build your children's lives on the firm foundation of the Word.

FROM GRIEF TO JOY

READ: John 16:16–22

*"Very truly I tell you, you will weep and
mourn while the world rejoices. You will grieve,
but your grief will turn to joy."* JOHN 16:20

KELLY'S PREGNANCY BROUGHT COMPLICATIONS, and doctors were concerned. During her long labor, they decided to whisk her away for a Cesarean section. But despite the ordeal, Kelly quickly forgot her pain when she held her newborn son. Joy had replaced anguish.

Scripture affirms this truth: "A woman giving birth to a child has pain because her time has come; but when her baby is born she forgets the anguish because of her joy that a child is born into the world" (John 16:21). Jesus used this illustration with His disciples to emphasize that though they would grieve because He would be leaving soon, that grief would turn to joy when they saw Him again (vv. 20–22).

Jesus was referring to His death and resurrection—and what followed. After His resurrection, to the disciples' joy, Jesus spent another forty days walking with and teaching them before ascending and leaving them once again (Acts 1:3). Yet Jesus did not leave them grief-stricken. The Holy Spirit would fill them with joy (John 16:7–15; Acts 13:52).

Though we have never seen Jesus face-to-face, as believers we have the assurance that one day we will. On that day, the anguish we face in this earth will be forgotten. But until then, the Lord has not left us without joy—He has given us His Spirit (Romans 15:13; 1 Peter 1:8–9). —ALYSON KIEDA

One day our sorrow will be turned to joy!

HE IS ENOUGH

READ: Matthew 14:22–33

But Jesus immediately said to them: "Take courage!
It is I. Don't be afraid." MATTHEW 14:27

SOMETIMES WE ARE OVERWHELMED by life. The crushing waves of disappointment, endless debt, debilitating illness, or trouble with people can cause hopelessness, depression, or despair. It happened to Jesus's disciples. And it has happened to me.

Three statements by the Lord beginning with the words "It is . . ." offer us comfort, reassurance, and hope that Jesus is enough. The first is in Matthew 4 and is repeated three times: "It is written" (vv. 4, 7, 10). In responding to the three temptations of Satan, Jesus gave us proof enough that the Word of God is true and that it overcomes the most powerful forms of temptation and pressure.

The second statement, "It is I" (Matthew 14:27), was spoken when Jesus told His terrified disciples that He himself was presence enough to stop the howling storm and calm the raging seas.

Jesus spoke the third "It is" from the cross: "It is finished!" (John 19:30). He assured us that His death was provision enough to pay the debt for our sins and set us free.

Whatever our circumstances, Jesus is present with His love, compassion, and grace. He is proof, presence, and provision enough to carry us safely through. —DAVID EGNER

God's love does not keep us from trials;
it helps us get through them.

HE WALKED IN OUR SHOES

READ: Hebrews 2:10–18

Because he himself suffered when he was tempted, he is able to help those who are being tempted. HEBREWS 2:18

To HELP HIS STAFF of young architects understand the needs of those for whom they design housing, David Dillard sends them on "sleepovers." They put on pajamas and spend twenty-four hours in a senior living center in the same conditions as people in their eighties and nineties. They wear earplugs to simulate hearing loss, tape their fingers together to limit manual dexterity, and exchange eyeglasses to replicate vision problems. Dillard says, "The biggest benefit is [that] when I send twenty-seven-year-olds out, they come back with a heart ten times as big. They meet people and understand their plights" (Rodney Brooks, *USA Today*).

Jesus lived on this earth for thirty-three years and shared in our humanity. He was made like us, "fully human in every way" (Hebrews 2:17), so He knows what it's like to live in a human body on this earth. He understands the struggles we face, so He comes alongside us with understanding and encouragement.

"Because [Jesus] himself suffered when he was tempted, he is able to help those who are being tempted" (v. 18). The Lord could have avoided the cross. Instead, He obeyed His Father. Through His death, He broke the power of Satan and freed us from our fear of death (vv. 14–15).

In every temptation, Jesus walks beside us to give us courage, strength, and hope along the way.   —DAVID MCCASLAND

Jesus understands.

UNFIT

READ: Mark 2:13–17

*On hearing this, Jesus said to them, "It is not the
healthy who need a doctor, but the sick. I have not come
to call the righteous, but sinners."* MARK 2:17

HEALTH CLUBS OFFER MANY different programs for those who want
to lose weight and stay healthy. One fitness center caters only to
those who want to lose at least fifty pounds and develop a healthy
lifestyle. One member says that she quit her previous fitness club
because she felt the slim and fit people were staring at her and
judging her out-of-shape body. She now works out five days a week
and is achieving healthy weight loss in a positive and welcoming
environment.

Two thousand years ago, Jesus came to call the spiritually unfit
to follow Him. Levi was one such person. Jesus saw him sitting in
his tax collector's booth and said, "Follow me" (Mark 2:14). His
words captured Levi's heart, and he followed Jesus. Tax collectors
were often greedy and dishonest in their dealings and were considered religiously unclean. When the religious leaders saw Jesus
having dinner at Levi's house with other tax collectors, they asked,
"Why does he eat with tax collectors and sinners?" (2:16). Jesus
replied, "I have not come to call the righteous, but sinners" (2:17).

Jesus came to save sinners, which includes all of us. He loves us,
welcomes us into His presence, and calls us to follow Him. As we
walk with Him, we grow more and more spiritually fit.

—MARVIN WILLIAMS

Jesus's arms of welcome are always open.

KEEP YOUR EYES ON HIM

READ: Hebrews 12:1–3

*For the joy set before him he endured the cross,
scorning its shame, and sat down at the right
hand of the throne of God.* HEBREWS 12:2

A GREAT ARTIST KEPT a number of beautiful gems on his easel. The sparkling sapphires, emeralds, and rubies always caught the eye of his patrons. He kept the jewels there to keep the brilliance of their colors in mind as he painted. He was afraid his paints might fade, and he would forget the brilliance of the original colors. He retained his eyesight keen and perceptive by constantly referring to the original colors of the jewels, for they never fade.

Similarly, in matters of the spirit, we are in danger of toning down our spiritual perception by looking at earthly things—things that fade. How important it is, therefore, to keep our eyes on Jesus. The brilliance of the crucified Christ will heighten our spiritual insight and stimulate our heart and life. This will help us to "live as Jesus did" (1 John 2:6). Let us never allow the eyes of our soul to grow dim.

When we look at human frailty and earthly trial, it is so easy to lose our confidence, but if we look to Jesus our faith will be strengthened. Let's keep our eyes on Jesus. If we do, the brightness of our life in Him will never fade. —HENRY BOSCH

*Look at self and circumstances, and you will have
doubts and discouragement; look to Jesus and
you will be safe, satisfied, and blessed!*

LIGHT FOR EACH STEP

READ: Proverbs 6:16–23

Your word is a lamp for my feet,
a light on my path. PSALM 119:105

THOSE OF US WHO have received the Lord Jesus as Savior know where we are going and are assured of a safe arrival. A dark shroud of the unknown, however, obscures our pathway. It is this mystery of the immediate future, along with the possibility of lurking dangers and our own errors, that can upset us and rob us of the peace our Lord intended for us to enjoy.

But if we refuse to worry about tomorrow and instead trust Jesus for help today, we find grace and guidance for each step of the way.

Someone has commented, "He who carries a lantern on a dark road at night sees only one step ahead. When he takes that one, the lamp moves forward and another is made plain. He finally reaches his destination in safety without once walking in darkness. All the way is lighted, but only a single step at a time."

The writer of Proverbs tells us, "In all your ways submit to him, and he will make your paths straight" (Proverbs 3:6). Even as a lantern illuminates each new step on the dark road at night, so the lamp of God's Word is a light upon your pathway.

It isn't necessary for us to see beyond what the Lord reveals. If we simply follow as He leads, we'll find enough light for each step of the way!   —RICHARD DEHAAN

God will never lead you where
His Word will not light you!

THE GREATEST THING

READ: Luke 10:38–42

*She had a sister called Mary, who sat at the Lord's
feet listening to what he said.* LUKE 10:39

DURING A CHURCH SERVICE I spotted an infant several rows ahead. As the baby peeked over his father's shoulder, his eyes were wide with wonder as he looked at the members of the congregation. He grinned at some people, drooled, and chewed his chunky fingers, but never quite found his thumb. The pastor's words grew distant as my eyes kept sliding back to that sweet baby.

Distractions come in all shapes and sizes. For Martha, distraction took the form of cooking and cleaning—trying to serve Christ instead of listening to Him and talking with Him. Mary refused to be sidetracked. "Mary . . . sat at the Lord's feet listening to what he said" (Luke 10:39). When Martha grumbled because Mary wasn't helping her, Jesus said, "Mary has chosen what is better, and it will not be taken away from her" (v. 42).

Jesus's words remind us that our relationship with Him is more important than any of the good things that might temporarily capture our attention. It has been said that good things are the enemies of great things. For followers of Jesus, the greatest thing in this life is to know Him and to walk with Him.

—JENNIFER BENSON SCHULDT

*Teach me, Lord, to get to know you, for that's when
I'll learn to love you more than anything.*

RES AND PRIORITIES

READ: John 11:1–7

*gdom and his righteousness, and all these
iven to you as well.* MATTHEW 6:33

ᴠɪsɪᴛɪɴɢ ᴀ ғʀɪᴇɴᴅ's office, I noticed that the standard In-Out baskets had been replaced by a five-tiered set of trays labeled Critical, Urgent, Important, Back-burner, and Long-term. Those trays reminded me that unless I have God's perspective each day, pressures will always determine my priorities.

John 11:1–7 reminds us of how radically different God's sense of urgency is from our own. Notice the chain of events: Lazarus was sick. His two sisters, Mary and Martha, sent word of his illness to Jesus. Then we see two seemingly incompatible statements: "Jesus loved Martha and her sister and Lazarus. So when he heard that Lazarus was sick, he stayed where he was two more days" (vv. 5–6).

A dying man—a delaying Lord. Jesus's priorities were determined not by pressure but by perfect communion with His heavenly Father.

"But I'm not Jesus," we are quick to say. "I drive the freeways and don't have enough hours in the day." But Christ calls us to consult Him in every urgency and emergency, to listen for His wise direction, and to make time for the truly important things of life.

What priorities need our attention today?

—DAVID MCCASLAND

Focusing on Christ puts everything else in perspective.

WALK THE WALK

READ: 1 Timothy 4:6–16

Don't let anyone look down on you because you are young,
but set an example for the believers in speech, in conduct,
in love, in faith and in purity. 1 TIMOTHY 4:12

THE PREACHER WAS SPEAKING tongue-in-cheek when he complained, "My wife is absolutely unreasonable. She actually expects me to live everything I preach!" It's so much easier to tell someone what is right than to practice it personally.

When my son and I play golf together, I can tell him exactly how to play the hole and hit the shots. But my own ability to hit those shots is sadly limited. I suppose this is what is meant when we refer to athletes who "talk the talk, but don't walk the walk." Anyone can talk a good game, but actually performing well is far more difficult.

This is particularly true in the challenge of following Jesus Christ. It is not enough for us to talk about faith; we must live out our faith. Perhaps that is why Paul, after giving instructions to his young protégé Timothy about how to preach, included this reminder: "Don't let anyone look down on you because you are young, but set an example for the believers in speech, in conduct, in love, in spirit, in faith and in purity. . . . Be diligent in these matters; give yourself wholly to them" (1 Timothy 4:12, 15).

As Christ's followers, we do not have the luxury of just talking a good game—we must live lives of exemplary faith in Jesus Christ. We must walk the walk.   —BILL CROWDER

We please God when our walk matches our talk.

CLOSE ON HIS HEELS

READ: Matthew 4:18–25

*"Come, follow me," Jesus said, "and I will send
you out to fish for people."* MATTHEW 4:19

STAN AND JENNIFER WERE speaking at a mission conference in
Marion, North Carolina, after their first term of service in overseas
ministry.

Jennifer told of a Bible study she had held with one woman. The
two were discussing Matthew 4:19, and the woman told Jennifer
about a word in her native language, which means *follow*. She said,
"It is the word for following closely, not at a distance."

To illustrate, Jennifer held up slippers used by the native women,
showing one far behind the other. Then she moved one slipper right
up against the back of the other one, and she said that the word
means "to follow right on one's heels." It suggests that we are to
follow Jesus as closely as possible.

Later, when Jennifer was reading over the journal she had been
keeping, she was surprised to see that she had often questioned,
"Is Jesus enough?" She had been working her way through culture
shock, loneliness, illness, and childlessness. At times she had felt
far from Christ. But when through prayer and faith she had drawn
as close to Him as she could, walking "right on His heels," He had
calmed her soul, restored her strength, and given her peace.

Are you feeling far from the Lord—empty, weak, and afraid?
It's time to follow close on His heels.   —DAVID EGNER

*The closer we walk with God,
the clearer we see His guidance.*

A COMPANION ON THE ROAD

READ: John 1:35-43

Finding Philip, [Jesus] said to him, "Follow me." JOHN 1:43

I LOVE TO WALK Idaho's paths and trails and enjoy its grandeur and picturesque beauty. I'm often reminded that these treks are symbolic of our spiritual journey, for the Christian life is simply walking—with Jesus alongside as our companion and guide. He walked through the land of Israel from one end to the other, gathering disciples, saying to them, "Follow me" (John 1:43).

The journey is not always easy. Sometimes giving up seems easier than going on, but when things get difficult, we can rest a while and renew our strength. In *Pilgrim's Progress*, John Bunyan describes the arbor on Hill Difficulty where Christian caught his breath before continuing the climb. His scroll provided comfort, reminding him of the Lord's continual presence and sustaining power. He got a second wind so he could walk a few more miles.

Only God knows where the path will take us, but we have our Lord's assurance, "I am with you always" (Matthew 28:20). This is not a metaphor or other figure of speech. He is real company. There is not one hour without His presence, not one mile without His companionship. Knowing He's with us makes the journey lighter.

—DAVID ROPER

As you travel life's weary road,
let Jesus lift your heavy load.

WORLD'S FASTEST WALKERS

READ: Luke 10:38–42

*She had a sister called Mary, who sat at the Lord's
feet listening to what he said.* LUKE 10:39

ACCORDING TO A STUDY measuring the pace of life of cities in thirty-two countries, people in the biggest hurry live in my home city of Singapore. We walk sixty feet in 10.55 seconds, compared to 12 seconds for New Yorkers and 31.6 seconds for those living in the African city of Blantyre, Malawi.

But regardless of where you live, the study shows that walking speeds have increased by an average of ten percent in the past twenty years. And if walking speed is any indicator for the pace of life, we are certainly much busier than before.

Are you caught up in the frenzy of a busy life? Pause and consider Jesus's words to Martha: "You are worried and upset about many things, but few things are needed—or indeed only one. Mary has chosen what is better, and it will not be taken away from her" (Luke 10:41–42).

Notice Jesus's gentle words. He didn't rebuke Martha for wanting to be a good host but rather reminded her about her priorities. Martha had allowed the necessary to get out of proportion. And, in the process, she was so busy doing good that she didn't take time to sit at Jesus's feet.

In our drive to be productive for the Lord, let's remember the one thing worth being concerned about—enjoying time with our Savior.   —POH FAN CHIA

Jesus longs for our fellowship even more than we long for His.

WALKING WITH THE LORD

READ: Psalm 37:23–32

*The LORD makes firm the steps of the one
who delights in him.* PSALM 37:23

A SMALL PAMPHLET I received from a friend was titled *An Attempt to Share the Story of 86 Years of Relationship with the Lord.* In it, Al Ackenheil noted key people and events in his journey of faith over nearly nine decades. What seemed to be ordinary choices at the time—memorizing Bible verses, meeting for prayer with others, telling his neighbors about Jesus—became turning points that changed the direction of his life. It was fascinating to read how God's hand guided and encouraged Al.

The psalmist wrote, "The LORD makes firm the steps of the one who delights in him" (Psalm 37:23). The passage continues with a beautiful description of God's faithful care for everyone who wants to walk with Him. "The law of his God is in his heart; None of his steps shall slide" (v. 31 NKJV).

Each of us could create a record of God's leading and faithfulness, reflecting on God's guidance—the people, places, and experiences that are landmarks on our pathway of faith. Every remembrance of the Lord's goodness encourages us to keep walking with Him and to thank someone who influenced us for good.

The Lord guides and guards all who walk with Him.

—DAVID MCCASLAND

You are headed in the right direction when you walk with God.

SUNSET HOURS

READ: Philippians 3:2–4:1

They will still bear fruit in old age, they will stay fresh and green. PSALM 92:14

IF YOU ARE STILL young and energetic, you may find it difficult to sympathize with the feelings that afflict many older people. But those who have long ago passed the midpoint on life's journey and have begun to descend the westering slope can appreciate what David said: "I was young and now I am old" (Psalm 37:25). And because aging often brings with it pain and loss, there may be those who vainly wish that their summertime days would never end.

But listen to Christian essayist and theologian F. W. Boreham: "Someday my life's little day will soften down to eventide. My sunset hours will come. . . . And then, I know there will arise, out of the dusk, a dawning fairer than any dawn that has yet broken upon me. Out of the last tints of sunset there shall rise a day such as I shall never have known before; a day that shall restore to me all that the other days have taken from me, a day that shall never fade into twilight."

So no matter where we are on the heavenward pilgrimage, if we are walking with Jesus we can rejoice. And since we know that our faithful Father will abide with us till our journey on earth is over, we can actually be thankful for the lengthening shadows and the setting sun.　　　　　　　　　　　　　　　　—VERNON GROUNDS

To live is Christ; to die is gain. —*Paul the apostle*

HOW TO WALK

READ: Ephesians 3:14–4:3

*I pray that out of his glorious riches he may
strengthen you with power through his Spirit
in your inner being.* EPHESIANS 3:16

DANA AND RICH WENT out for an afternoon bike ride expecting to come home refreshed. Instead, their lives were changed forever. As Rich rode down a hill, he lost control of his bike and crashed. His body was mangled, and he barely made it to the hospital alive.

Dana faithfully kept vigil by her husband's side. He couldn't feed himself, and he couldn't walk. One day, as the two of them sat under a shade tree outside the hospital, Rich turned to his wife and said, "Dana, I don't know if I'll ever walk again, but I'm learning to walk closer to Jesus, and that's what I really want." Instead of shaking his fist at God, Rich reached out and grabbed His hand. Sometimes in the midst of our trials, we need to think about someone like Rich to help us adjust our perspective—to remind us of the remarkable relationship we have with God through Jesus Christ. This is the relationship we need most when the going gets the toughest.

We are not equipped to handle all the problems we face, but God is. That's why He told us to give them all to Him—to "cast your cares on the LORD" (Psalm 55:22). As Rich found out, walking with Jesus doesn't depend on our legs. It depends on our heart.

—DAVE BRANON

*We can walk through the darkest trials when
we walk with God in the light.*

GIVING OTHERS A PUSH

READ: Acts 11:19–26

When he arrived and saw what the grace of God had done, he was glad and encouraged them all to remain true to the Lord with all their hearts. ACTS 11:23

WHEN JEAN WAS A teenager, she often walked through a park where she saw mothers sitting on benches talking. Their toddlers sat on the swings, wanting someone to push them. "I gave them a push," says Jean. "And you know what happens when you push a kid on a swing? Pretty soon he's pumping, doing it himself. That's what my role in life is—I'm there to give others a push."

Encouraging others along in life—that's a worthy purpose. Joses, a godly man mentioned in the book of Acts, had that gift as well. In the days of the early church, he sold some land and gave the money to the church to use for the less fortunate (4:36–37). He also traveled with Paul on missionary journeys and preached the gospel (11:22–26; 13:1–4). You may know Joses as "Barnabas," which is the name the apostles gave to the "Son of Encouragement." When the Jerusalem church heard that people in Antioch were coming to know Jesus as Savior, they sent Barnabas because "he was a good man, full of the Holy Spirit and faith" (11:24). He "encouraged them all to remain true to the Lord with all their hearts" (v. 23).

We too can give others a "push" of encouragement in their walk with the Lord. —ANNE CETAS

A little spark of encouragement can ignite great endeavors.

INTEGRITY 101

READ: Psalm 101

I will be careful to lead a blameless life—when will you come to me? I will conduct the affairs of my house with a blameless heart. PSALM 101:2

OFFICIALS IN PHILADELPHIA WERE astonished to receive a letter and payment from a motorist who had been given a speeding ticket in 1954. John Gedge, an English tourist, had been visiting the City of Brotherly Love when he was cited for speeding. The penalty was $15, but Gedge forgot about the ticket for more than fifty years until he discovered it in an old coat. "I thought, I've got to pay it," said Gedge who was eighty-four and living in a nursing home in East Sussex when he paid off the ticket fifty-two years late. "Englishmen pay their debts. My conscience is clear."

This story reminded me of the psalmist David's commitment to integrity. Although he made some terrible choices in his life, he declared his resolve to live blamelessly, according to Psalm 101. His integrity would begin in the privacy of his own house (v. 2) and extend to his choice of colleagues and friends (vv. 6–7). In sharp contrast to the corrupt lives of most kings of the ancient Near East, David's integrity led him to respect the life of his sworn enemy, King Saul (1 Samuel 24:4–6; 26:8–9).

As followers of Jesus, we are called to walk in integrity and to maintain a clear conscience. When we honor our commitments to God and to others, we will walk in fellowship with God. Our integrity will guide us (Proverbs 11:3) and help us walk securely (10:9).

—MARVIN WILLIAMS

There is no better test of a man's integrity than his behavior when he is wrong.

DORCAS: A WORTHY EXAMPLE

READ: Acts 9:36–43

*In Joppa there was a disciple named Tabitha
(in Greek her name is Dorcas); she was always
doing good and helping the poor.* ACTS 9:36

THE UNTIMELY DEATH OF Dorcas brought much sorrow to those
to whom she had faithfully served. When the apostle Peter arrived,
many widows "stood around him, crying and showing him the robes
and other clothing that Dorcas had made" (Acts 9:39). Through
God's power, Peter commanded her to arise from the dead, and he
presented her alive—to the joy of all. Her faithful devotion to the
Lord in commonplace things and her loving compassion for others
have made her a model we should emulate.

Dorcas's life of humble service reminds me of these thoughts
from an old poem: "I asked the Lord to let me do some mighty work
for Him; to fight amidst His battle hosts, then sung the victor's
hymn. I longed my ardent love to show but Jesus would not have
it so. He placed me in a quiet home, whose life was calm and still,
and gave me little things to do, my daily round to fill."

That is the way it is with most of us. We have not been given
mighty deeds and fame as a way of advancing the gospel. Instead,
it is the small thing, done faithfully, that accomplishes the tasks
God has called us to do.

May the worthy example of Dorcas spur us on to a Christian
walk that is characterized by a host of loving deeds that bring blessing to others and reflect credit on our Savior!   —HENRY BOSCH

---

*Making a living is measured by what we
get—making a life by what we give!*

"JESUS IS WITH ME"

READ: Acts 7:54–60

"Whoever has my commands and keeps them is the one who loves me. The one who loves me will be loved by my Father, and I too will love them and show myself to them." JOHN 14:21

ONE NIGHT DURING WORLD War II, Dr. Edward H. Friedman was on duty in an overseas army hospital. An American soldier by the name of Rothermel had just been brought in from the battlefield. His right leg was torn, his arms were twisted, and part of his face was gone. The pain was excruciating. As Friedman prepared for surgery, the young man said, "Don't worry, Doc, Jesus is with me!" Those words kept ringing through the surgeon's mind as he worked over that mangled body.

Later, the exhausted doctor lay on his bed and asked himself, "Is Rothermel's Jesus my Jesus?" After reading the New Testament, he accepted Christ as his Savior. After the war, Friedman informed his parents about his faith. They had told him earlier that if he ever made that decision, as far as they were concerned, he was dead, and they stuck to their objection. The words "Jesus is with me" sustained him as he walked that lonely pathway of being disowned.

In John 14:21, Jesus tells us that living in obedience to His commands is the secret of experiencing His marvelous presence. When we do His will, He assures us of His love and promises to manifest himself to us. Then whatever our situation, we will be able to say, "Jesus is with me!" —DENNIS DEHAAN

It is not the sense of Christ's presence but the fact of His presence that is our strength.

UNSEEN

READ: 1 Peter 1:3–8

Though you have not seen him, you love him; and even though you do not see him now, you believe in him and are filled with an inexpressible and glorious joy. 1 PETER 1:8

WE CAN TAKE GREAT comfort in what Jesus told Thomas, "Because you have seen me, you have believed; blessed are those who have not seen and yet have believed" (John 20:29). It's a joy to have faith in an unseen Savior and know that He lives within us by the Holy Spirit! That's even better than seeing Him perform miracles during His earthly ministry!

Nineteenth-century Scottish evangelist Henry Drummond told of a young lady whose grace and charm marked her as a beautiful person. She usually wore a dainty locket about her neck. Friends had repeatedly asked to see what was inside, but she never opened it for anyone. One day when she became quite ill, she gave permission to a dear friend to look in the locket. It contained a small slip of paper that bore these words, evidently written by her own hand, "Whom having not seen, I love." Someone commenting on this incident said, "Undoubtedly that's the secret of her poise and loveliness!" Having given her heart to the Lord Jesus, she made Him the primary object of her devotion.

Most of us know Christians whose radiance beams from their countenance and is reflected in their lives. They are in love! Their affection has been given to the Unseen One who dwells within them by the Holy Spirit, and His loveliness permeates all they do. This accounts for their inward glow.   —PAUL VAN GORDER

True worship and love meet only in God.

COME SIT A SPELL

READ: Luke 19:1–9

*When Jesus reached the spot, he looked up and said
to him, "Zacchaeus, come down immediately. I
must stay at your house today."* LUKE 19:5

WHEN I WAS A kid, our family made a monthly excursion from
Ohio to West Virginia to visit my maternal grandparents. Every
time we arrived at the door of their farmhouse, Grandma Lester
would greet us with the words, "Come on in and sit a spell." It was
her way of telling us to make ourselves comfortable, stay a while,
and share in some "catching-up" conversation.

Life can get pretty busy. In our action-oriented world, it's hard
to get to know people. It's tough to find time to ask someone to "sit
a spell" with us. We can get more done if we text each other and
get right to the point.

But look at what Jesus did when He wanted to make a difference
in the life of a tax collector. He went to Zacchaeus's house to "sit
a spell." His words, "I must stay at your house," indicate that this
was no quick stopover (Luke 19:5). Jesus spent time with him, and
Zacchaeus's life was turned around because of this time with Jesus.

On the front porch of my grandparents' house were several
chairs—a warm invitation to all visitors to relax and talk. If we're
going to get to know someone and to make a difference in their
life—as Jesus did for Zacchaeus—we need to invite them to "come
sit a spell."   —DAVE BRANON

The best gift you can give to others may be your time.

THE PERFECT MODEL

READ: Philippians 2:5–11

*Follow my example, as I follow the example
of Christ.* 1 CORINTHIANS 11:1

WHEN WE PLACE OUR trust in Christ for salvation, we are given a new life and a new destiny. In God's sight we are clothed in Christ's perfect righteousness. In our daily living, however, learning to imitate our Savior will take some time. As we walk in obedience to His will, we become more and more like Him and bring honor and glory to His name.

In his book *How to Begin the Christian Life*, George Sweeting tells this story. "In an Italian city stands a statue of a Grecian maiden with a beautiful face, a graceful figure, and a noble expression. One day a poor little peasant girl came face-to-face with the statue. She stood and stared, and then went home to wash her face and comb her hair. The next day she came again to stand before the statue, and then to return home once more. This time she mended her tattered clothing. Day by day she changed, her form grew more graceful, and her face more refined, till she greatly reflected the famous statue. She was transformed in appearance!" Sweeting commented, "Just so, the spiritual man must each day seek to conform to the perfect image of our Lord and Savior Jesus Christ."

During His time on earth, our Lord was humble, loving, patient, forgiving, compassionate, submissive, obedient, courageous, and holy. No wonder Paul claimed to be an imitator of Christ. The Lord is our perfect model. —RICHARD DEHAAN

*God's children should be recognized by a growing
likeness to their heavenly Father.*

PRACTICING CHRIST'S PRESENCE

READ: Matthew 28:16–20

"My Presence will go with you." EXODUS 33:14

"I am with you always." MATTHEW 28:20

AS A YOUNG BOY I remember hearing a preacher say, "I once counseled with a member of my church who found it difficult to sense God's presence when praying. He always thought of Him as being far away and unreachable.

"To make him realize that the Savior is near at hand, I said, 'Think of the Lord riding beside you in the car, and sitting next to you in an empty chair at the table.' Taking my advice, he soon learned to converse with Christ as 'friend with Friend.' Later when he became terminally ill, he always wanted an empty chair beside his bed. He would turn that way whenever he talked with the Savior.

"One morning his wife came into his room and found that he had died in the night. His hand lay palm up on the chair as if he had rested it in the hand of the Lord in his final moments."

Perhaps you do not feel the need to be as literal as that man in following the preacher's counsel. Yet one thing is sure: practicing the presence of Christ will revolutionize your life and make fellowship with Him more intimate and blessed. —HENRY BOSCH

———

Christ's pardon brings the soul to heaven; His presence brings heaven to the soul.

THROUGH EYES OF COMPASSION

READ: Matthew 25:31-46

*"The King will reply, 'Truly I tell you, whatever you
did for one of the least of these brothers and sisters
of mine, you did for me.'"* MATTHEW 25:40

ONE DAY I WENT into a grocery store with my wife. As I stood near the checkout lanes, I overheard a clerk telling a young mother that she couldn't use her food stamps to buy the socks her daughter had selected. I saw disappointment on the child's face, so I impulsively stepped over, handed her a few dollars, and quickly walked away. I didn't dare look at the mother because I was afraid I might have embarrassed her. I was only trying to practice the principle of Matthew 25:40.

We sometimes find it difficult to see the poor through eyes of compassion. For instance, have you ever heard affluent Christians telling stories about people buying steaks with food stamps, yet having cash for beer and cigarettes? Some of these stories may be true, but there are so many other well-deserving people who do need help. Rather than dwelling on the exceptions, we need the attitude expressed by Andrew W. Blackwood Jr. He wrote: "Jesus, why didn't you tell me you were hungry? Why didn't you tell me you were thirsty? Why didn't you tell me those were your toes sticking through cracked shoes? I didn't know you needed Medicaid; why didn't you tell me they had sent you to jail? I want to open the door and invite you in; please tell me who you are next time you knock."

Lord, help us see through eyes of compassion.

—HERB VANDER LUGT

*Life takes on new interest when we
forget self and think of others.*

WALKING IN HIS DUST

READ: Mark 1:16–20

*Without delay he called them, and they left
their father Zebedee in the boat with the hired
men and followed him.* MARK 1:20

IN THE FIRST CENTURY, a Jewish man who wanted to become a
disciple of a rabbi (teacher) was expected to leave family and job
to join his rabbi. They would live together twenty-four hours a
day—walking from place to place, teaching and learning, studying
and working. They discussed and memorized the Scriptures and
applied them to life.

The disciple's calling, as described in early Jewish writings about
basic ethics, was to "cover himself in the dust of [the rabbi's] feet,"
drinking in his every word. He followed his rabbi so closely that
he would "walk in his dust." In doing so, he became like the rabbi,
his master.

Simon, Andrew, James, and John knew that this was the type
of relationship to which Jesus was calling them (Mark 1:16–20).
So immediately they walked away from their work and "followed
him" (v. 20). For three years they stayed close to Him—listening
to His teaching, watching His miracles, learning His principles,
and walking in His dust.

As Jesus's followers today, we too can "walk in His dust." By
spending time studying and meditating on His Word and applying
its principles to life, we'll become like our rabbi—Jesus.

—ANNE CETAS

*Faith in Christ is not just a single step—
it's a lifelong walk with Him.*

WORDS OF LIGHT

READ: John 8:12–20

When Jesus spoke again to the people, he said, "I am the light of the world. Whoever follows me will never walk in darkness, but will have the light of life." JOHN 8:12

JESUS, AN ITINERANT RABBI from the town of Nazareth, asserted that He was the light of the world. That was an incredible claim in first-century Galilee, an obscure region in the Roman Empire. It could not boast of any impressive culture and had no famous philosophers, noted authors, or gifted sculptors. And we have no record that Jesus had any formal education.

More than that, Jesus lived before the invention of the printing press, radio, television, and email. How could He expect His ideas to be circulated around the globe? The words He spoke were committed to the memories of His followers. Then the Light of the world was snuffed out by the darkness—or so it seemed.

Centuries later we still listen with amazement to Jesus's words, which His Father has miraculously preserved. His words lead us out of darkness into the light of God's truth; they fulfill His promise, "Whoever follows me will never walk in darkness, but will have the light of life" (John 8:12).

I encourage you to read the words of Jesus in the Gospels. Ponder them. Let them grip your mind and change your life. You'll exclaim as His contemporaries did: "No one ever spoke the way this man does!" (John 7:46).   —VERNON GROUNDS

Because Jesus is the Light of the world, we don't need to be in the dark about God.

AS IS

READ: 2 Corinthians 5:14–21

Therefore, if anyone is in Christ, the new creation has come: The old has gone, the new is here! 2 CORINTHIANS 5:17

THE BEAT-UP OLD CAR sits on the used-car lot, rusty and forsaken. Years of abuse and hard driving have taken their toll on the formerly shiny automobile.

A man walks onto the lot and is attracted to this rust bucket. He plunks down cash and the salesperson hands over the keys while saying, "I'm selling you this car 'as is.'" The new owner just smiles; he knows his cars, and he's about to restore this castoff to its former beauty.

Across town, a troubled woman sits in forlorn sadness, contemplating where she went wrong. Years of abuse and hard living have taken their toll on what was once a vibrant young girl. She's been mistreated by others so many times that she feels she has little value anymore. And after making her own mistakes and living with her own bad choices, she's sure she will be left on life's junk heap forever.

But then someone tells her about Jesus. Someone mentions that Jesus specializes in castoffs, that He is waiting to transform anyone who trusts Him—even her. Someone tells her that Jesus will take her "as is." She believes. She trusts. And Jesus begins to restore another lost person to the abundant life He has promised.

—DAVE BRANON

Salvation is not turning over a new leaf, but receiving a new life.

HIS FRIENDS KNOW

READ: John 15:13–17

"I no longer call you servants, because a servant does not know his master's business. Instead, I have called you friends, for everything that I learned from my Father I have made known to you." JOHN 15:15

RENÉ LACOSTE, THE WORLD'S top tennis player in the late 1920s, won seven major singles titles during his career, including multiple victories at Wimbledon, the US Open, and the French Open. His friends called him "Le Crocodile," an apt term for his tenacious play on the court.

Lacoste accepted the nickname and had a tiny crocodile embroidered on his tennis blazer. When he added it to a line of shirts he designed, the symbol caught on. While thousands of people around the world wore "crocodile shirts," the emblem always had a deeper significance for Lacoste's friends, who knew its origin and meaning.

The cross, an emblem of Christianity, holds special meaning for every friend of Christ. Whenever we see a cross, it speaks to us of Christ's tenacious determination to do His Father's will by dying for us on Calvary. What a privilege to know Him and be included in His words to His disciples: "I no longer call you servants, . . . instead, I have called you friends" (John 15:15).

I can picture a friend of Lacoste seeing the little crocodile on someone's shirt and saying, "I know the story behind that emblem. Lacoste is my friend." And I can picture a friend of Jesus seeing a cross and doing the same. —DAVID MCCASLAND

Because of the cross of Christ,
we can become friends of Christ.

PEACELESS IN PITTSBURGH

READ: Matthew 6:25–34

"Therefore do not worry about tomorrow, for tomorrow will worry about itself. Each day has enough trouble of its own." MATTHEW 6:34

A FOLLOWER OF CHRIST can find a lot to worry about these days— the moral degeneration of society, the stock market, anti-Christian sentiment, social turmoil, and on and on. Often we are troubled about what could happen in the future, or we spend way too much time dwelling on the past. Our minds whirl and emotions rise because of some sin we committed or a sad event that occurred years ago.

Because we can neither change the past nor manipulate the future, we are peaceless in Pittsburgh, fretful in Fresno, or worried in Washington. How fruitless! How wasteful!

Author Jean-Pierre de Caussade said that every day we can experience the peace of God when we stop stewing about what might be or what might have been and focus on what is. He wrote, "It is necessary to be disengaged from all we feel and do, in order to walk with God in the duty of the present moment. . . . Each moment imposes a virtuous obligation on us which committed souls faithfully obey."

But how can we walk with the Lord and experience His peace when we're paralyzed with worry about the past or the future? We can't! No wonder Jesus told us, "Do not worry" (Matthew 6:34).

—DAVID EGNER

Worry is like a rocking chair—it will give you something to do, but it won't get you anywhere.

HE HUMBLED HIMSELF

READ: Philippians 2:1–9

*In your relationships with one another, have the same
mindset as Christ Jesus.* PHILIPPIANS 2:5

BILL, A COLLEGE STUDENT, was a new Christian. According to
author Rebecca Manley Pippert, one Sunday he visited a church
near campus. He walked in barefoot and was wearing a T-shirt and
jeans. The service had already started, so he walked down the aisle
looking for a seat. Finding none, he sat down cross-legged on the
floor—right in front of the pulpit!

The congregation became noticeably uneasy. Then, from the
back of the church, an elderly deacon got up and with his cane
slowly made his way to the front. Every eye followed him. The
minister paused and there was total silence. As the old gentleman
approached Bill, he dropped his cane and with great effort lowered
himself and sat down beside him so the young man wouldn't have
to worship alone. Many in the congregation were deeply moved.

Paul wrote that Christ, being equal with God, set aside His
reputation and became obedient unto death—the ultimate act of
humility (Philippians 2:6–8). Why? To come to us in our loneliness,
to forgive our sins, and to teach us a new way to live and worship.

When we learn to think as Jesus thought, we see people through
the same eyes as that godly deacon. May we learn how to humble
ourselves for the benefit of others.　　　　—DENNIS DEHAAN

---

*We can do great things for the Lord if we are
willing to do little things for others.*

ARE YOU READY?

READ: Matthew 24:36–46

"So you also must be ready, because the Son of Man will come at an hour when you do not expect him." MATTHEW 24:44

WHEN JESUS PROMISED HIS disciples that He would one day return to earth, He said He would come at a time they did not expect (Matthew 24:44). Therefore, people today who set dates for Christ's second coming are wasting their time. Jesus never told His followers how to calculate the day of His return. Rather, He emphasized that our main priority is to make sure we're ready for Him and that we are occupied in His service when He comes (vv. 45–46).

A woman who lived by this teaching was shopping in a small country store. Several young people were just standing around doing nothing. Knowing she was a Christian, they began ridiculing her. "We hear you're expecting Jesus to come back," they jeered. "That's right," she replied brightly. "Do you really believe He's coming?" they asked. "Absolutely," she answered. They said, "Well, you'd better hurry home and get ready. He might be on the way!" Facing them, she said, "I don't have to get ready—I keep ready!"

Are you ready for the arrival of God's Son? Will you be glad to see Jesus when He returns? If not, get ready now. Without delay, turn away from your sin and trust Jesus Christ as your Lord and Savior. Then keep ready by walking in His will every day.

—JOANIE YODER

The hope of Christ's returning can keep us going.

"NO" POWER

READ: Romans 7:1–6

But now, by dying to what once bound us, we have been released from the law so that we serve in the new way of the Spirit, and not in the old way of the written code. ROMANS 7:6

I REMEMBER SEEING A newspaper photograph of three signs nailed to a big oak tree. Their message was obvious. On the top sign were printed the words, "No Trespassing," on the middle one, "No Hunting," and on the bottom, "No Nothing."

The newspaper's accompanying comment read, " 'No Trespassing,' 'No Hunting,' well, that's a landowner's prerogative. But 'No Nothing' makes you want to beep your horn, shout out the window—anything to resist a little."

The apostle Paul was very familiar with the urge behind such a response. In Romans 7 he pointed out that the law actually awakens rebellious desires within us (v. 5). Being told not to do something excites our sinful nature to express itself.

Our rebellious response to negative rules points out our need for a strong, compelling motivation to do what's right. Paul said that we can go beyond a list of dos and don'ts to a love relationship with Christ himself (v. 6). The law carries with it the sentence of death because of our inability to keep it (v. 10). But being united to Christ results in life.

By daily walking and talking with our Lord and Savior Jesus Christ, we can go from "no" power in the law to all power in Him.

—MART DEHAAN

In Christ, God's love was expressed
and His law was satisfied.

RUNNING IN THE RIGHT DIRECTION

READ: John 6:53–69

*Simon Peter answered him, "Lord, to whom shall we
go? You have the words of eternal life." JOHN 6:68*

ONE OF THE MOST difficult experiences in my years as a pastor was
telling a member of our church that her husband, her son, and her
father-in-law had all drowned in a boating accident. I knew the
news would shatter her life.

In the days following their tragic loss, I was amazed as she
and her family responded with unusual faith. Sure, there was deep
brokenness, haunting doubt, and confusion. But when nothing
else made sense, they still had Jesus. Rather than deserting Him
in the midst of their desperately difficult days, they ran to Him as
the only source of hope and confidence.

This reminds me of the reaction of the disciples to Jesus. After
some of them "turned back and no longer followed him" because
He was hard to understand (John 6:66), Jesus turned to His inner
circle, and asked, "You don't want to leave too, do you?" (v. 67).
Peter got it right when he responded, "Lord, to whom shall we go?
You have the words of eternal life" (v. 68).

Whatever you face today, be encouraged by the words of Peter
and by the example of a family who went through the fire with their
faith intact. As long as you're running in the right direction—to
Jesus—you'll find the grace and strength you will need.

—JOE STOWELL

*When all is lost, remember that you
haven't lost Jesus. Run to Him.*

POPULARITY

Read: John 6:60–69

*From this time many of his disciples turned back
and no longer followed him.* John 6:66

Popularity is fickle. Just ask a politician. Many of them watch their ratings to see how their constituents view their policies. They may start with a high rating, but then it steadily declines during their term.

Jesus also experienced a sharp decline in popularity. His popularity reached its peak after He fed the 5,000 (John 6:14–15). It plummeted when He told His listeners that He had "come down from heaven" (v. 38). Their response to His stupendous claim was, essentially, "Who does this guy think He is?!" (See v. 41).

Jesus's popularity continued to dip when He explained how they could have Him as spiritual bread (vv. 51–52). Perplexed by what they heard, they said, "This is a hard teaching. Who can accept it?" (v. 60). As a result, many left Him.

The crowds followed Jesus conditionally. They were happy only as long as Jesus supplied their needs and met their wants. They balked when He asked for commitment.

Jesus's question to His disciples was "You do not want to leave too, do you?" (v. 67). Peter answered, "Lord, to whom shall we go? You have the words of eternal life" (v. 68). Will you, like Peter, choose to ignore the world's rating of Jesus and follow Him daily?

—C. P. Hia

Commitment to Christ is a daily calling that challenges us.

WHERE DO I START?

READ: Luke 11:1–10

*I call on the LORD in my distress, and
he answers me.* PSALM 120:1

SEVERAL YEARS AGO, I was driving down the freeway when my car died. I pulled over to the side of the road, got out of the car, and opened the hood. As I looked at the engine I thought, *A lot of good this does me. I know nothing about cars. I don't even know where to start!*

That's how we might sometimes feel about prayer: Where do I start? That's what the disciples wanted to know when they asked Jesus, "Teach us to pray" (Luke 11:1). The best place to look for instruction is in the example and teaching of Jesus. Two questions you may have are:

Where should we pray? Jesus prayed in the temple, in the wilderness (Luke 4), in quiet places (Matthew 14:22–23), in the garden of Gethsemane (Luke 22), and on the cross (Luke 23:34, 46). He prayed alone and with others. Look at His life, follow His example, and pray wherever you are.

What should we pray? In the Lord's Prayer, Jesus taught us to ask that God's name be honored and that His will be done on earth as it is in heaven. Ask Him for your daily provisions, for forgiveness of sin, and for deliverance from temptation and evil (Luke 11:2–4).

So if you're looking for a good place to start, follow the example of the Lord's Prayer. —ANNE CETAS

If Jesus needed to pray, how can we do less?

A FRIEND TO THE END

READ: Proverbs 18:14–24

One who has unreliable friends soon comes to ruin, but there is a friend who sticks closer than a brother. PROVERBS 18:24

TRADITIONALLY, MEDICAL SCHOOLS HAVE trained their students to help patients live while offering little instruction in helping them face death. But that is changing with the addition of courses in end-of-life care. Physicians are now taught that when they have used all their medical expertise without achieving a cure, they should seize the opportunity to stand compassionately beside their dying patients and be a friend.

Death frightens many of us and makes us feel awkward in the presence of a terminally ill person. But our greatest opportunities to help someone in Jesus's name may come during a person's final days on earth.

The Bible speaks of a friendship that knows no limits. "A friend loves at all times," said the wise man (Proverbs 17:17). And "there is a friend who sticks closer than a brother" (18:24). Jesus said, "Greater love has no one than this: to lay down one's life for one's friends" (John 15:13).

Jesus is both our Great Physician and our Friend, and He promised that He would never leave us nor forsake us (Hebrews 13:5). He calls us to stand with our friends and family in His name as their earthly journey nears its end. That's what a true friend would do.

—DAVID MCCASLAND

A true friend stays true to the end.

CHRIST LIVING IN US

READ: Galatians 2:15–21

I have fought the good fight, I have finished the race, I have kept the faith. Now there is in store for me the crown of righteousness, which the Lord, the righteous Judge, will award to me on that day—and not only to me, but also to all who have longed for his appearing. 2 TIMOTHY 4:7–8

THE IRONMAN TRIATHLON CONSISTS of a 2.4-mile swim, a 112-mile bike ride, and a 26.2-mile run. It is not an easy feat for anyone to accomplish. But Dick Hoyt participated in the race and completed it with his physically disabled son Rick. When Dick swam, he pulled Rick in a small boat. When Dick cycled, Rick was in a seat-pod on the bike. When Dick ran, he pushed Rick along in a wheelchair. Rick was dependent on his dad in order to finish the race. He couldn't do it without him.

We see a parallel between their story and our own Christian life. Just as Rick was dependent on his dad, we are dependent on Christ to complete our Christian race.

As we strive to live a God-pleasing life, we realize that in spite of our best intentions and determination, we often stumble and fall short. By our strength alone, it is impossible. Oh, how we need the Lord's help! And it has been provided. Paul declares it with these insightful words, "I no longer live, but Christ lives in me. The life I now live in the body, I live by faith in the Son of God" (Galatians 2:20).

We cannot finish the Christian race on our own. We have to do so by depending on Jesus living in us.   —ALBERT LEE

Faith connects our weakness to God's strength.

PEACE IN CRISIS

READ: John 14:19–27

"Peace I leave with you; my peace I give you. I do not give to you as the world gives. Do not let your hearts be troubled and do not be afraid." JOHN 14:27

TED, ONE OF THE elders in our church, used to be a police officer. One day after responding to a report of violence, he said the situation turned life-threatening. A man had stabbed someone and then menacingly turned the blade toward Ted. A fellow officer had taken a position and fired his weapon at the assailant as he attacked Ted. The criminal was subdued, but Ted was shot in the crossfire. As he was driven by ambulance to the hospital, he felt deep waves of peace flowing over his soul from the Holy Spirit. Ted felt so tranquil that he was able to offer words of comfort to the other law enforcement officer, who was emotionally distraught over the crisis.

The Lord Jesus promised us peace in crisis. Just hours before His own crucifixion, Christ comforted His disciples with these words: "Peace I leave with you; my peace I give you. I do not give to you as the world gives. Do not let your hearts be troubled and do not be afraid" (John 14:27).

What is your worst fear? If you should have to face it, Christ will be there with you. Trusting Him through prayer makes available the "peace of God, which transcends all understanding," and it "will guard your hearts and your minds through Christ Jesus" (Philippians 4:7). —DENNIS FISHER

The secret of peace is to give every anxious care to God.

A WORK IN PROGRESS

READ: John 15:9–17

*But grow in the grace and knowledge of our Lord
and Savior Jesus Christ. To him be glory both
now and forever! Amen.* 2 PETER 3:18

PABLO CASALS WAS CONSIDERED to be the preeminent cellist of the first half of the twentieth century. When he was still playing his cello in the middle of his tenth decade of life, a young reporter asked, "Mr. Casals, you are ninety-five years old and the greatest cellist that ever lived. Why do you still practice six hours a day?"

Mr. Casals answered, "Because I think I'm making progress."

What a great attitude! As believers in Christ, we should never be satisfied to think we have reached some self-proclaimed pinnacle of spiritual success, but rather continue to "grow in the grace and knowledge of our Lord and Savior Jesus Christ" (2 Peter 3:18). Jesus reminds us in John 15:16 that He chose us to "go and bear fruit." The result of healthy growth is continuing to bear spiritual fruit throughout our lives. Our Lord promises: "I am the vine, you are the branches. If you remain in me and I in you, you will bear much fruit" (v. 5).

In a steady and faithful progression to become more and more like the One we love and serve, we can be confident that He who began "a good work" in us will continue it until it is finally finished on the day when He returns (Philippians 1:6).

—CINDY HESS KASPER

*God's unseen work in our hearts
produces fruit in our lives.*

FOR THE CHILDREN

READ: Psalm 68:5; Mark 10:13–16

When Jesus saw this, he was indignant. He said to them, "Let the little children come to me, and do not hinder them, for the kingdom of God belongs to such as these." MARK 10:14

AS THE TEENAGERS LEFT Robin's Nest orphanage near Montego Bay, Jamaica, many of them were in tears.

"It's just not fair," one girl said after their too-brief visit. "We have so much, and they don't have anything." In the two hours we visited, handing out stuffed animals and playing with the kids, she had been holding a sad little girl who never smiled. We learned that before she was rescued she had been abused by her parents.

Multiply this little girl's plight by the millions, and it's easy to feel overwhelmed. My teenage friends were right. It's not fair. Abuse, poverty, and neglect have turned the lives of millions of little ones into a nightmare.

How this must grieve God's heart! Jesus, who said, "Let the little children come to me" (Mark 10:14), is surely saddened by the way these children are treated.

What can we do? In Jesus's name, we can give monetary support to good orphanages. When possible, we can offer physical help. If we feel led, we can seek to provide homes for these precious children. And all of us can pray—beseeching God to help those for whom life is so unfair.

Let's show children the love of God through our hearts and our hands. —DAVE BRANON

Be Jesus to a child today.

LOSING TO FIND

READ: Matthew 10:37–42

*Whoever finds their life will lose it, and whoever loses
their life for my sake will find it.* MATTHEW 10:39

WHEN I MARRIED MY English fiancé and moved to the United Kingdom, I thought it would be a five-year adventure in a foreign land. I never dreamed I'd still be living here nearly twenty years later, or that at times I'd feel like I was losing my life as I said good-bye to family and friends, work, and all that was familiar. But in losing my old way of life, I've found a better one.

The upside-down gift of finding life when we lose it is what Jesus promised to His apostles. When He sent out the twelve disciples to share His good news, He asked them to love Him more than their mothers or fathers, sons or daughters (Matthew 10:37). His words came in a culture where families were the cornerstone of the society and highly valued. But He promised that if they would lose their life for His sake, they would find it (v. 39).

We don't have to move abroad to find ourselves in Christ. Through service and commitment—such as the disciples going out to share the good news of the kingdom of God—we find ourselves receiving more than we give through the lavish love the Lord showers on us. Of course, He loves us no matter how much we serve, but we find contentment, meaning, and fulfillment when we pour ourselves out for the well-being of others.   —AMY BOUCHER PYE

*Every loss leaves a space that can
be filled with God's presence.*

DOES CHRIST LIVE HERE?

READ: Mark 9:1–8

When they looked up, they saw no
one except Jesus. MATTHEW 17:8

SIR ISAAC NEWTON (1643–1727) was eager to solve an optical problem, so he found it necessary to gaze intently at the sun in its noonday splendor. When he had finished his observations, the effect of the sun stayed with him. For a while, he "saw" that luminous body wherever he looked.

This reminds me a bit of Saul of Tarsus, who was traveling to Damascus when he saw a light that was brighter than the sun (Acts 9:1–20). Saul became Paul—and Jesus completely filled his vision. If, like the apostle, we have caught a glimpse of the Savior, we too will always have Him in our line of vision.

A pastor and his wife serving in a small village visited a home for the first time, and only the wife who lived there was home. Later, when her husband came home from work, she said, "The new preacher and his wife came by today." "And what did he say?" "He asked, 'Does Christ live here?' I didn't know how to answer." The husband, a bit irritated, asked, "Why didn't you tell him we go to church, say our prayers, and read our Bible?" "He didn't inquire about any of those things," she replied. "He only asked, 'Does Christ live here?'"

If our eyes are properly focused on Jesus, then like Paul and the disciples we will see "Jesus only!" It will be clear that in our homes, Jesus lives there.   —HENRY BOSCH

Gazing on Jesus and adoring Him works in us the
same mind, and we are changed into His image.

LET HONOR MEET HONOR

READ: Matthew 6:1–6

*"Be careful not to practice your righteousness in front
of others to be seen by them. If you do, you will have no
reward from your Father in heaven."* MATTHEW 6:1

I'VE ALWAYS BEEN IMPRESSED by the solemn, magnificent simplicity of the Changing of the Guard at the Tomb of the Unknowns at Arlington National Cemetery. The carefully choreographed event is a moving tribute to soldiers whose names—and sacrifice—are "known but to God." Equally moving are the private moments of steady pacing when the crowds are gone: back and forth, hour after hour, day by day, in even the worst weather.

In September 2003, Hurricane Isabel was bearing down on Washington, DC, and the guards were told they could seek shelter during the worst of the storm. Surprising almost no one, the guards refused! They unselfishly stood their post to honor their fallen comrades even in the face of a hurricane.

Underlying Jesus's teaching in Matthew 6:1–6, I believe, is His desire for us to live with an unrelenting, selfless devotion to Him. The Bible calls us to good deeds and holy living, but these are to be acts of worship and obedience (vv. 4-6), not orchestrated acts for self-glorification (v. 2). The apostle Paul endorses this whole-life faithfulness when he pleads with us to make our bodies "a living sacrifice" (Romans 12:1).

May our private and public moments speak of our devotion and wholehearted commitment to you, Lord. —RANDY KILGORE

The more we serve Christ, the less we will serve self.

FRIENDSHIP WITH JESUS

READ: 1 Corinthians 1:1–9

God is faithful, who has called you into fellowship with his Son, Jesus Christ our Lord. 1 CORINTHIANS 1:9

MANY PEOPLE WERE LED to faith in Christ through the witness of John Gilmour, a godly Englishman of days gone by. He would fill his pockets with gospel books to use as God directed him.

One day he was walking in a village when he came across an old Irishman selling kettles and saucepans. At first, Gilmour thought, *There's no use speaking to him.* But prompted by the Spirit, he changed his mind. So he said, "Good morning, how is business today?" "Oh," said the Irishman, "I cannot complain."

Pursuing his desire to witness for Christ, Gilmour said, "Well now, what a grand thing it is to be saved!" The old man looked intently at him and replied, "I know something better than that." "Something better than being saved? I would like to know what that is." With a warm smile, the old Irishman responded, speaking of Jesus: "The companionship of the Man who saved me, sir."

Songwriter Horatius Bonar wrote, "Friendship with Jesus, fellowship divine; Oh, what blessed sweet communion! Jesus is a friend of mine." Christ wants us to experience fellowship with Him every day. This holy intimacy is ours through confessing our sin and yielding to Christ. Each day we can enjoy His satisfying companionship. —PAUL VAN GORDER

Christ's friendship prevails when human friendship fails.

APPROACHING GOD

READ: Hebrews 4:14–16

But as for me, it is good to be near God.
I have made the Sovereign LORD my refuge;
I will tell of all your deeds. PSALM 73:28

A WOMAN DESIRING TO pray grabbed an empty chair and knelt before it. In tears, she said, "My dear heavenly Father, please sit down here; you and I need to talk!" Then, looking directly at the vacant chair, she prayed. She demonstrated confidence in approaching the Lord; she imagined He was *sitting* on the chair and believed He was listening to her petition.

A time with God is an important moment when we engage the Almighty. God comes near to us as we draw near to Him in a mutual involvement (James 4:8). He has assured us, "I am with you always" (Matthew 28:20). Our heavenly Father is always waiting for us to come to Him, always ready to listen to us.

There are times when we struggle to pray because we feel tired, sleepy, sick, and weak. But Jesus sympathizes with us when we are weak or face temptations (Hebrews 4:15). Therefore we can "approach God's throne of grace with confidence, so that we may receive mercy and find grace to help us in our time of need" (v. 16).

—LAWRENCE DARMANI

God is everywhere, is available
every time, and listens always.

SEEING GOD

READ: John 14:1–12

*Philip said, "Lord, show us the Father and
that will be enough for us."* JOHN 14:8

AUTHOR AND PASTOR ERWIN Lutzer recounts a story about television show host Art Linkletter and a little boy who was drawing a picture of God. Amused, Linkletter said, "You can't do that because nobody knows what God looks like."

"They will when I get through!" the boy declared.

We may wonder, *What is God like? Is He good? Is He kind? Does He care?* The simple answer to those questions is Jesus's response to Philip's request: "Lord, show us the Father." Jesus replied, "Don't you know me, Philip, even after I have been among you such a long time? Anyone who has seen me has seen the Father" (John 14:8–9).

If you ever get hungry to see God, look at Jesus. "The Son is the image of the invisible God," said Paul (Colossians 1:15). Read through the four Gospels in the New Testament: Matthew, Mark, Luke, and John. Think deeply about what Jesus did and said. "Draw" your own mental picture of God as you read. You'll know much more of what He's like when you're through.

A friend of mine once told me that the only God he could believe in is the one he saw in Jesus. If you look closely, I think you'll agree. As you read about Him, your heart will leap, for though you may not know it, Jesus is the God you've been looking for all your life.   —DAVID ROPER

*The clearer we see God, the clearer we see
ourselves. —Erwin Lutzer*

"ME AND THE KING"

READ: Colossians 2:20–3:4

*Since, then, you have been raised with Christ, set
your hearts on things above, where Christ is, seated
at the right hand of God.* COLOSSIANS 3:1

THE STORY IS TOLD of a convict who had been in prison for many years. Finally, he received a pardon from the king. When the time came for him to be released, he walked boldly to the prison gate and said with confidence, "Me and the king say you have to open the doors and set me free." He then produced the papers signed by the ruler. His identification with the king guaranteed his freedom.

In a much deeper sense, we as Christians are identified with Jesus, our King. Through faith we are actually united with Him, and this union not only gives us liberty but also power to live a new life. Because we are "in Christ," (Romans 6:11) we are reconciled forever to God.

An old tract called "The Seven Togethers" summarizes the completeness of our union with Christ. It says we are (1) crucified together with Christ (Galatians 2:20); (2) dead together with Christ (Colossians 2:20); (3) buried together with Christ (Romans 6:4); (4) made alive together with Christ (Ephesians 2:5); (5) raised together with Christ (Colossians 3:1); (6) sufferers together with Christ (Romans 8:17); and (7) glorified together with Christ (Romans 8:17).

Let's live free! Let's exercise the liberty and power that comes through being identified with the King of kings and Lord of lords.

—DAVID EGNER

*Only those who are bound to Christ
know freedom from sin.*

WHO IS THIS?

Read: Luke 19:28-40

"Blessed is the king who comes in the name of the Lord!"
"Peace in heaven and glory in the highest!" LUKE 19:38

IMAGINE STANDING SHOULDER TO shoulder with onlookers by a dirt road. The woman behind you is on her tiptoes, trying to see who is coming. In the distance, you glimpse a man riding a donkey. As He approaches, people toss their coats onto the road. Suddenly, you hear a tree crack behind you. A man is cutting down palm branches, and people are spreading them out ahead of the donkey.

Jesus's followers zealously honored Him as He entered Jerusalem a few days before His crucifixion. The multitude rejoiced and praised God for "all the miracles they had seen" (Luke 19:37). Jesus's devotees surrounded Him, calling out, "Blessed is the king who comes in the name of the Lord!" (v. 38). Their enthusiastic honor affected the people of Jerusalem. When Jesus finally arrived, "the whole city was stirred and asked, 'Who is this?'" (Matthew 21:10).

Today, people are still curious about Jesus. Although we can't pave His way with palm branches or shout praises to Him in person, we can still honor Him. We can discuss His remarkable works, assist people in need (Galatians 6:2), patiently bear insults (1 Peter 4:14–16), and love each other deeply (v. 8). Then we must be ready to answer the onlookers who ask, "Who is Jesus?"

—JENNIFER BENSON SCHULDT

We honor God's name when we call Him
our Father and live like His Son.

THE LAND OF FAR DISTANCES

READ: Isaiah 33:17–22

*Your eyes will see the king in his beauty and view
a land that stretches afar.* ISAIAH 33:17

AMY CARMICHAEL (1867–1951) IS known for her work of rescuing orphaned girls in India and giving them a new life. In the midst of this exhausting work there were times she called "moments of vision." In her book *Gold by Moonlight*, she wrote, "In the midst of a crowded day we are given almost a glimpse of 'the land of far distances,' and we stand still, arrested on the road."

The prophet Isaiah spoke of a time when God's rebellious people would turn back to Him. "Your eyes will see the king in his beauty and view a land that stretches afar" (Isaiah 33:17). To view this "land of far distances" is to be lifted above the circumstances of the immediate present and to gain an eternal perspective. During difficult times, the Lord enables us to see our lives from His viewpoint and regain hope. "For the LORD is our judge, the LORD is our lawgiver, the LORD is our king; it is he who will save us" (v. 22).

Each day, we can choose to look down in discouragement or lift our eyes to "the land of far distances," to the Lord who is "our Mighty One" (v. 21).

Amy Carmichael spent more than fifty years in India helping young women in great need. How did she do it? Each day she fixed her eyes on Jesus and placed her life in His care. And so can we.

—DAVID MCCASLAND

Fix your eyes on Jesus.

TAKE THE TIME

READ: Luke 19:1–10

*When Jesus reached the spot, he looked up and said
to him, "Zacchaeus, come down immediately.
I must stay at your house today." LUKE 19:5*

RIMA, A SYRIAN WOMAN who had recently moved to the United
States, tried to explain to her tutor with hand motions and limited
English why she was upset. Tears trickled down her cheeks as she
held up a beautifully arranged platter of *fatayer* (meat, cheese, and
spinach pies) that she had made. Then she said, "One man," and made
a swishing sound as she pointed from the door to the living room and
then back to the door. The tutor pieced together that several people
from a nearby church were supposed to visit Rima and her family and
bring some gifts. But only one man had shown up. He had hurried
in, dropped off a box of items, and rushed out. He was busy taking
care of a responsibility, while she and her family were lonely and
longed for community and to share their *fatayer* with new friends.

Taking time for people is what Jesus was all about. He attended
dinner parties, taught crowds, and took time for interaction with
individuals. He even invited himself to one man's house. Zacchaeus,
a tax collector, climbed a tree to see Him, and when Jesus looked
up, He said, "Come down immediately. I must stay at your house
today" (Luke 19:5). And Zacchaeus's life was changed forever.

Because of other responsibilities, we won't always be able to take
the time. But when we do, we have a wonderful privilege of being
with others and watching the Lord work through us.

—ANNE CETAS

The best gift you can give to others may be your time.

THE PEACE-FILLED LIFE

READ: John 14:27–15:7

"Peace I leave with you; my peace I give you. I do not give to you as the world gives. Do not let your hearts be troubled and do not be afraid." JOHN 14:27

WHEN H. B. MACARTNEY, an Australian pastor, visited Hudson Taylor in China, he was amazed at the missionary's peacefulness in spite of his many burdens and his busy schedule. Macartney commented, "You are occupied with millions, I with tens. Your letters are pressingly important, mine of comparatively little value. Yet I am worried and distressed while you are always calm. Tell me, what makes the difference?" Taylor replied, "I could not possibly get through the work I have to do without the peace of God, which passes all understanding keeping my heart and mind." Macartney later wrote, "He was in God all the time, and God was in him. It was the true abiding spoken of in John 15."

Do you feel as if your life is more like Macartney's than Taylor's? Do you desire the peace Jesus promised? The secret is to abide in Christ as Hudson Taylor did. Abiding in Christ means to be in touch with Him continually so the composure He experienced while on earth rules your life.

We need not agonize or plead or try to work up a certain feeling. The path to abiding in Him is that of confessing and rejecting all known sin, surrendering completely, and looking trustfully to the Lord Jesus for strength. It's a continual depending on Him. We too can enjoy the serenity of a peace-filled life if we will learn to abide in Christ. —HERB VANDER LUGT

Peace floods the soul when Christ rules the heart.

A GLIMPSE OF GLORY

READ: Acts 7:54–60

*But Stephen, full of the Holy Spirit, looked up
to heaven and saw the glory of God, and Jesus
standing at the right hand of God.* ACTS 7:55

DEATH IS OUR LAST great enemy. Jesus has removed its sting, which is sin (1 Corinthians 15:56), but it still creates apprehension in us as we think about it.

This was illustrated in the life of the great evangelist Dwight L. Moody (1837–1899). When he was on his deathbed at the very end of the nineteenth century, family and friends gathered to say goodbye. Thinking that the end had come, they silently began to leave the room. Just then a stirring was heard. Turning, they found Moody's eyes open and his mind apparently clear. Someone began to pray, but Moody interrupted, "Do not pray that I may live. I have seen Dwight and Irene [two grandchildren who had died]. I have seen the face of Jesus, and I am satisfied. Earth is receding; heaven is opening. God is calling me. This is my coronation day!"

Before being stoned to death for preaching the gospel, Stephen saw Jesus standing at the Father's right hand. How this must have strengthened him! I have heard of dying saints who voiced disappointment when, after lapsing into unconsciousness, they revived briefly and found that they were still on earth instead of in heaven.

Whatever our circumstances, if we have trusted Christ as Savior, He will be with us when we pass from this world and catch our first glimpse of Glory. —DENNIS DEHAAN

*For the Christian, death is the last shadow
before heaven's dawn.*

HOW TO BE FREE

READ: Proverbs 16:16–33

*The evil deeds of the wicked ensnare them; the cords
of their sins hold them fast.* PROVERBS 5:22

THE GREATLY LOVED BIBLE teacher Henrietta Mears (1890–1963)
knew the secret of true freedom, and she wanted her students to
know it too. She told them, "A bird is free in the air. Place a bird
in the water and he has lost his liberty. A fish is free in the water,
but leave him on the sand and he perishes. He is out of his realm.
Likewise, the Christian is free when he does the will of God and is
obedient to God's command. This is as natural a realm for God's
child as the water is for the fish, or the air for the bird."

Freedom is one theme of the book of Proverbs. Solomon urged
his son to understand that true freedom is possible only within the
sphere of God-centered living for which all men are created. By
contrast, bondage follows, predictably and inescapably, for anyone
who ignores God's truth. Proverbs 16, for example, describes the
liberty and satisfaction that results from practicing humility, trust,
careful conversation, and self-control. But it also warns about the
inevitable bondage that always comes to those governed by willful
rebellion, pride, arrogance, strife, and malicious troublemaking.

The New Testament introduces us to Jesus—the ultimate source
of our freedom. It was He, our Creator and Redeemer, who said, "If
you hold to my teaching, you are really my disciples. Then you will
know the truth, and the truth will make you free" (John 8:31–32).

—MART DEHAAN

*True freedom is not in having your own
way, but in yielding to God's way.*

CUT-FLOWER CHRISTIANS

READ: John 15:1–8

*"I am the vine; you are the branches. If you remain
in me and I in you, you will bear much fruit; apart
from me you can do nothing."* JOHN 15:5

ALMOST EVERY WOMAN LIKES to receive a bouquet of cut flowers.
After admiring and smelling them, she wastes no time getting them
into water. Even though fresh and beautiful when she gets them,
their days are numbered. Because they've been severed from their
life source, they will soon wither and die. One day she will have to
throw them away.

Author Lloyd Ogilvie sees in this a picture of the Christian
whose spiritual vitality has faded and shriveled. Such a person has
become a "cut-flower Christian." This is similar to the illustration
Jesus used in describing the vine and the branches. Just as a branch
can't bear fruit by itself, He explained, we can't bear spiritual fruit
unless we abide in Him, the true vine (John 15:4).

If a branch could speak, it wouldn't apologize for its need to
depend on the vine for bearing fruit. It would say instead, "For this
I was made!" Jesus likewise knew we were made for dependence on
Him, our life source—no apology needed! In fact, such dependence
is the only way to avoid becoming a "cut-flower Christian."

Let's embrace His declaration, "Without Me you can do nothing." He is really saying, "With Me you can do everything I appoint
for you, including bearing much fruit!"   —JOANIE YODER

Fellowship with Christ is the secret of fruitfulness.

DON'T LEAVE HIM ON THE CROSS

READ: Matthew 28:1–10

*If Christ has not been raised, our preaching is useless
and so is your faith.* 1 CORINTHIANS 15:14

WHEN THE DISCIPLES RECOGNIZED the awful truth that Jesus was dead, their hopes were crushed. They had believed their miracle-working Friend was sent by God to establish a kingdom. Yet His body lay in Joseph's tomb. And their dreams, like Christ, were dead.

Miraculously, the Lord Jesus left His cave-like prison in a glorified body. Hope was revived as His followers realized that their dead leader had become the risen Lord. He was alive!

Sadly, many people today fail to recognize the fact that Christ literally arose from the grave. While my wife and I were on an extended stay in one country, we observed traditional Good Friday presentations. We watched as a man who portrayed Jesus was strapped to a cross between two others. As the drama unfolded, the man "died." When he did, the crowds simply turned and walked away. No reference was made to Christ's resurrection. The following Easter Sunday was hauntingly somber. To many of these people, Christ's death was the end of the story. They knew of a dead Christ, but they knew nothing of a risen Savior.

The gospel is incomplete without Christ's resurrection. Consider the impact of that great event on your life and eternal destiny by reading 1 Corinthians 15:12–28. Then list three results that instill hope in your heart. Don't leave Christ on the cross.

—DAVE BRANON

The Victim of crucifixion became the Victor in resurrection.

JESUS'S INVITATION

READ: Mark 8:34–38

Then he called the crowd to him along with his disciples and said: "Whoever wants to be my disciple must deny themselves and take up their cross and follow me." MARK 8:34

DURING WORLD WAR II, B-17 bombers made long flights from the US mainland to the Pacific island of Saipan. When they landed there, the planes were met by a jeep bearing the sign: "Follow Me!" That little vehicle guided the giant planes to their assigned places in the parking area.

One pilot, who by his own admission was not a religious man, made an insightful comment: "That little jeep with its quaint sign always reminds me of Jesus. He was [a lowly] peasant, but the giant men and women of our time would be lost without His direction."

Centuries after our Savior walked the streets and hills of Israel, the world with all its advances still needs His example and instruction. When His ways aren't followed, numerous problems and evils arise in our world—including immorality, crime, and greed.

How do we follow Jesus's ways? First of all, we turn from our sin and entrust our lives to Him as our Savior and Lord. Then we seek His will in His Word each day and put it into practice by the power of the Holy Spirit within us. We learn to deny our selfish desires and give ourselves completely to following Jesus (Mark 8:34–35).

If you want to get in line with the purposes of God, respond to Jesus's invitation: "Follow Me!"   —VERNON GROUNDS

To find your way through life, follow Jesus.

MORE THAN INFORMATION

READ: John 15:1–13

*"Remain in me, as I also remain in you. No branch can
bear fruit by itself; it must remain in the vine. Neither can
you bear fruit unless you remain in me."* JOHN 15:4

HOW IS BEHAVIOR ALTERED? In his book *The Social Animal*, David
Brooks notes that some experts have said people just need to be
taught the long-term risks of bad behavior. For example, he writes:
"Smoking can lead to cancer. Adultery destroys families, and lying
destroys trust. The assumption was that once you reminded people
of the foolishness of their behavior, they would be motivated to stop.
Both reason and will are obviously important in making moral
decisions and exercising self-control. But neither of these character
models has proven very effective." In other words, information alone
is not powerful enough to transform behavior.

As Jesus's followers, we want to grow and change spiritually.
More than two millennia ago, Jesus told His disciples how that
can happen. He said, "Remain in me, as I also remain in you. No
branch can bear fruit of itself; it must remain in the vine. Neither
can you bear much fruit unless you remain in me" (John 15:4).
Jesus is the Vine and we, His followers, are the branches. If we're
honest, we know we're utterly helpless and spiritually ineffective
apart from Him.

Jesus transforms us spiritually and reproduces His life in us—as
we abide in Him.   —MARVIN WILLIAMS

A change in behavior begins with Jesus changing our heart.

A FRIEND HE COULDN'T FORGET

READ: John 15:9–15

*"I have called you friends, for everything
that I learned from my Father I have
made known to you."* JOHN 15:15

WHEN SEVENTEENTH-CENTURY CLERGYMAN BISHOP Beveridge was on his deathbed, he could no longer recognize anyone. The man who had been his associate minister for years visited him and inquired, "Bishop, do you know me?" "No, who are you?" said Beveridge. Another person entered who knew him well and received the same response. Finally, one of them said, "Bishop, do you still know the Lord Jesus Christ?" Hearing those words, he brightened. "Oh yes, I've known Him for forty years. He's my dearest Friend!"

It's not unusual for someone who is ill and dying to lapse into a state where most memories seem to be erased. Yet if the name of Jesus is mentioned, he may perk up and exclaim, "He's my Savior!" I know of a young girl who lay in a coma for many months. The doctors said she would never speak again. Yet just before she died, she whispered the entire twenty-third Psalm. She still knew the Good Shepherd.

When Jesus said to His disciples, "You are my friends" (John 15:14), He was affirming a relationship that would remain strong even in the last flickering moments of our life. As we cultivate that relationship through obedience, we'll find it to be the greatest friendship in all the world! —HENRY BOSCH

*Christ is the only Friend you'll ever find
without a fault—is He yours?*

UNIQUE PRIVILEGES

READ: Romans 8:12–17

He predestined us for adoption to sonship through Jesus Christ,
in accordance with his pleasure and will. EPHESIANS 1:5

IN *Forever Young: My Friendship with John F. Kennedy, Jr.*, Billy Noonan recalls the life experiences he shared with the son of President John Kennedy.

In 1980, as one of the stories goes, John Jr. and Billy were invited aboard the *USS John F. Kennedy* aircraft carrier. On a guided tour of the ship, the two young men and their guide inadvertently entered a restricted area. When an officer stopped them, the guide pointed to John and said, "This is his father's ship." Snapping to attention, the officer saluted John. He explained his understanding that when a US Navy ship is named for someone, it is considered that person's ship. Thus, as the son of the man for whom the ship was named, John Jr. had unique privileges.

This illustrates a vital spiritual principle. As adopted children in God's family, we who have been saved possess the position of sonship. Paul wrote that as believers we are "predestined . . . for adoption to sonship through Jesus Christ" (Ephesians 1:5). By virtue of this sonship, we have the unique privileges that belong to the children of the King of kings.

In life's challenging voyage, we can take courage that our "Abba, Father" (Romans 8:15) owns the ship and shares all with us. Praise God, we are joint-heirs with Christ!   —DENNIS FISHER

A Christian's inheritance is guaranteed forever!

A BLIND MAN'S PLEA

READ: Luke 18:35–43

*He called out, "Jesus, Son of David,
have mercy on me!"* LUKE 18:38

SOME YEARS AGO A traveling companion noticed that I was straining to see objects at a distance. What he did next was simple but life-changing. He took off his glasses and said, "Try these." When I put his glasses on, surprisingly my blurred vision cleared up. Eventually, I went to an optometrist who prescribed glasses to correct my vision problem.

Today's reading in Luke 18 features a man with no vision at all. Living in total darkness had forced him to beg for a living. News about Jesus, the popular teacher and miracle worker, had reached the blind beggar's ears. So when Jesus's travel route took Him by where the blind man was sitting, hope was ignited in his heart. "Jesus, Son of David, have mercy on me!" (v. 38) he called. Though without sight physically, the man possessed spiritual insight into Jesus's true identity and faith in Him to meet his need. Compelled by this faith, "He shouted all the more, 'Son of David, have mercy on me!'" (v. 39). The result? His blindness was banished, and he went from begging for his living to blessing God because he could see (v. 43).

In moments or seasons of darkness, where do you turn? Upon what or to whom do you call? Eyeglass prescriptions help improve vision, but it's the merciful touch of Jesus, God's Son, that brings people from spiritual darkness to light.   —ARTHUR JACKSON

The Father's delight is to give sight to those who ask Him.

A MUTUAL FRIEND

READ: John 15:9–17

*"As the Father has loved me,
so have I loved you."* JOHN 15:9

IMAGINE BEING A VISITOR in a foreign land, showing up unannounced at a gathering of people you have never met and who have never heard of you—and then being allowed to address that group just a few minutes later. That can only happen if something breaks down barriers—something like mutual friends.

It happened when I took a missions team to a church service in Discovery Bay, Jamaica. Before we left the US, my friend Dorant Brown, a Jamaican pastor, recommended a church to attend. So when we arrived at the church, and I mentioned Pastor Brown, we were not only welcomed, but I was also asked to speak briefly and our team was asked to sing.

While sharing Dorant's name was vital, I really don't think it was that mutual friend who got us such a warm welcome. I think it was our shared Friend and Savior Jesus who opened our Jamaican friends' hearts to our visit.

Have you experienced a connection with someone you just met when you tell them you too know Jesus? He's a friend who laid down His life for us (John 15:13), and He makes brothers and sisters of all who believe (1 Peter 2:17).

Jesus. Our Savior. Our mutual Friend. He joins hearts around the world under the banner of His love.　　　　—DAVE BRANON

———

Those who are drawn to Christ are drawn to each other.

I SPY!

READ: John 21:1–7

Then the disciple whom Jesus loved said to Peter, "It is the Lord!" As soon as Simon Peter heard him say, "It is the Lord," he wrapped his outer garment around him (for he had taken it off) and jumped into the water. JOHN 21:7

MY WIFE AND I have some friends who used to play a game with their children called "I Spy." If a family member saw what appeared to be God at work in their surroundings, he or she would call out, "I spy!" It might be a beautiful sunset or some special blessing. These experiences reminded them of God's presence in the world and in their lives.

That game reminds me of Jesus's disciples and their futile fishing endeavor recorded in John 21:1–7. Early in the morning they saw through the mist a man standing on the shore, but they didn't know it was Jesus. "Friends, haven't you any fish?" He asked. "No," they replied.

"Throw the net on the right side of the boat," He said, "and you will find some." The disciples obeyed, and their net was filled with so many fish they couldn't draw it in. "It is the Lord!" exclaimed John. It was an "I spy" moment, and it was John, "the disciple whom Jesus loved," who was the first to recognize Him.

Ask God to give you eyes to "see" Jesus, whether in the extraordinary events or the everyday affairs of your life. If you pay attention, you will see His hand at work where others see nothing. Try playing "I spy" today and let the Lord's presence reassure you of His love and care. —DAVID ROPER

Eyes of faith can see God at work.

A TIME TO CRY

READ: John 11:1–7, 32–36

Jesus wept. JOHN 11:35

MY FATHER, RICHARD DEHAAN, had been battling a debilitating disease for many years. We asked the Lord to take him home. But as I knelt by his bed and watched him take that last breath, the tears I had choked back on other occasions came out like a flood. As my brothers and my mother hugged and prayed, the finality was overwhelming.

That event helped me understand the significance of the shortest verse in the Bible: "Jesus wept" (John 11:35). God the Son wept! He knew the reality of heaven. He was the source of all hope of a future day of resurrection. And yet, Jesus cried. He loved His friends Mary and Martha and Lazarus so much that Jesus "was deeply moved in spirit and troubled" (v. 33). Jesus truly felt their heartache.

When someone we love dies, we struggle with a wide range of emotions. If a young person dies, we ask "Why?" When death comes after long-term suffering, we struggle to understand why the Lord waited so long to bring relief. We begin to think of God as distant, untouched by our sorrow. We may question His wisdom or His goodness. Then we read, "Jesus wept." God is deeply touched by our anguish.

When a painful situation invades your life, remember the Bible's shortest verse. Jesus shed tears too.   —KURT DEHAAN

———

If you doubt that Jesus cares, remember His tears.

GETTING IN THE WAY

READ: John 14:1–6

*Jesus answered, "I am the way and the truth and the life.
No one comes to the Father except through me."* JOHN 14:6

THE ANCIENT ROMANS WERE known for their roads, which criss-crossed their empire with wide, heavily traveled highways. It's what Jesus's audience would have pictured when He claimed, "I am the way" in John 14:6.

While this verse indicates that He is the way to heaven, there's really more to His statement. Cutting through the underbrush of the dense jungle of our world, Jesus is our trail guide who makes a new way for us to live. While many follow the way of the world by loving their friends and hating their enemies, Jesus carves out a new way: "Love your enemies and pray for those who persecute you" (Matthew 5:44). It's easy to judge and criticize others, but Jesus the Way-maker says to take the plank out of our own eye first (7:3–4). And He cuts a path for us to live with generosity instead of greed (Luke 12:13–34).

When Jesus said, "I am the way," He was calling us to leave the old ways that lead to destruction and to follow Him in His new way to live. In fact, the word *follow* (Mark 8:34) literally means "to be found in the way" with Him. You and I can make the choice to travel the familiar and ultimately destructive ways, or we can follow Him and be found in the way with the One who is the way!

—JOE STOWELL

*We don't need to see the way if we're
following the One who is the Way.*

DOCTOR JESUS

READ: Hebrews 13:1–9

Keep your lives free from the love of money and be content with what you have, because God has said, "Never will I leave you; never will I forsake you." HEBREWS 13:5

OM SENG WAS AN elderly Cambodian woman who was widowed and separated from her children by a long and bitter war. When she walked into the emergency room of a missionary hospital in a Thai refugee camp, she asked to see "Doctor Jesus." She was having terrible pain in her eyes and was haunted by nightmarish memories of cruelty and death.

Although the woman was dressed in the white robes of a Buddhist nun, she was deeply troubled about what would happen to her when she died. The doctors diagnosed her eye condition and cured her. When they told her about Doctor Jesus, she put her trust in Him and found inner healing also.

Om Seng became a shining witness in that refugee camp and formed a church that met in her bamboo-and-thatch house. When it was time for her to return to Cambodia, thirty-seven converts had been baptized. Seng was thankful for everything God had done, but she was apprehensive about what it would be like back in her own country. Would she be free to worship God, or would there be persecution? Her fear turned into peace when she realized that Doctor Jesus would be going back with her.

Jesus is always at our side as Savior, Protector, and Helper. What a wonderful reality! —HERB VANDER LUGT

You need not be afraid of where you're going when you know God's going with you.

LIKE A LAMB

READ: John 15:9–17

He was oppressed and afflicted, yet he did not open his mouth; he was led like a lamb to the slaughter, and as a sheep before its shearers is silent, so he did not open his mouth. ISAIAH 53:7

IN 1602, ITALIAN ARTIST Caravaggio produced a painting called *The Taking of Christ.* This work, an early example of the Baroque style, is compelling. Created in dark hues, it allows the viewer to contemplate Jesus's arrest in the Garden of Gethsemane. Two main elements of the scene depicted in the painting demand the observer's attention. The first is Judas as he delivers the traitor's kiss. Immediately, however, the viewer's focus is drawn toward Jesus's hands, which are passively clasped together to show that He offered no resistance to this injustice. Although He possessed the power to create a universe, Christ gave himself up voluntarily to His captors and to the waiting cross.

Long before this scene took place, Jesus told His listeners that no one could take His life from Him—He would lay it down willingly (John 10:18). This heart of voluntary surrender was prophesied by Isaiah, who wrote, "He was led like a lamb to the slaughter, and as a sheep before its shearers is silent, so he did not open his mouth" (Isaiah 53:7).

Christ's lamblike self-sacrifice is a grand indicator of His powerful love. Jesus explained, "Greater love has no one than this: to lay down one's life for one's friends" (John 15:13). Think of it. Jesus loved you that much! —BILL CROWDER

The nail-pierced hands of Jesus reveal the love-filled heart of God.

TELL IT!

READ: Mark 5:1–20

So the man went away and began to tell in the
Decapolis how much Jesus had done for him. And
all the people were amazed. MARK 5:20

THE YEAR WAS 1975 and something significant had just happened to me. I needed to find my good friend Francis and tell him about it. I found him in his apartment hurriedly preparing to go out, but I slowed him down. The way he stared at me, he must have sensed that I had something important to tell him. "What is it?" he asked. So I told him simply, "Yesterday I surrendered my life to Jesus!"

Francis looked at me, sighed heavily, and said, "I've felt like doing the same for a long time now." He asked me to share what happened, and I told him that the previous day someone had explained the gospel to me and that I asked Jesus to come into my life. I still remember the tears in his eyes as he too prayed to receive Jesus's forgiveness. No longer in a hurry, he and I talked and talked about our new relationship with Christ.

After Jesus healed the man with an evil spirit, He told him, "Go home to your own people and tell them how much the Lord has done for you, and how he has had mercy on you" (Mark 5:19). The man didn't need to preach a powerful sermon; he simply needed to share his story.

No matter what our conversion experience is, we can do what that man did: "[He] went away and began to tell . . . how much Jesus had done for him."   —LAWRENCE DARMANI

"Let the redeemed of the LORD tell their story."
—Psalm 107:2

SEEING WELL

READ: John 15:12–17

"You are my friends if you do what I command." JOHN 15:14

RALEIGH LOOKS LIKE A powerful dog—he is large and muscular and has a thick coat of fur. And he weighs over 100 pounds! Despite his appearance, Raleigh connects well with people. His owner takes him to nursing homes and hospitals to bring people a smile.

Once, a four-year-old girl spotted Raleigh across a room. She wanted to pet him but was afraid to get close. Eventually, her curiosity overcame her sense of caution and she spent several minutes talking to him and petting him. She discovered that even though he is powerful, he is a gentle creature.

The combination of these qualities reminds me of what we read about Jesus in the New Testament. Jesus was approachable—He welcomed little children (Matthew 19:13–15). He was kind to an adulterous woman in a desperate situation (John 8:1–11). Compassion motivated Him to teach crowds (Mark 6:34). At the same time, Jesus's power was astounding. Heads turned and jaws dropped as He subdued demons, calmed violent storms, and resurrected dead people! (Mark 1:21–34; 4:35–41; John 11).

The way we see Jesus determines how we relate to Him. If we focus only on His power, we may treat Him with the detached worship we'd give a comic book superhero. Yet, if we overemphasize His kindness, we risk treating Him too casually. The truth is that Jesus is both at once—great enough to deserve our obedience yet humble enough to call us friends. —JENNIFER BENSON SCHULDT

*What we think of Jesus shows
in how we relate with Him.*

PRAYING FOR YOU TODAY

READ: Romans 8:22–34

In the same way, the Spirit helps us in our weakness. We do not know what we ought to pray for, but the Spirit himself intercedes for us through wordless groans. . . . Who then is the one who condemns? No one. Christ Jesus who died—more than that, who was raised to life—is at the right hand of God and is also interceding for us. ROMANS 8:26, 34

WHEN WE FACE A perplexing situation or a tough problem, we often ask our brothers and sisters in Christ to pray for us. It's a great encouragement to know that others who care are holding us up to God in prayer. But what if you don't have close Christian friends? Perhaps you live where the gospel of Christ is opposed. Who will pray for you?

Romans 8, one of the great, triumphant chapters of the Bible, declares, "We do not know what we ought to pray for, but the Spirit himself intercedes for us through wordless groans. . . . The Spirit intercedes for God's people in accordance with the will of God" (Romans 8:26–27). The Holy Spirit is praying for you today.

In addition, "Christ Jesus who died—more than that, who was raised to life—is at the right hand of God and is also interceding for us" (v. 34). The living Lord Jesus Christ is praying for you today.

Think of it! The Holy Spirit and the Lord Jesus Christ mention your name and your needs to God the Father, who hears and acts on your behalf.

No matter where you are or how confusing your situation, you do not face life alone. The Spirit and the Son are praying for you today!   —DAVID MCCASLAND

The Holy Spirit and Jesus are always praying for you.

ISN'T HE WONDERFUL!

READ: Luke 1:26–33

For to us a child is born, to us a son is given, and the government will be on his shoulders. And he will be called Wonderful Counselor, Mighty God, Everlasting Father, Prince of Peace. ISAIAH 9:6

EVERYTHING ABOUT JESUS IS remarkable!

One author exclaimed with wonder and adoration: "Christ came from the bosom of the Father to the bosom of a woman. He put on humanity that we might put on divinity. (See 2 Peter 1:4.) He became a man that we might become the sons of God. In infancy He startled a king; in boyhood He puzzled the scholars; in manhood He ruled the course of nature. He walked upon the storms, hushed the sea to sleep, and healed the multitudes without medicine. He never wrote a book; yet the libraries of the world are filled with volumes that have been written about Him. He never penned a musical note; yet He is the theme of more lyrics than any other subject in the world. Great men have come and gone; yet He lives on. Herod could not kill Him, Satan could not seduce Him, death could not destroy Him, the grave could not hold Him. All others have failed in some way, but not Jesus!"

Not only is Christ matchless in His person and accomplishments but He is also absolutely thrilling to know as Savior and Friend. With Isaiah and millions of redeemed souls, I can testify that Jesus is truly wonderful!   —HENRY BOSCH

*How awe-inspiring is the name of "Immanuel"—
the wonder of God with us!*

GROWING IN THE WIND

READ: Mark 4:36–41

*They were terrified and asked each other, "Who is this?
Even the wind and the waves obey him!"* MARK 4:41

IMAGINE A WORLD WITHOUT wind. Lakes would be calm. Falling leaves wouldn't blow in the streets. But in still air, who would expect trees to suddenly fall over? That's what happened in a three-acre glass dome built in the Arizona desert. Trees growing inside a huge windless bubble called Biosphere 2 grew faster than normal until suddenly collapsing under their own weight. Project researchers eventually came up with an explanation. These trees needed wind stress to grow strong.

Jesus let His disciples experience gale-force winds to strengthen their faith (Mark 4:36–41). During a night crossing of familiar waters, a sudden storm proved too much even for these seasoned fishermen. Wind and waves were swamping their boat while an exhausted Jesus slept in the stern. In a panic they woke Him. *Didn't it bother their Teacher that they were about to die? What was He thinking?* Then they began to find out. Jesus told the wind and waves to be quiet—and asked His friends why they still had no faith in Him.

If the wind had not blown, these disciples would never have asked, "Who is this? Even the winds and the waves obey him!" (Mark 4:41).

Today, life in a protective bubble might sound good. But how strong would our faith be if we couldn't discover for ourselves His reassuring "be still" when the winds of circumstance howl?

—MART DEHAAN

God never sleeps.

PAIN WITH A PURPOSE

READ: John 16:17–24

"So with you: Now is your time of grief, but I will see you again and you will rejoice, and no one will take away your joy." JOHN 16:22

I ASKED SEVERAL FRIENDS what their most difficult, painful experience in life had been. Their answers included war, divorce, surgery, and the loss of a loved one. My wife's reply was, "The birth of our first child." It was a long and difficult labor in a lonely army hospital. But looking back, she said she considers it joyful "because the pain had a big purpose."

Just before Jesus went to the cross, He told His followers they were about to go through a time of great pain and sorrow. The Lord compared their coming experience to that of a woman during childbirth when her anguish turns to joy after her child is born (John 16:20–21). "So with you: Now is your time of grief, but I will see you again and you will rejoice, and no one will take away your joy" (v. 22).

Sorrow comes to us all along the road of life. "For the joy set before him [Jesus] endured the cross, scorning its shame" (Hebrews 12:2) and purchasing forgiveness and freedom for all who open their hearts to Him. His painful sacrifice accomplished God's eternal purpose of opening the way to friendship and fellowship with Him.

The joy of our Savior outweighed His suffering, just as the joy He gives us overshadows all our pain.   —DAVID McCASLAND

Suffering can be like a magnet that draws the Christian close to Christ.

TWO PORTRAITS

READ: John 16:19–24

"You will grieve, but your grief will turn to joy." JOHN 16:20

CLUTCHING TWO FRAMED PHOTOGRAPHS, the proud grandmother showed them to friends in the church foyer. The first picture was of her daughter back in her homeland of Burundi. The second was of her grandson, born recently to that daughter. But the daughter wasn't holding her newborn. She had died giving birth to him. A friend approached and looked at the pictures. Reflexively, she reached up and held that dear grandmother's face in her hands. All she could say through her own tears was, "I know. I know."

And she did know. Two months earlier she had buried a son.

There's something special about the comfort of others who have experienced our pain. They *know*. Just before Jesus's arrest, He warned His disciples, "You will weep and mourn while the world rejoices." But in the next breath He comforted them: "You will grieve, but your grief will turn to joy" (John 16:20). In mere hours, the disciples would be devastated by Jesus's arrest and crucifixion. But their crushing grief soon turned to a joy they could not have imagined when they saw Him alive again.

Isaiah prophesied of the Messiah, "Surely he took up our pain and bore our suffering" (Isaiah 53:4). We have a Savior who doesn't merely know *about* our pain; He lived it. He knows. He cares. One day our grief will be turned into joy. —TIM GUSTAFSON

When we put our cares into His hands,
He puts His peace into our hearts.

THE LAST WORD

READ: John 11:17–27

*Jesus said to her, "I am the resurrection and the
life. He who believes in Me, though he may
die, he shall live."* JOHN 11:25 (NKJV)

WHEN WALTER BOUMAN, a retired seminary professor, learned
that the cancer in his body had spread and that he had perhaps
nine months to live, he pondered many things. One was comedian
Johnny Carson's quip: "It is true that for several days after you die,
your hair and fingernails keep on growing, but the phone calls
taper off." He found that humor to be a wonderful tonic, but it was
something far deeper that sustained his soul.

In Bouman's newspaper column, he wrote of his greatest source
of encouragement: "The Christian good news is that Jesus of Nazareth has been raised from death, that death no longer has dominion
over Him. I have bet my living, and now I am called to bet my
dying, that Jesus will have the last word."

In John 11, we read what Jesus said to Martha, a close friend
who was grieving the death of her brother. He said: "I am the
resurrection and the life. He who believes in Me, though he may
die, he shall live. And whoever lives and believes in Me shall never
die" (vv. 25–26 NKJV).

For each "today" we are given, and for the inevitable "tomorrow"
that will come, we don't have to be afraid. Jesus Christ is with all
who trust Him, and He will have the last word.

—DAVID MCCASLAND

*Because Jesus has risen from the dead,
He has the last word in life and in death.*

INTERRUPTED FELLOWSHIP

READ: Matthew 27:32–50

About three in the afternoon Jesus cried out in a loud voice,
"Eli, Eli, lema sabachthani?" (which means "My God, my
God, why have you forsaken me?"). MATTHEW 27:46

THE LOUD, SORROWFUL CRY pierced the dark afternoon air. I imagine it drowning out the sound of mourning from friends and loved ones gathered at Jesus's feet. It must have overwhelmed the moans of the dying criminals who flanked Jesus on both sides. And surely startled all who heard it.

"*Eli, Eli, lema sabachthani?*" Jesus cried out in agony and in utter despondency as He hung on that cross of shame on Golgotha (Matthew 27:45–46).

"My God," He said, "my God, why have you forsaken me?"

I cannot think of more heart-wrenching words. Since eternity, Jesus had been in perfect fellowship with God the Father. Together they had created the universe, had fashioned mankind in their image, and planned salvation. Never in the eons past had they not been in total fellowship with each other.

And now, as the anguish of the cross continued to bring devastating pain on Jesus, He for the first time lost the awareness of God's presence as He carried the burden of the sins of the world.

It was the only way. Only through this time of interrupted fellowship could our salvation be provided for. And it was only because Jesus was willing to experience this sense of being forsaken on the cross that we humans could gain fellowship with God.

Thank you, Jesus, for experiencing such pain so we could be forgiven.
—DAVE BRANON

The cross reveals God's heart for the lost.

WITH US ALWAYS

READ: Isaiah 41:8–13

So do not fear, for I am with you; do not be dismayed, for I am your God. I will strengthen you and help you; I will uphold you with my righteous right hand. ISAIAH 41:10

AN OLD STORY IS told of a timid prisoner who committed a minor infraction and was sentenced to spend the night in a dark, isolated cell—deep inside the prison walls. As the man was led down to it, the loathsome air seemed to choke him. The heavy door clanked shut, and he knew a long, lonely night was before him—far beyond the sound of any human voice.

As he sank to the floor in despair, he heard the sound of footsteps. Then a voice said softly, "I'm the prison chaplain. I knew you could not stand it alone, so I've come to be with you. I will be here as long as you are." Because the prisoner knew that another person was with him in the darkness, his lonely chamber became a place of rest.

Whenever we must walk the dark and solitary roads of anguish and heartache, we have someone by our side: Jesus Christ. True, we may sorrow. But when we do, we have the assurance of the unseen presence of Jesus himself. He has promised to be with us always. He will never leave us alone.   —DAVID EGNER

*No danger can come so near the
Christian that God is not nearer.*

HUMBLE LOVE

READ: Philippians 2:1–11

The greatest among you will be your servant.
MATTHEW 23:11

WHEN BENJAMIN FRANKLIN WAS a young man, he made a list of twelve virtues he desired to grow in over the course of his life. He showed it to a friend, who suggested he add "humility" to it. Franklin liked the idea. He then added some guidelines to help him with each item on the list. Among Franklin's thoughts about humility, he held up Jesus as an example to emulate.

Jesus shows us the ultimate example of humility. God's Word tells us, "In your relationships with one another, have the same mindset as Christ Jesus: Who, being in very nature God, did not consider equality with God something to be used to his own advantage; rather, he made himself nothing by taking the very nature of a servant" (Philippians 2:5–7).

Jesus demonstrated the greatest humility of all. Though eternally with the Father, He chose to bend beneath a cross in love so that through His death He might lift any who receive Him into the joy of His presence.

We imitate Jesus's humility when we seek to serve our heavenly Father by serving others. Jesus's kindness helps us catch a breathtaking glimpse of the beauty of setting ourselves aside to attend to others' needs. Aiming for humility isn't easy in our "me first" world. But as we rest securely in our Savior's love, He will give us everything we need to follow Him.   —JAMES BANKS

We can serve because we are loved.

MANY BEAUTIFUL THINGS

READ: Mark 14:1–9

*"Leave her alone," said Jesus. "Why are you bothering her?
She has done a beautiful thing to me."* MARK 14:6

JUST BEFORE HER DEATH, artist and missionary Lilias Trotter looked out a window and saw a vision of a heavenly chariot. According to her biographer, a friend asked, "Are you seeing many beautiful things?" She answered, "Yes, many, many beautiful things."

Trotter's final words reflect God's work in her life. Not only in death, but throughout her life, He revealed much beauty to her and through her. Although a talented artist, she chose to serve Jesus as a missionary in Algeria. John Ruskin, a famous painter who tutored her, is said to have commented, "What a waste," when she chose the mission field over a career in art.

Similarly, in the New Testament when a woman came to Simon the Leper's house with an alabaster jar and poured perfume on Jesus's head, those present saw it as a waste. This expensive perfume was worth a year's common wages, so some of the people present thought it could have been used to help the poor. However, commending this woman's deep devotion to Him, Jesus said, "She has done a beautiful thing to me" (Mark 14:6).

Every day we can choose to let Christ's life shine in our lives and display His beauty to the world. To some, it may seem a waste, but let us have willing hearts to serve Him. May Jesus say we have done many beautiful things for Him.　　　　—KEILA OCHOA

May our lives display the beauty of God.

MAN OF CONTRASTS

READ: Revelation 5:8–14

Then I heard every creature in heaven and on earth and under the earth and on the sea, and all that is in them, saying: "To him who sits on the throne and to the Lamb be praise and honor and glory and power, for ever and ever!" REVELATION 5:13

JESUS IS THE MOST unusual person ever to walk on earth. He is the God-man, fully God and fully man. His life was marked by striking contrasts that reflect both His genuine humanity and His full deity.

Someone has written of Jesus: "He who is the Bread of Life began His ministry hungering. He who is the Water of Life ended his ministry thirsting. Christ hungered as man, yet fed the hungry as God. He was weary, yet He is our rest. He paid tribute, yet He is the King. He was called a devil, but He cast out demons. He prayed, yet He hears prayer. He wept and He dries our tears. He was sold for thirty pieces of silver, yet He redeems sinners. He was led as a lamb to the slaughter, yet He is the Good Shepherd. He gave His life, and by dying He destroyed death."

Jesus came to earth to reveal the Father and to provide our redemption. Speaking of the incarnation of Christ, John wrote, "In the beginning was the Word, and the Word was with God, and the Word was God. . . . The Word became flesh and made his dwelling among us. We have seen his glory, the glory of the one and only Son, who came from the Father, full of grace and truth" (John 1:1, 14).

Yes, Jesus is the heart of our faith, and He deserves our heartfelt praise. —RICHARD DEHAAN

We can never praise Jesus too much.

THE POWER OF INFLUENCE

READ: 2 Chronicles 22:1–9

You foolish Galatians! Who has bewitched you?
Before your very eyes Jesus Christ was clearly
portrayed as crucified. GALATIANS 3:1

ALL THOSE YEARS OF training in good grammar couldn't stand up to a few hours of being with a friend who mangles the language. That was my observation many years ago when I overheard my then second-grade son Steven talking with one of his friends.

I had listened as Steven's buddy used poor English again and again. I was surprised by his word choices, but I was really taken aback when I heard Steven talking the same way. He didn't usually talk like that—at least he didn't until a little peer pressure got to him.

It was another illustration of the power of others to change the way we think. We carefully guide our children to use proper speech patterns, but the influence of one friend can undo all that.

Think about how this principle affects much more important choices. Consider Ahaziah in 2 Chronicles 22. He was influenced by his mother to do wrong (v. 3). As a result, "He did evil in the eyes of the LORD" (v. 4). His godly grandfather Jehoshaphat surely had some influence on Ahaziah, but it was the evil persuasion of Athaliah that marked his course.

We can be manipulated! So we must be careful about who or what influences us and stay close to our Father, the source of all that is good and right.   —DAVE BRANON

Choose your companions with care—
you may become what they are.

MISTAKEN IDENTITY

READ: Matthew 16:13–20

*"But what about you?" he asked. "Who do
you say I am?"* MATTHEW 16:15

MY YOUNGEST BROTHER, SCOTT, was born when I was a senior in high school. This age difference made for an interesting situation when he grew to college age. On his first trip to his college campus, I went along with him and our mom. When we arrived, people thought we were Scott Crowder and his dad and his grandmom. Eventually, we gave up correcting them. No matter what we said or did, our actual relationships were overridden by this humorous case of mistaken identity.

Jesus questioned the Pharisees about His identity: "What do you think about the Messiah? Whose son is he?" They replied, "The son of David" (Matthew 22:42). The identity of Messiah was critical, and their answer was correct but incomplete. The Scriptures had affirmed that Messiah would come and reign on the throne of His father David. But Jesus reminded them that though David would be Christ's ancestor, He would also be more—David referred to Him as "LORD" (See Psalm 110:1).

Faced with a similar question, Peter rightly answered, "You are the Messiah, the Son of the living God" (Matthew 16:16). Still today, the question of Jesus's identity rises above the rest in significance—and it is eternally important that we make no mistake in understanding who He is.   —BILL CROWDER

*No mistake is more dangerous than
mistaking the identity of Jesus.*

FOR OUR FRIENDS

READ: John 15:5–17

*"He cuts off every branch in me that bears no fruit,
while every branch that does bear fruit he prunes so
that it will be even more fruitful."* JOHN 15:2

IN EMILY BRONTË'S NOVEL *Wuthering Heights*, a cantankerous man
who often quotes the Bible to criticize others is memorably described
as "the wearisomest self-righteous Pharisee that ever ransacked a Bible
to rake [apply] the promises to himself and fling the curses to his
neighbours."

It's a funny line, and it may even bring particular people to
mind. But aren't we *all* a bit like this—prone to condemn others'
failures while excusing our own?

In Scripture some people amazingly did the exact opposite; they
were willing to give up God's promises for them and even be cursed
if it would save others. Consider Moses, who said he'd rather be
blotted out of God's book than to see the Israelites be unforgiven
(Exodus 32:32). Or Paul, who said he'd choose to be "cut off from
Christ" if it meant his people would find Him (Romans 9:3).

As self-righteous as we can be, Scripture highlights those who love
others more than themselves. Because ultimately, such love points to
Jesus. "Greater love has no one than this," Jesus taught, than "to lay
down one's life for one's friends" (John 15:13). Even before we knew
Him, Jesus loved us "to the end" (13:1)—choosing death to give us life.

Now we are invited into the family of God, to love and be loved
like this (15:9–12). And as we pour into others Christ's unimagi-
nable love, the world will catch a glimpse of Him.

—MONICA BRANDS

When we love Christ, we love others.

IT'S A FACT

READ: Ephesians 4:1–6

*"That all of them may be one, Father, just as you are in me
and I am in you. May they also be in us so that the world
may believe that you have sent me."* JOHN 17:21

IN DOING RESEARCH FOR his epic story *Roots*, Alex Haley embarked
on the freighter *African Star*, sailing from Monrovia, Liberia, to
Jacksonville, Florida. He did so to better understand the travails of
his ancestors, who were brought in chains to America.

Haley descended into the ship's hold, stripped himself of protective clothing, and tried to sleep on some thick, rough-hewn bracing.
After the third miserable night, he gave up and returned to his
cabin. But he could now write with some small degree of empathy
of the sufferings of his forebears.

It's one thing to say we believe that Jesus Christ, the second Person of the holy Trinity, identifies himself with us. It's quite another
to feel the blessed experience of our identification with Him. But
we need not resort to extreme measures to grasp the truth of that
oneness, for Christ himself has endured the most extreme of all
measures to identify with us. He went to the cross to reconcile a
sinful human race to himself (Romans 5:10–11).

Reading Scripture, praying, and partaking of the Lord's Supper
can help us gain at least some awareness of our identification with
our Lord and Savior. But regardless of how we feel, our unity with
Him is a fact that we must grasp in faith.   —VERNON GROUNDS

The just shall live by faith—not by feeling.

RESEMBLING CHRIST

READ: Matthew 5:12–16, 43–48

*When he found him, he brought him to Antioch. So for
a whole year Barnabas and Saul met with the church
and taught great numbers of people. The disciples were
called Christians first at Antioch.* ACTS 11:26

JESUS'S DISCIPLES WERE SUCH enthusiastic witnesses of His teachings that those who lived in Antioch nicknamed them "Christians," or "Christ ones." Their unusual character and zeal quickly identified them as His followers. They were continually preaching, praying, and showing forth the grace of God with earnestness and love. Filled with the power of His Spirit, they reminded everyone of Jesus.

You have probably observed that elderly couples who have been married for many years resemble each other both in looks and mannerisms. So too the intimate followers of Jesus, having been in close fellowship with the Savior for three transforming years, revealed to others His tender compassion and holy attitudes.

If we love Jesus as the disciples did, seeking to "live as Jesus did" (1 John 2:6), the world will notice before long that our lives have taken on His characteristics and virtues. They will see Jesus in us!

At home, at work, and at school, can others see our Savior demonstrated in us by what we say and by how we act? Just how much do we resemble Christ? —HENRY BOSCH

*Christians, like mirrors, should reflect the light
and glory of Christ to a dark world.*

A PIERCING THORN

READ: Isaiah 53:1–6

He was pierced for our transgressions, he was crushed for our iniquities; the punishment that brought us peace was on him, and by his wounds we are healed. ISAIAH 53:5

THE THORN PRICKED MY index finger, drawing blood. I hollered and then groaned, drawing back my hand instinctively. But I shouldn't have been surprised: trying to prune a thorny bush without gardening gloves was a recipe for exactly what had just happened.

The pain throbbing in my finger—and the blood flowing from it—demanded attention. And as I searched for a bandage, I found myself unexpectedly thinking about my Savior. After all, soldiers forced Jesus to don an entire crown of thorns (John 19:1–3). *If one thorn hurt this much*, I thought, *how much agony would an entire crown of them inflict?* And that's just a small portion of the physical pain He suffered. A whip flogged His back. Nails penetrated His wrists and ankles.

But Jesus endured spiritual pain too. Verse 5 of Isaiah 53 tells us, "But he was pierced for our transgressions, he was crushed for our iniquities; the punishment that brought us peace was on him." The "peace" Isaiah talks about here is another way of talking about forgiveness. Jesus allowed himself to be pierced—by nails, by a crown of thorns—to bring us spiritual peace with God. His sacrifice, His willingness to die on our behalf, paved the way to make a relationship with the Father possible. And He did it, Scripture tells us, for me, for you.　　　　　　　　　　　—ADAM HOLZ

Jesus allowed himself to be pierced to bring us spiritual peace with God.

PIGEON WALK

READ: Daniel 6:1–10

Three times a day [Daniel] got down on his knees and prayed, giving thanks to his God. DANIEL 6:10

HAVE YOU EVER WONDERED why a pigeon walks so funny? It's so that it can see where it's going. Because a pigeon's eyes can't focus as it moves, the bird actually has to bring its head to a complete stop between steps in order to refocus. So it proceeds clumsily—head forward, stop, head back, stop.

In our spiritual walk with the Lord, we have the same problem as the pigeon: We have a hard time seeing while we're on the go. We need to stop between steps—to refocus on the Word and the will of God. That's not to say we have to pray and meditate about every little decision in life. But certainly our walk with the Lord needs to have built into it a pattern of stops that enable us to see more clearly before moving on.

Daniel's practice of praying three times a day was an essential part of his walk with God. He realized that there's a certain kind of spiritual refocusing that we can't do without stopping. His stops gave him a very different kind of walk—one that was obvious to those around him.

What about us? At the risk of being thought of as different, as Daniel was, let's learn this valuable lesson from the pigeon: "Looking good" isn't nearly as important as "seeing well."

—MART DEHAAN

Time in Christ's service requires time out for renewal.

SEEING JESUS

READ: Isaiah 53:1–6

He grew up before him like a tender shoot, and like a root out of dry ground. He had no beauty or majesty to attract us to him, nothing in his appearance that we should desire him. ISAIAH 53:2

WHEN I WAS YOUNG, I thought I knew exactly what Jesus looked like. After all, I saw Him every day whenever I looked at some pictures in my bedroom. One showed Jesus knocking at a door and the other depicted Him as a Shepherd with His sheep.

What I didn't know was that a mere decade before I was born, those pictures of Jesus didn't exist. Warner Sallman painted the well-known *Head of Christ* and other portraits of Jesus in the 1940s. Those images were just one man's idea of what Jesus might have looked like.

The Bible never gives a physical description of Jesus. Even the men who saw Him every day didn't tell us what He looked like. In fact, the only clue we have is a passage in Isaiah that says: "He had no beauty or majesty to attract us to him" (53:2). It seems that Jesus's human form was deliberately de-emphasized. He looked like an ordinary man. People weren't drawn to Him because of a regal appearance but because of what He said and did and because of the message of love He came to give (John 3:16).

But the next time Jesus comes to earth, it will be different. When our Savior returns, we will recognize Him as the sovereign King of kings and Lord of lords! (1 Timothy 6:14–15).

—CINDY HESS KASPER

To see Jesus will be heaven's greatest joy.

JESUS AT THE CENTER

READ: Zechariah 12:10–14

*"And I will pour out on the house of David and the inhabitants
of Jerusalem a spirit of grace and supplication. They will look
on me, the one they have pierced, and they will mourn for
him as one mourns for an only child, and grieve bitterly for
him as one grieves for a firstborn son."* ZECHARIAH 12:10

HAVE YOU HEARD OF the "Christocentric Principle" of biblical
understanding? Simply put, it means that everything we know
about God, angels, Satan, human hopes, and the whole universe is
best understood when viewed in relationship to Jesus Christ. He
is at the center.

Recently, I discovered that one of the less familiar Old Testament
books, Zechariah, is one of the most Christocentric. This book is
a good example because it speaks of Christ's humanity (6:12), His
humility (9:9), His betrayal (11:12), His deity (12:8), His crucifixion
(12:10), His return (14:4), and His future reign (14:8–21).

One especially meaningful passage is Zechariah 12:10, which
says, "They will look on me, the one they have pierced." The piercing
refers to Israel's historic rejection of Jesus as Messiah—resulting in
His crucifixion. But this verse also predicts a future generation of
Jews who will accept Him as their Messiah. At the second coming
of Jesus, a remnant of Israel will recognize the crucified One and
turn to Him in faith.

This marvelous book should encourage us to look for more
Christ-centered truths—both in other parts of the Bible and in all
of life. Keep Jesus in the middle of everything. Live a Christocentric
life.   —DENNIS FISHER

Jesus Christ is the Key that unlocks the Word of God.

A PORTRAIT OF JESUS

READ: Isaiah 53:4–12

*We all, like sheep, have gone astray, each of us has
turned to our own way; and the LORD has laid
on him the iniquity of us all.* ISAIAH 53:6

IN *Portraits of Famous American Women*, Robert Henkes writes, "A portrait is not a photograph, nor is it a mirror image." A portrait goes beyond the outer appearance to probe the emotional depth of the human soul. In a portrait, a true artist tries "to capture what the person is really about."

Over the centuries, many portraits have been painted of Jesus. Perhaps you've seen them in a church or museum of art or even have one in your home. Not one of these is a true portrait, of course, because we have no photograph or mirror image of our Lord's physical appearance. We do, however, have a magnificent word portrait of Him in Isaiah 53. This God-inspired description captures in vivid detail what He is all about: "Surely he took up our pain and bore our suffering . . . . But he was pierced for our transgressions, he was crushed for our iniquities; . . . and by his wounds we are healed" (vv. 4–5).

This passage enables us to see love and sorrow, anguish and pain on Jesus's face. But His lips do not accuse or condemn. He has no sins of His own to grieve; only ours to bear. And deep inside, He knows that "He shall see the labor of His soul, and be satisfied" (v. 11 NKJV).

What a portrait of our Savior!   —DAVID MCCASLAND

Love was when God became a man.

CLOSE ASSOCIATION

READ: Acts 4:13–22

*When they saw the courage of Peter and John
and realized that they were unschooled, ordinary
men, they were astonished and they took note that
these men had been with Jesus.* ACTS 4:13

IN HER BOOK *Acting Like Christians*, Ruth Huston told this story: "A beautiful but non-fragrant plant was delivered to a home from a florist shop. To the surprise of the lady who received it, the plant had the delicious, pungent fragrance of heliotrope. In a few days the odor disappeared entirely. The owner contacted the florist. She concluded that the gift plant had been placed next to a heliotrope plant in the greenhouse, and it had absorbed its pleasant fragrance. Later, separated from the heliotrope, the odorless plant gradually lost the perfume and returned to its natural state."

The Scripture says of Peter and John that the Sanhedrin "took note that these men had been with Jesus" (Acts 4:13). Their boldness in proclaiming the gospel resulted from their close association and fellowship with the risen Lord. This gave a heavenly fragrance to their lives.

It is our privilege to have daily sweet communion with our blessed Lord. As we linger long in His presence, the holy aroma of His person will permeate our entire life.   —PAUL VAN GORDER

*There will be more reflection of Jesus when
there is more reflection on Jesus.*

LOOK WHAT JESUS HAS DONE

READ: Luke 8:1–8

But since you excel in everything—in faith, in speech,
in knowledge, in complete earnestness and in the
love we have kindled in you—see that you also excel
in this grace of giving. 2 CORINTHIANS 8:7

THE LITTLE BOY WAS only eight when he announced to his parents' friend Wally, "I love Jesus and want to serve God overseas someday." During the next ten years or so, Wally prayed for him as he watched him grow up. When this young man later applied with a mission agency to go to Mali, Wally told him, "It's about time! When I heard what you wanted to do, I invested some money and have been saving it for you, waiting for this exciting news." Wally has a heart for others and for getting God's good news to people.

Jesus and His disciples needed financial support as they traveled from one town and village to another, telling the good news of His kingdom (Luke 8:1–3). A group of women who had been cured of evil spirits and diseases helped to support them "out of their own means" (v. 3). One was Mary Magdalene, who had been freed from the presence of seven demons. Another was Joanna, the wife of an official in Herod's court. Nothing is known about Susanna and "many others" (v. 3), but we know that Jesus had met their spiritual needs. Now they were helping Him and His disciples through giving their financial resources.

When we consider what Jesus has done for us, His heart for others becomes our own. Let's ask God how He wants to use us.

—ANNE CETAS

Jesus gave His all; He deserves our all.

JESUS LOVES MAYSEL

READ: 1 John 4:7–16

This is love: not that we loved God, but that he loved us and sent his Son as an atoning sacrifice for our sins. 1 JOHN 4:10

WHEN MY SISTER MAYSEL was little, she would sing a familiar song in her own way: "Jesus loves me, this I know, for the Bible tells Maysel." This irritated me to no end! As one of her older, "wiser" sisters, I knew the words were "me so," not "Maysel." Yet she persisted in singing it her way.

Now I think my sister had it right all along. The Bible does indeed tell Maysel, and all of us, that Jesus loves us. Over and over again we read that truth. Take, for example, the writings of the apostle John, "the disciple whom Jesus loved" (John 21:7, 20). He tells us about God's love in one of the best-known verses of the Bible: John 3:16, "For God so loved the world that he gave his one and only Son, that whoever believes in him shall not perish but have eternal life."

John reinforces that message of love in 1 John 4:10: "This is love: not that we loved God, but that he loved us and sent his Son as an atoning sacrifice for our sins." Just as John knew Jesus loved him, we too can have that same assurance: Jesus does love us. The Bible tells us so.　　　　　　　　　　　　　　　　　—ALYSON KIEDA

Jesus loves me! This I know.

TAKE ANOTHER LOOK AT JESUS

READ: Hebrews 3:1–6

Christ is faithful as the Son over God's house. And we are his house, if indeed we hold firmly to our confidence and the hope in which we glory. HEBREWS 3:6

IF THERE EVER WAS a faithful person, it was Brother Justice. He was committed to his marriage, dedicated to his job as a postal worker, and each Sunday stood at his post as a leader in our local church. I visited my childhood church recently, and perched on the upright piano was the same bell that Brother Justice rang to notify us that the time for Bible study was about to end. The bell has endured the test of time. And although Brother Justice has been with the Lord for years, his legacy of faithfulness also endures.

Hebrews 3 brings a faithful servant and a faithful Son to the readers' attention. Though the faithfulness of Moses as God's "servant" is undeniable, Jesus is the one believers are taught to focus on. "Therefore, holy brothers and sisters . . . fix your thoughts on Jesus" (v. 1). Such was the encouragement to all who face temptation (2:18). Their legacy could come only from following Jesus, the faithful One.

What do you do when the winds of temptation are swirling all around you? When you are weary and worn and want to quit? The text invites us to, as one paraphrase renders it, "Take a good hard look at Jesus" (3:1 MSG). Look at Him again—and again and again. As we reexamine Jesus, we find the trustworthy Son of God who gives us courage to live in His family.   —ARTHUR JACKSON

Looking to Jesus can give us courage to face the challenges in our lives.

A BOY'S LUNCH

READ: John 6:1–14

Then Jesus declared, "I am the bread of life. Whoever comes to me will never go hungry, and whoever believes in me will never be thirsty." JOHN 6:35

ONCE I MADE THE mistake of thinking I could single-handedly finish a twenty-eight-ounce steak at a restaurant. I had the remainder boxed up to take home. I thought, *At least it will give me another feast to look forward to.*

As I left the restaurant, a homeless man approached me, asking for money. At first I refused. But struck by sudden guilt, I called him back, gave him five dollars, and blessed him in Jesus's name. Having done my Christian duty, I was happy to go on my way, boxed-up steak in hand, until he asked, "What about the box?" I have to admit, I had a hard time parting with my steak.

One of my favorite stories in the New Testament is about the little boy who brown-bagged it to a revival service (John 6:1–14). If he was like most boys, his lunch was a very important commodity. Yet he was willing to give his lunch of five barley loaves and two small fish to the Lord. I think he may have known that by putting his lunch in the hands of Jesus, He could do something extraordinary with it. And He did. He fed thousands of hungry people.

Jesus is still looking for a few common folk like you and me who are willing to commit out-of-the-ordinary, intentional acts of selfless sacrifice so that He can turn our offering into His glory. Commit such an act today!   —JOE STOWELL

Let Jesus share with others what you want to keep for yourself.

A FRESH START

READ: Luke 5:17–26

Jesus answered them, "It is not the healthy who need a doctor, but the sick." LUKE 5:31

IN MANY COUNTRIES, HEALTH laws prohibit reselling or reusing old mattresses. Only landfills will take them. Tim Keenan tackled the problem and today his business employs a dozen people to extract the individual components of metal, fabric, and foam in old mattresses for recycling. But that's only part of the story. Journalist Bill Vogrin wrote, "Of all the items Keenan recycles . . . it's the people that may be his biggest success" (*The Gazette*, Colorado Springs). Keenan hires men from halfway houses and homeless shelters, giving them a job and a second chance. He says, "We take guys nobody else wants."

Luke 5:17–26 tells how Jesus healed the body and the soul of a paralyzed man. Following that miraculous event, Levi answered Jesus's call to follow Him and then invited his fellow tax collectors and friends to a banquet in honor of the Lord (vv. 27–29). When some people accused Jesus of associating with undesirables (v. 30), He reminded them that healthy people don't need a doctor—adding, "I have not come to call the righteous, but sinners to repentance" (v. 32).

To everyone who feels like a "throwaway" headed for the landfill of life, Jesus opens His arms of love and offers a fresh beginning. That's why He came!　　　　　　　　　　—DAVID MCCASLAND

Salvation is receiving a new life.

WANTED

READ: Luke 19:29–40

They replied, "The Lord needs it." LUKE 19:34

AS JESUS APPROACHED JERUSALEM for the last time, He sent two disciples into the city to obtain a donkey for Him. He told them, "If anyone asks you, 'Why are you untying it?' say, 'The Lord needs it'" (Luke 19:31).

People who have reached what are sometimes called the "sunset years" in life may ask themselves, "Can I still be useful to God? Is there some service I can render that will fill my days with significance? Am I needed?"

Of course you are! God needs you just as He needed the donkey to carry Him through the streets of Jerusalem. He has always needed something or someone to get His work done. He still has useful work for you to do.

Perhaps your work will be one brief task, like the donkey's single act of service. Or it may be some activity that will fully occupy your years until your Master calls you home. It may be an opportunity to share your faith with someone, to intercede for him, or to love him through quiet acts of mercy, friendly visits, or to extend some small courtesy. There will always be something for you to do.

In the meantime, you and I must stand and wait, preparing ourselves through prayer, Bible reading, and quiet listening—ready for the moment when our Lord needs us.

Will you be ready when He needs you?   —DAVID ROPER

God has work for all His children, regardless of age or ability.

FOR THIS I HAVE JESUS

READ: Psalm 66

*You let people ride over our heads;
we went through fire and water, but you brought
us to a place of abundance.* PSALM 66:12

IN A BYGONE ERA, an evangelist was speaking in Ireland about what it means to trust Jesus in every test and trial. To drive his point home, he ended by saying, "It means that in every circumstance you remind yourself: 'For this I have Jesus.'" He then opened the meeting for testimonies from those present.

One young lady arose and said, "I have just been informed that I have to leave. During the message, I was handed this telegram." Unfolding it she read, "Mother is very ill; take train home immediately." Immediately, my heart prompted me to say, 'For this I have Jesus.' Peace and strength flooded over me." She continued, "I have never before traveled a great distance alone, 'but for this I have Jesus.' For all strain that goes with the thought of my mother's severe illness, 'I praise God, I have Jesus.'"

A few weeks later, the evangelist received a letter from this woman. She wrote, "Thank you for that message. I have come to realize that no matter what life brings, 'For this I have Jesus.'" The Lord often leads us through fire and through water still He eventually brings us out into a "place of abundance" (Psalm 66:12).

Are you enduring a great trial? Remember, "for this you have Jesus!" —HENRY BOSCH

*Those who see God's hand in everything are
content to leave everything in God's hand!*

NOWHERE TO HIDE

READ: Genesis 3:6–13, 22–24

*Jesus Christ, who is the faithful witness,
the firstborn from the dead, and the ruler of the
kings of the earth.* REVELATION 1:5

I SMELLED SOMETHING BURNING, so I hurried to the kitchen. Nothing was on the stove or in the oven. I followed my nose through the house. From room to room I went, eventually arriving downstairs. My nose led me to my office and then to my desk. I peeked beneath it and there, peering back at me with big eyes pleading for help, was Maggie, our very "fragrant" dog. What smelled like something burning when I was upstairs now had the distinct odor of skunk. Maggie had gone to the farthest corner of our house to escape the foul smell, but she couldn't get away from herself.

Maggie's dilemma brought to mind the many times I have tried to run away from unpleasant circumstances only to discover that the problem was not the situation I was in but me. Since Adam and Eve hid after sinning (Genesis 3:8), we've all followed their example. We run away from situations thinking we can escape the unpleasantness—only to discover that the unpleasantness is us.

The only way to escape ourselves is to stop hiding, acknowledge our waywardness, and let Jesus wash us clean (Revelation 1:5). I am grateful that when we do sin, Jesus is willing to give us a brand-new start.   —JULIE ACKERMAN LINK

———

Sin's contamination requires the Savior's cleansing.

PACE YOURSELF

READ: Mark 6:30–36

*Then, because so many people were coming and
going that they did not even have a chance to eat,
he said to them, "Come with me by yourselves to
a quiet place and get some rest."* MARK 6:31

NOT LONG AGO I developed a physical problem. My left shoulder
and arm were aching, I had a painful rash on my forearm and
thumb, and I struggled daily with fatigue. When I finally went to
the doctor, I learned that I had a case of shingles. The doctor put
me on antiviral medication and said it would take several weeks
for the disease to run its course.

Because of this illness, I had to force myself into a new routine.
A short nap in the morning and one in the afternoon were necessary to give me the strength to be productive. Until I recovered, I
had to learn to pace myself.

At one point when Jesus sent His representatives out to teach in
His name, they were so excited with all they were doing that they
neglected to take time to eat and rest properly. When they returned,
Christ told them: "Come with me by yourselves to a quiet place
and get some rest" (Mark 6:31).

Everyone needs rest, and if we go too long without it, we will
suffer physically and emotionally. We also will be unable to carry
out our responsibilities as well as we should. Is the Lord encouraging you to "come . . . and get some rest"? Sometimes a few more
rest stops with Him may be necessary.   —DENNIS FISHER

To avoid a breakdown, take a break for rest and prayer.

FILTERED LIGHT

READ: 2 Corinthians 4:1–12

For God, who said, "Let light shine out of darkness," made his light shine in our hearts to give us the light of the knowledge of God's glory displayed in the face of Christ. 2 CORINTHIANS 4:6

THE PAINTING *A Trail of Light* by Colorado Springs artist Bob Simpich shows a grove of aspen trees with golden leaves lit by the autumn sun. The topmost leaves are brilliantly illuminated while the ground beneath the trees is a mixture of sunlight and shadows. The painter said of this contrast, "I can't resist the light filtered through to the forest floor. It weaves a special magic."

The apostle Paul wrote to the followers of Jesus in Corinth, "For God, who said, 'Let light shine out of darkness,' made his light shine in our hearts to give us the light of the knowledge of God's glory displayed in the face of Christ" (2 Corinthians 4:6). Paul goes on to describe the reality of life in which "we are hard pressed on every side, but not crushed; perplexed, but not in despair; persecuted, but not abandoned; struck down, but not destroyed" (vv. 8–9).

There are times when it seems that the light of God's face is dimmed because of our difficulty, sorrow, or loss. Yet, even in these dark shadows, we can see evidence of His presence with us.

If we walk in filtered light today, may we discover anew that God's light—Jesus—is always shining in our hearts.

—DAVID MCCASLAND

In dark circumstances, God's light is still shining in our hearts.

THE LAST WILL BE FIRST

READ: Mark 9:30–37

Sitting down, Jesus called the Twelve and said, "Anyone who wants to be first must be the very last, and the servant of all." MARK 9:35

AS A HUNDRED THOUSAND fans watched, Richard Petty ended his forty-five-race losing streak at the Daytona 500 and picked up stock car racing's biggest purse—$73,500. Petty's win, however, was a complete surprise.

Going into the last lap, he was running thirty seconds behind the two leaders. When the second-place car tried to pass No. 1 on the final stretch, the first car drifted inside and forced the challenger onto the infield grass. The offended driver pulled his car back onto the track, caught up with the leader, and forced him into the outside wall. Both vehicles came to a screeching halt. The two drivers jumped out and quickly got into a slugging match. Meanwhile, third-place Petty cruised by for the win.

This incident brings to mind our Lord's words to His disciples. They had been disputing among themselves about who should be the greatest. So Jesus told them that the one who selfishly struggles for first place now is sure to miss it later. He must follow a different strategy. Rather than reaching for top honors, he must willingly run in last place for a while. He should seek opportunities to serve others for Christ's sake.

Such meekness from God's point of view isn't self-defeating. It's the only way to keep from coming in last—at the last.

—MART DEHAAN

*He who would take a high place before men
must take a low place before God.*

KNOWING AND LOVING

READ: John 10:7–16

"My sheep listen to my voice; I know them,
and they follow me." JOHN 10:27

"JESUS LOVES ME, THIS I know, for the Bible tells me so" is the message of one of Christian music's most enduring songs, particularly for children. Written by Anna B. Warner in the 1800s, this lyric tenderly affirms our relationship with Him—we are loved.

Someone gave my wife a plaque for our home that gives these words a fresh twist by flipping that simple idea. It reads, "Jesus knows me, this I love." This provides a different perspective on our relationship with Him—we are known.

In ancient Israel, loving and knowing the sheep distinguished a true shepherd from a hired hand. The shepherd spent so much time with his sheep that he developed an abiding care for and a deep knowledge of his lambs. Little wonder then that Jesus tells His own, "I am the good shepherd; I know my sheep and my sheep know me. . . . My sheep listen to my voice; I know them, and they follow me" (John 10:14, 27).

He knows us and He loves us! We can trust Jesus's purposes for us and rest in the promise of His care because His Father "knows what [we] need before [we] ask him" (Matthew 6:8). As you deal with the ups and downs of life today, be at rest. You are known and loved by the Shepherd of your heart. —BILL CROWDER

The wonder of it all—just to think that Jesus loves me!

STRENGTH IN SUFFERING

READ: 1 Peter 2:11–13

*Christ suffered for you, leaving you an example, that
you should follow in his steps.* 1 PETER 2:21

WHEN EIGHTEEN-YEAR-OLD SAMMY RECEIVED Jesus as Savior, his
family rejected him because their tradition was of a different faith.
But the Christian community welcomed him, offering encouragement and financial resources for his education. Later, when his
testimony was published in a magazine, his persecution intensified.

But Sammy did not stop seeing his family. He visited whenever
he could and talked with his father, even though his siblings cruelly
prevented him from participating in family affairs. When his father
fell ill, Sammy overlooked his family's slighting and attended to
him, praying his father would get well. When God healed him, the
family began to warm up toward Sammy. Over time, his loving
witness softened their attitude toward him—and some of his family
members became willing to hear about Jesus.

Our decision to follow Christ may cause us difficulties. Peter
wrote, "It is commendable if someone bears up under the pain of
unjust suffering because they are conscious of God" (1 Peter 2:19).
When we undergo discomfort or suffering because of our faith, we
do so because "Christ suffered for [us], leaving [us] an example, that
[we] should follow in his steps" (v. 21).

Even when others hurled insults at Jesus, "he did not retaliate;
when he suffered, he made no threats. Instead, he entrusted himself
to him who judges justly" (v. 23). Jesus is our example in suffering.
We can turn to Him for strength to continue.

—LAWRENCE DARMANI

When we suffer for Jesus, He comes to walk us through it.

OFFICER MIGLIO'S HEART

READ: Matthew 18:1–10

*"See that you do not despise one of these little ones. For
I tell you that their angels in heaven always see the
face of my Father in heaven."* MATTHEW 18:10

BACK AT THE POLICE station, Officer Miglio slumped wearily against
a wall. A domestic violence call had just consumed half his shift.
Its aftermath left a boyfriend in custody, a young daughter in the
emergency room, and a shaken mother wondering how it had come
to this. This call would wear on the young officer for a long time.

"Nothing you could do, Vic," said his sergeant sympathetically.
But the words rang hollow. Some police officers seem able to leave
their work at work. Not Vic Miglio. Not the tough cases like this one.

Officer Miglio's heart reflects the compassion of Jesus. Christ's
disciples had just come to Him with a question: "Who, then, is
the greatest in the kingdom of heaven?" (Matthew 18:1). Calling
a small child to Him, He told His disciples, "Unless you change
and become like little children, you will never enter the kingdom
of heaven" (v. 3). Then He gave a stern warning to anyone who
would harm a child (v. 6). In fact, children are so special to Him
that Jesus told us, "Their angels in heaven always see the face of my
Father in heaven" (v. 10).

How comforting, then, that Jesus's love for children is connected to His love for us all! That's why He invites us, through
childlike faith, to become His sons and daughters.

—TIM GUSTAFSON

---

*Our earthly families may fail us, but our
heavenly Father never will.*

LOVE CHANGES US

READ: Acts 9:1–22

*At once he began to preach in the synagogues
that Jesus is the Son of God.* ACTS 9:20

BEFORE I MET JESUS, I'd been wounded so deeply that I avoided close relationships in fear of being hurt more. My mom remained my closest friend until I married Alan. Seven years later and on the verge of divorce, I toted our kindergartener, Xavier, into a church service. I sat near the exit door, afraid to trust but desperate for help.

Thankfully, believers reached out, prayed for our family, and taught me how to nurture a relationship with God through prayer and Bible reading. Over time, the love of Christ and His followers changed me.

Two years after that first church service, Alan, Xavier, and I asked to be baptized. Sometime later, during one of our weekly conversations, my mom said, "You're different. Tell me more about Jesus." A few months passed and she too accepted Christ as her Savior.

Jesus transforms lives . . . lives like Saul's, one of the most feared persecutors of the church until his encounter with Christ (Acts 9:1–5). Others helped Saul learn more about Jesus (vv. 17–19). His drastic transformation added to the credibility of his Spirit-empowered teaching (vv. 20–22).

Our first personal encounter with Jesus may not be as dramatic as Saul's. Our life transformation may not be as quick or drastic. Still, as people notice how Christ's love is changing us over time, we'll have opportunities to tell others what He did for us.

—XOCHITL DIXON

A life changed by Christ's love is worth talking about.

STEADY OR ERRATIC?

After he became the father of Methuselah, Enoch walked faithfully with God 300 years and had other sons and daughters. GENESIS 5:22

HOW WOULD YOU DESCRIBE your spiritual life? Is it marked by steady growth as you walk in fellowship with Jesus and learn from Him each day? Or is it an up-and-down kind of roller-coaster ride with times of intensity followed by seasons of indifference?

Too many people are "religious only by fits and starts," remarked the noted American pastor Jonathan Edwards. Used by God to spearhead a powerful revival in colonial New England, Edwards said churchgoers are "like the waters in the time of a shower of rain, which during the shower, and a little after, run like a brook and flow abundantly, but they are presently quite dry, and when another shower comes, then they will flow again. Whereas a true saint is like a stream from a living spring which, though it may be greatly increased by a shower of rain and diminished in time of drought, yet constantly runs."

If someone were to monitor our lives, would our discipleship be characterized as "fits and starts" or like "a stream from a living spring"? Could we say that we, like Enoch, "walked faithfully with God"? (Genesis 5:22).

If our discipleship has been like a roller coaster, let's prayerfully begin a steady walk with our Lord.　　　—VERNON GROUNDS

Discipleship demands discipline.

TOO MUCH TO DO?

READ: Luke 10:38–42

One thing I ask from the LORD, this only do I seek; that I may dwell in the house of the LORD all the days of my life, to gaze on the beauty of the LORD and to seek him in his temple. PSALM 27:4

I'M USUALLY A HAPPY person. Most of the time I can take on as much work as anyone can give me. But some days there just seems to be too much to do. The schedule may be so full of meetings, appointments, and deadlines that there's no room to breathe. Life often contains too much work, parenting, home improvement, and other responsibilities for one person to handle.

When that happens to me—as it may happen to you—I have some options. I can retreat into a shell of inactivity and leave everyone who is depending on me out in the cold. I can slug my way through, moaning as I go and making everyone wish I had chosen option one. Or I can get my perspective realigned by reminding myself what Jesus said to Martha (Luke 10:38–42).

Jesus told Martha that she had become "distracted by all the preparations that had to be made" (v. 40). He reminded her that her sister Mary had chosen the one thing that would never be taken away (v. 42). Like many of us, Martha got so wrapped up in her service that she forgot the most important thing—fellowship with her Lord.

Are you overwhelmed? Don't lose sight of your priorities. Spend time with the Lord. He will lift your load and give you the right perspective.   —DAVE BRANON

To keep your life in balance, lean on the Lord.

LONELINESS

READ: Hebrews 13:1–6

Keep your lives free from the love of money and be content with what you have, because God has said, "Never will I leave you; never will I forsake you." HEBREWS 13:5

FROM TIME TO TIME, lonely people call me to share their problems. One man, who professes faith in Christ, is struggling to live a pure life. Whenever he falls into sin, he needs reassurance of God's forgiveness.

Another person who calls is a woman who has had some bad experiences with men. She has to be assured that God still loves her.

Then there's a young woman with a physical disability. She lives alone because she is treated badly at home.

All these people have two things in common: they've felt the pain of rejection, and they are lonely. But it's loneliness that stands out as their greatest problem.

Loneliness can't be cured just by being with people, seeing a counselor, or talking on the phone. What's needed is friendship. That's where we who are not lonely can help. We must befriend lonely people.

Just waiting for someone to become a friend, however, is not the way to find the cure for loneliness. Hebrews 13:1–6 does not mention this problem, but it does give the answer. We must focus our attention on Jesus Christ. He promises to be a helper who will never leave nor forsake us (vv. 5–6).

Jesus always listens and always cares. He will help you make it through any situation. —HERB VANDER LUGT

Jesus cares.

A TRUE FRIEND

READ: John 15:9–17

*A friend loves at all times, and a brother is born
for a time of adversity.* PROVERBS 17:17

I HAVE A FRIEND named Nelson. We work together, play together, cry together, and often laugh together. Our friendship keeps growing.

Recently Nelson said he wanted me to conduct his funeral if he died before I did. I said, "Hold off on that request for a few years. I might disappoint you, and you might change your mind." "Oh no," he quipped, "that won't happen. You can't disappoint me any more than you already have."

We had a good laugh, but I began pondering his comment. Isn't that what it means to be a true friend—knowing the disappointing side of a person's life yet continuing to accept him? Solomon described such a friend as one who "sticks closer than a brother," one who "loves at all times" (Proverbs 18:24; 17:17). We all need someone like that in our lives.

Jesus wants to be that kind of friend to us. When we admit our sinful disobedience, ask for His forgiveness, and submit to Him, He becomes our Savior and Friend. Because He took the penalty of our sins upon himself on the cross, nothing we've done, or may do, will turn Him away.

Jesus is one friend you can't afford to be without. Is He your Friend? —DENNIS DEHAAN

Christ is the truest friend you can have.

HEARTS AND STARS

READ: Psalm 147:1–11

*He determines the number of the stars and calls
them each by name.* PSALM 147:4

ASTRONOMERS USED AUSTRALIA'S LARGEST optical telescope to
map 100,000 galaxies that surround our own galaxy, the Milky
Way. The three-dimensional map covers five percent of the sky
and allows us to see four billion light-years deep into space. The
number of stars included defies our imagination while enhancing
our knowledge of God.

How amazing to read, "He determines the number of the stars
and calls them each by name. Great is our Lord and mighty in
power; his understanding has no limit" (Psalm 147:4–5).

Even more amazing, though, is the psalmist's affirmation that
God, who is far greater than the universe He created, cares about
our sorrows. Instead of being remote and aloof, He is close at hand
with love and mercy for His own. "He heals the brokenhearted and
binds up their wounds," wrote the psalmist. "The LORD sustains the
humble, but casts the wicked to the ground" (vv. 3, 6).

Jesus Christ, the creator of the galaxies, visited our planet to
pay the penalty for our sin and open the way to friendship and
fellowship with Him. Today He stands ready to bring healing and
wholeness to our deeply wounded spirits. From naming stars to
mending hearts, nothing is too hard for God.

—DAVID MCCASLAND

*In creation we see God's hand;
in redemption we see His heart.*

BREAD!

READ: John 6:34–51

"I am the bread of life." JOHN 6:48

I ONCE LIVED IN a small Mexican city where every morning and evening you can hear a distinctive cry: "Bread!" A man with a huge basket on his bike offers a great variety of fresh sweet and salty breads for sale. I used to live in a bigger city, where I had to go to the bakery to buy bread. So I enjoy having fresh bread brought to my door.

Moving from the thought of feeding physical hunger to spiritual hunger, I think of Jesus's words: "I am the living bread that came down from heaven. Whoever eats this bread will live forever" (John 6:51).

Someone has said that evangelism is really one beggar telling another beggar where he found bread. Many of us can say, "Once I was spiritually hungry, spiritually starving because of my sins. Then I heard the good news. Someone told me where to find bread: in Jesus. And my life changed!"

Now we have the privilege and the responsibility of pointing others to this Bread of Life. We can share Jesus in our neighborhood, in our workplace, in our school, or in our places of recreation. We can talk about Jesus in the waiting room, on the bus, or on the train. We can take the good news to others through doors of friendship.

Jesus is the Bread of Life. Let's tell everybody where to find Bread! —KEILA OCHOA

Share the Bread of Life wherever you are.

PERFECT PEACE

READ: John 14:25–31

"Peace I leave with you; my peace I give you. I do not give to you as the world gives. Do not let your hearts be troubled and do not be afraid." JOHN 14:27

A FRIEND SHARED WITH me that for years she searched for peace and contentment. She and her husband built up a successful business, so she was able to buy a big house, fancy clothes, and expensive jewelry. But these possessions didn't satisfy her inner longings for peace, nor did her friendships with influential people. Then one day, when she was feeling low and desperate, a friend told her about the good news of Jesus. There she found the Prince of Peace, and her understanding of true peace and contentment was forever changed.

Jesus spoke words of such peace to His friends after their last supper together (John 14), when He prepared them for the events that would soon follow: His death, resurrection, and the coming of the Holy Spirit. Describing a peace—unlike anything the world can give—He wanted them to learn how to find a sense of well-being even in the midst of hardship.

Later, when the resurrected Jesus appeared to the frightened disciples after His death, He greeted them, saying, "Peace be with you!" (John 20:19). Now He could give them, and us, a new understanding of resting in what He has done for us. As we do, we can find the awareness of a confidence far deeper than our ever-changing feelings. —AMY BOUCHER PYE

Jesus came to usher peace into our lives and our world.

STAY IN THE SUNSHINE

READ: John 15:5–17

*"If you keep my commands, you will remain in my
love, just as I have kept my Father's commands
and remain in his love."* JOHN 15:10

IN HIS BOOK *The Best Is Yet to Be*, Henry Durbanville told the story
of a little girl in London who won a prize at a flower show. Her
entry was grown in an old, cracked teapot and had been placed in
the rear attic window of a rundown tenement house. When asked
how she managed to raise such a lovely flower in such an unlikely
environment, she said she moved it around so it would always be
in the sunlight.

Durbanville then reminded his readers of Jesus's words, "As
the Father loved me, so have I loved you. Now remain in my love"
(John 15:9). We learn from this that we too must keep ourselves
continually in the warmth of Christ's love.

We abide in Christ's love when we show love to others. Jesus
made this clear when He said, "If you keep my commands, you
will remain in my love. . . . My command is this: Love each other
as I have loved you. Greater love has no one than this: to lay down
one's life for one's friends" (vv. 10, 12–13).

We feel the warmth of Christ's love when we obey His commandment to love and serve others. That's the way to stay in the
sunshine!   —RICHARD DEHAAN

Our love for God is seen in our love for others.

CHRIST'S RESURRECTING TOUCH

READ: Luke 7:11–16

*Then he went up and touched the bier they were
carrying him on, and the bearers stood still. He said,
"Young man, I say to you, get up!"* LUKE 7:14

IN LUKE 7 WE read the dramatic story of a widow who was on her
way to the cemetery to bury her only son. When Jesus saw the
funeral procession, compassion filled His heart. He approached the
grieving woman and said, "Weep not." Then, walking over to the
coffin, He touched it and said, "Young man, I say to you, get up!"
Immediately "the dead man sat up and began to talk" (Luke 7:15).
Imagine the emotions that must have swept over the mourners!

This incident can picture for us what happens to a person who
turns to Jesus for salvation. Until people come into contact with the
Savior, they are "dead in [their] transgressions and sins" (Ephesians
2:1) and headed for the "second death" (Revelation 20:6). They face
being eternally separated from God's love unless they are "born
again" (John 3:3).

But when Jesus touches the needy sinner through the convict-
ing power of the Holy Spirit, instantly that person receives new life
through faith in Him. What happiness and blessing follows! In fact,
the gladness over such a miracle of grace extends all the way to the
throne room of heaven (see Luke 15:10).

Have you experienced the resurrecting touch of Jesus? He alone
can take away the deadness of your soul and give you a thrilling
awakening that leads to heaven and eternal life.

—HENRY BOSCH

*The darkness of sin and death gives way to the light
of life when the soul is converted to Christ.*

AN INVITATION TO FRIENDSHIP

READ: John 15:9–17

"I no longer call you servants, because a servant does not know his master's business. Instead, I have called you friends, for everything that I learned from my Father I have made known to you." JOHN 15:15

I GREW UP IN a home with lots of wall plaques. One had a quotation by poet Claude Mermet that stands out in my mind: "Friends are like melons; let me tell you why: To find a good one, you must one hundred try!"

Most of us can identify with that. It's hard to find good friends.

I wonder if God ever feels that way about us? Out of all the people in the Old Testament, only two were ever called His friend. In Isaiah 41:8, God says that He chose Jacob, who was an offspring of "Abraham my friend." And in Exodus 36:11, we watch as God speaks to Moses "as one speaks to a friend." Pretty exclusive club! So you can imagine how shocking it was for the disciples to hear Jesus say, "I no longer call you servants, . . . Instead, I have called you friends" (John 15:15).

Better yet, He is saying that to us as well. So, what does friendship with Jesus look like? It starts with commitment. As He said, "You are my friends if you do what I command you" (v. 14). Then He added the dynamic of communication. He promised to tell us all that the Father has told Him (v. 15).

Are we listening? Jesus welcomes us to the privilege of friendship with Him! Imagine that! A friend of Jesus.   —JOE STOWELL

Welcome to the privilege of friendship with God.

A SPECIAL SEAT

READ: Luke 10:38–42

*She had a sister called Mary, who sat at the Lord's
feet listening to what he said.* LUKE 10:39

I'VE NEVER SAT IN the first-class section of an airplane. But I still hold out the hope that someday I'll get on the plane and the flight attendant will stop me and say, "Come with me. I have a special seat for you."

That's why I was pretty excited when a friend gave my sister some tickets for an event and we realized that they were for box seats. Instead of sitting shoulder to shoulder with strangers all around us, we sat in a private compartment where we could see and hear everything perfectly. That evening, we felt privileged and special.

Remember Jesus's friends, Mary and Martha? Although Martha had the opportunity to enjoy having Jesus as her guest, she soon became frustrated with her sister Mary and overwhelmed with the busyness of her preparations. That is certainly understandable to a lot of us! Jesus made it clear to her, however, that sometimes it's necessary to step away from the unending pressures of life and spend undistracted time with Him. God has given us the opportunity to have personal moments with Him. By taking the time just to be with the Lord, we are fed, refreshed, and renewed.

Jesus commended Mary for taking time to sit and learn at her Savior's feet (Luke 10:42). As it turned out—she had the best seat in the house! —CINDY HESS KASPER

---

*Jesus longs for our fellowship even
more than we long for His.*

THE HONOR OF YOUR FRIENDSHIP

READ: John 15:9–17

"I no longer call you servants, because a servant does not know his master's business. Instead, I have called you friends, for everything that I learned from my Father I have made known to you." JOHN 15:15

DURING THE MARRIAGE CEREMONY of a British couple, the best man remained motionless. Even after vows were exchanged, he didn't move.

The still figure was a racecar driver who was trying to be in two places at one time. Because of contractual commitments, Andy Priaulx, three-time world touring-car champion, had to break his promise to participate in his friend's wedding. So he sent a life-size cardboard cutout of himself, as well as a prerecorded speech. The bride said she was moved by his effort to honor their marriage.

Priaulx's gesture was certainly creative, and we shouldn't second-guess his actions. But Jesus gave us another standard by which to gauge friendship.

Jesus asked His disciples to show their friendship to Him by loving one another as He had loved them. Then, He raised the bar. In anticipation of His death on the cross, He said, "Greater love has no one than this: to lay down one's life for one's friends" (John 15:13).

This depth of friendship isn't merely about doing the right thing. It's about sacrifice, and it springs out of a relationship with the One who truly did lay down His life for us.

Are we showing others that we have been loved by Jesus as He is loved by His Father? (v. 9).   —MART DEHAAN

———

Love is more than a sentiment, it's putting another's needs ahead of your own.

THE ONLY ONE STANDING

READ: Daniel 3:8–25

Whoever does not fall down and worship will immediately be thrown into a blazing furnace. DANIEL 3:6

I WAS VISITING A church in another city. The opening hymn was announced, and I jumped to my feet to sing. Everyone else stayed seated. Imagine my embarrassment. I was the only one standing!

Shadrach, Meshach, and Abednego also stood alone, but for a far different reason. King Nebuchadnezzar had built a ninety-foot-tall statue, set it in the plain of Dura, and ordered the people to bow down and worship it when music began.

The gold statue was gleaming in the afternoon sun. The music sounded, and all the people put their foreheads in the dust. Right? Wrong! The three young men from Israel were still standing. They would not break the second commandment of Jehovah their God by worshiping an idol.

You know what happened next. The king was furious. He ordered the furnace to be heated seven times hotter than usual and commanded that the rebels be thrown in. But they didn't burn up. They were seen walking around in the midst of the flames—and they were not alone. Someone else was in the fire with them.

As a follower of Jesus, when everyone else is bowing to idols of pride or greed or lust or prejudice, take your stand for righteousness. He will be with you, even when you are the only one standing!

—DAVID EGNER

He who takes his stand for Christ is not likely to fall for the devil.

SUBTLE WISDOM

READ: Mark 8:34–38

*"Whoever serves me must follow me; and where
I am, my servant also will be. My Father will
honor the one who serves me."* JOHN 12:26

WHEN I WAS IN college, my coworker Bud, a fork-truck driver, often enriched my life with his pithy wisdom. We were eating lunch one day, sitting on the back of his fork truck, when I announced that I was transferring to another school.

"Why?" he asked.

"All my friends are transferring," I answered.

Bud chewed his sandwich for a moment and then replied quietly and with subtle irony, "I guess that's one way to pick a school."

His words struck me with rare force. Of course, I thought. But is this the only way to choose a school? Will I follow my friends for the rest of my days, or will I follow Jesus? Will I seek His face and His will and go where He wants me to go?

Several times in the New Testament, Jesus said to His disciples, "Follow me." In Mark 8:34, He said, "Whoever wants to be my disciple must deny themselves and take up their cross and follow me." No matter what others do or what direction their lives may take, we must do what He asks us to do.

The world sometimes seems like a wilderness of decisions and possible directions. But Jesus knows the way. All we have to do is follow. —DAVID ROPER

To find your way through life, follow Jesus.

DISCIPLESHIP 101

READ: Mark 3:13–19

*He appointed twelve that they might be with him and
that he might send them out to preach.* MARK 3:14

BECAUSE I AM NOT a "fix it" kind of guy, I had to call a friend who
is a great handyman to make some repairs in my home recently. He
came over, and I gave him my list. But to my surprise, he told me I
would be doing the repairs myself! He modeled for me how to do
it, instructed me along the way, and stayed with me. I followed his
example and successfully made the repairs. This modeling seems
close to what Jesus did when He called His first disciples.

When Jesus called those men to follow Him, He wanted them
to be with Him and to teach the good news of the kingdom of God
(Mark 1:14, 39; 6:12). The first job would require being under the
immediate supervision of Jesus—learning His words and interpretation of the Scriptures and watching His behavior. For the second
task, Jesus sent them out to preach (Mark 3:14–15)—to say what
He said and to do what He did. As they carried out these tasks,
they were to be dependent on Jesus.

Today, Jesus is still calling His followers to this simple, yet
powerful process of discipleship—being with Him, following His
instructions, and living His example. Let's strive to be dependent
on Him as we follow Him today.   —MARVIN WILLIAMS

Discipleship is relational and experiential.

FRIENDING

READ: John 15:9–17

"You are my friends if you do what I command." JOHN 15:14

FACEBOOK WAS LAUNCHED IN 2004 as a way for college students to connect with each other online. It is now open to people of all ages, and currently there are more than two billion users. Each user has an individual page with photos and personal details that can be viewed by "friends." To "friend" a person means opening the door to communication and information about who you are, where you go, and what you do. Facebook friendships may be casual or committed, but each one is "by invitation only."

Just before Jesus was crucified, He told His disciples: "You are my friends if you do what I command you. I no longer call you servants, because a servant does not know his master's business. Instead, I have called you friends, for everything that I learned from my Father I have made known to you" (John 15:14–15).

Unselfishness, oneness of purpose, and confident trust are the hallmarks of true friendship, especially in our relationship with the Lord. Christ has taken the initiative by giving His life for us and inviting us to know and follow Him.

Have we responded to the Lord Jesus's invitation of friendship by opening our hearts to Him with nothing held back?

—DAVID MCCASLAND

Jesus longs to be our Friend.

HE CALLS ME FRIEND

READ: John 15:9–17

"You did not choose me, but I chose you and appointed you so that you might go and bear fruit—fruit that will last—and so that whatever you ask in my name the Father will give you." JOHN 15:16

SOMEONE HAS DEFINED FRIENDSHIP as "knowing the heart of another and sharing one's heart with another." We share our hearts with those we trust, and we trust those who care about us. We confide in our friends because we have confidence that they will use the information to help us, not harm us. They in turn confide in us for the same reason.

We often refer to Jesus as our friend because we know that He wants what is best for us. We confide in Him because we trust Him. But have you ever considered that Jesus confides in His people?

Jesus began calling His disciples "friends" rather than "servants" because He had entrusted them with everything He had heard from His Father (John 15:15). Jesus trusted the disciples to use the information for the good of His Father's kingdom.

Although we know that Jesus is our friend, can we say that we are His friends? Do we listen to Him? Or do we only want Him to listen to us? Do we want to know what's on His heart? Or do we only want to tell Him what's on ours? To be a friend of Jesus, we need to listen to what He wants us to know and then use the information to bring others into friendship with Him.

—JULIE ACKERMAN LINK

Christ's friendship calls for our faithfulness.

YOU'VE GOT A FRIEND

READ: Psalm 23

"I no longer call you servants, because a servant does not know his master's business. Instead, I have called you friends, for everything that I learned from my Father I have made known to you." JOHN 15:15

ONE OF THE IRONIC consequences of the sweeping growth of social media is that we often find ourselves more personally isolated. One online article warns: "Those who oppose leading one's life primarily or exclusively online claim that virtual friends are not adequate substitutes for real-world friends, and . . . individuals who substitute virtual friends for physical friends become even lonelier and more depressive than before."

Technology aside, all of us battle with seasons of loneliness, wondering if anyone knows, understands, or cares about the burdens we carry or the struggles we face. But followers of Christ have an assurance that brings comfort to our weary hearts. The comforting presence of the Savior is promised in words that are undeniable, for the psalmist David wrote, "Even though I walk through the darkest valley, I will fear no evil, for you are with me; your rod and your staff, they comfort me" (Psalm 23:4).

Whether isolated by our own choices, by the cultural trends that surround us, or by the painful losses of life, all who know Christ can rest in the presence of the Shepherd of our hearts. What a friend we have in Jesus! —BILL CROWDER

Those who know Jesus as their Friend are never alone.

OUR BEST FRIEND

READ: Hebrews 10:19–23

Yet to all who did receive him, to those who believed in his name, he gave the right to become children of God. JOHN 1:12

WHEN I WAS TWELVE years old, our family moved to a town in the desert. After gym classes in the hot air at my new school, we rushed for the drinking fountain. Being skinny and young for my grade, I sometimes got pushed out of the way while waiting in line. One day my friend Jose, who was big and strong for his age, saw this happening. He stepped in and stuck out a strong arm to clear my way. "Hey!" he exclaimed, "You let Banks get a drink first!" I never had trouble at the drinking fountain again.

Jesus understood what it was like to face the ultimate unkindness of others. The Bible tells us, "He was despised and rejected by mankind" (Isaiah 53:3). But Jesus was not just a victim of suffering; He also became our advocate. By giving His life, Jesus opened a "new and living way" for us to enter into a relationship with God (Hebrews 10:20). He did for us what we could never do for ourselves, offering us the free gift of salvation when we repent of our sins and trust in Him.

Jesus is the best friend we could ever have. He said, "Whoever comes to me I will never drive away" (John 6:37). Others may hold us at arm's length or even push us away, but God has opened His arms to us through the cross. How strong is our Savior!

—JAMES BANKS

God's free gift to us cost Him dearly.

THE ONE WHO UNDERSTANDS

READ: John 1:1–18

The Word became flesh and made his dwelling among us. We have seen his glory, the glory of the one and only Son, who came from the Father, full of grace and truth. JOHN 1:14

JOHN BABLER IS THE chaplain for the police and fire departments in his Texas community. During a sabbatical from his job, he attended police academy training so he could better understand the situations law enforcement officers face. Through learning about the intense challenges of the profession, Babler gained a new sense of humility and empathy. In the future, he hopes to be more effective as he counsels police officers who struggle with emotional stress, fatigue, and loss.

We know that God understands the situations we face because He made us and sees everything that happens to us. We also know He understands because He "became flesh and made his dwelling among us" in the person of Jesus Christ (John 1:14).

Jesus's earthly life included a wide range of difficulty. He felt the searing heat of the sun, the pain of an empty stomach, and the uncertainty of homelessness. Emotionally, He endured the tension of disagreements, the burn of betrayal, and the ongoing threat of violence.

Jesus experienced the joys of friendship and family love, as well as the worst problems that we face here on earth. He is the Wonderful Counselor who patiently listens to our concerns with insight and care (Isaiah 9:6). He is the One who can say, "I've been through that. I understand." —JENNIFER BENSON SCHULDT

God understands the struggles we face.

RUTH'S STORY

READ: Romans 10:1–13

*Everyone who calls on the name of the
Lord will be saved.* ROMANS 10:13

RUTH COULD NOT TELL her story without tears. In her mid-eighties and unable to get around much anymore, Ruth did not appear to be a central figure in our church's life.

But when she told us her story of salvation—as she did often—Ruth stood out as a remarkable example of God's grace. Back when she was in her thirties, a friend had invited her to go to a meeting. Ruth didn't know she was going to hear a preacher. "I wouldn't have gone if I knew," she would say. She already had "religion," and it wasn't doing her any good. But go she did. And she heard the good news about Jesus that night.

More than fifty years later, she would cry tears of joy when she told how Jesus transformed her life. So many years ago, she had become a child of God, and when she died in 2018, she was welcomed into heaven. Her story never grew old.

It doesn't matter if our story is similar to Ruth's or not. What does matter is that we take the simple step of putting our faith in Jesus and His death and resurrection. The apostle Paul said, "If you declare with your mouth, 'Jesus is Lord,' and believe in your heart that God raised him from the dead, you will be saved" (Romans 10:9).

That's what Ruth did and it changed everything. You can do that too. Jesus redeems, transforms, and gives us new life.

—DAVE BRANON

Belonging to Christ is not rehabilitation; it's re-creation.

GOD HEARS

Be joyful in hope, patient in affliction, faithful in prayer. ROMANS 12:12

DIANE LISTENED AS THE others in the group asked for prayers for their family members and friends facing challenges or illness. She had a family member who had been struggling with an addiction for years. But Diane kept her request silent. She couldn't bear to see the looks on people's faces or hear the questions or advice that often followed whenever she spoke the words aloud. She felt that this request was usually better left unspoken. Others simply didn't understand how her loved one could be a believer in Jesus and still struggle daily.

Although Diane didn't share her request with that group, she did have a few trusted friends she asked to pray with her. Together they asked God to set her loved one free from the very real bondage of addiction that he might experience freedom in Christ—and that God would give Diane the peace and patience she needed. As she prayed, she found comfort and strength from her relationship with Him.

Many of us have earnest, persistent prayers that seem to go unanswered. But we can be assured that God does care and He does hear all our requests. He urges us to continue to walk closely with Him, being "joyful in hope, patient in affliction, faithful in prayer" (Romans 12:12). We can lean on Him. —ALYSON KIEDA

Let us draw near to God with a sincere heart and with the full assurance that faith brings. —Hebrews 10:22

THE MARKS OF FRIENDSHIP

READ: John 15:9–17

"You are my friends if you do what I command." JOHN 15:14

AS A LITTLE BOY growing up in Ghana, I enjoyed holding my father's hand and walking with him in crowded places. He was both my father and my friend, for holding hands in my culture is a mark of true friendship. Walking along, we would talk about a variety of subjects. Whenever I felt lonely, I found consolation with my father. How I valued our companionship!

The Lord Jesus called His followers "friends," and He showed them the marks of His friendship. "As the Father has loved me, so I have loved you," He said (John 15:9), even laying down His life for them (v. 13). He showed them His kingdom business (v. 15). He taught them everything God had given Him (v. 15). And He gave them opportunity to share in His mission (v. 16).

As our Companion for life, Jesus walks with us. He listens to our heartaches and our desires. When we're lonely and downhearted, our Friend Jesus keeps company with us.

And our companionship with Jesus is tighter when we love each other and obey His commands (vv. 10, 17). As we obey His commands, we will bear "fruit that will last" (v. 16).

Walking through the crowded alleys and dangerous roadways of our troubled world, we can count on the Lord's companionship. It's a mark of His friendship.   —LAWRENCE DARMANI

———

You'll never find a better friend than Jesus.

HOPE IN GOD

READ: Luke 24:13–32

*Then their eyes were opened and they recognized him,
and he disappeared from their sight.* LUKE 24:31

WHEN I WAS NINETEEN, one of my close friends was killed in a car accident. In the following weeks and months, I walked each day in a tunnel of grief. The pain of losing someone so young and wonderful clouded my vision, and at times I even felt unaware of what was going on around me. I felt so blinded by pain and grief that I simply could not see God.

In Luke 24, two disciples, confused and brokenhearted after Jesus's death, didn't realize they were walking with their resurrected Teacher himself, even as He explained from Scripture why the promised Savior had to die and rise again. Only when He took bread and broke it was it revealed that this was Jesus (vv. 30–31). Although the followers of Jesus had faced death in all its horror when Jesus died, through His resurrection from the dead God showed them how to hope again.

Like those disciples, we might feel weighed down with confusion or grief. But we can find hope and comfort in the reality that Jesus is alive and at work in the world—and in us. Although we still face heartache and pain, we can welcome Christ to walk with us in our tunnel of grief. As the Light of the world (John 8:12), He can bring rays of hope to brighten our fog.

—AMY BOUCHER PYE

Though we grieve, we have hope in Jesus.

TO BE WITH HIM IS HEAVEN!

READ: 2 Corinthians 5:1–8

*We are confident, I say, and would prefer to be away from
the body and at home with the Lord.* 2 CORINTHIANS 5:8

A MAN LAY SERIOUSLY ill in the small-town hospital. When his
doctor who, like the man, was a Christian, made a special trip to
the hospital to check on him, the patient said, "Doctor, I'm afraid
to die. Exactly what happens in the hour of death?" The physician
replied, "I'm afraid I can't give you an exact answer!"

After the doctor completed his examination and was ready to
leave, he heard scratching and whining at the door. He realized
that he had left his car window open too far, and his little dog had
jumped out and found him. With the patient's permission, he let
the dog in, and it leaped into the doctor's arms with eager gladness.

In a flash the doctor thought of a scriptural truth. Turning to
the sick man, he said, "Did you see how my dog acted? He's never
been in this room before. He had no idea what was inside; yet when
I opened the door, he sprang in without fear, for he knew I was here!
That's how heaven will be for us."

As Christians, we don't know much about what awaits us on
the other side. But we know this: Jesus is there, and that is enough!

To be "away from the body" is to be "at home with the Lord."
This truth should give every believer comfort in the hour of death.

—HENRY BOSCH

---

*Jesus is the joy and heart of heaven; therefore, we long
for glory only in the measure that we love Him.*

IN ALL KINDS OF WEATHER

READ: Acts 18:9–11

*"[Teach] them to obey everything I have commanded
you. And surely I am with you always, to the
very end of the age."* MATTHEW 28:20

WHEN JESUS SENT HIS disciples out He gave them this promise: "I am with you always, to the very end of the age" (Matthew 28:20). Literally, the word *always* means "all the days," according to Greek scholars Jamieson, Fausset, and Brown.

Jesus didn't simply say "always," but "all the days." That takes into account all our various activities, the good and bad circumstances surrounding us, the varied responsibilities we have through the course of our days, the storm clouds, and the sunshine.

Our Lord is present with us no matter what each day brings. It may be a day of joy or of sadness, of sickness or of health, of success or of failure. No matter what happens to us today, our Lord is walking beside us, strengthening us, loving us, filling us with faith, hope, and love. As He envelops us with quiet serenity and security, our foes, fears, afflictions, and doubts begin to recede. We can bear up in any setting and circumstance because we know the Lord is at hand, just as He told Paul in Acts 18:10, "I am with you."

Practice God's presence, stopping in the midst of your busy day to say to yourself, "The Lord is here." And pray that you will see Him who is invisible—and see Him everywhere.

—DAVID ROPER

*Seek the Lord while he may be found;
call on him while he is near.* —*Isaiah 55:6*

A BEAUTIFUL MELODY

READ: 1 Peter 2:9–12

You are a chosen people, a royal priesthood, a holy nation, God's special possession, that you may declare the praises of him who called you out of darkness into his wonderful light. 1 PETER 2:9

IN THE SPRING OF 2009, Susan Boyle took the stage of *Britain's Got Talent*. Compared to the other contestants, she was plain-looking. No one expected much when she raised the microphone to her lips. But then she began to sing. Spellbound, the judges were clearly taken with the beauty and power of the voice that filled the auditorium as the audience stood to their feet cheering with delight. All were surprised that such a rivetingly beautiful song came from such an unlikely source.

All of us can be unlikely sources when it comes to the beauty of Jesus flowing out of us. But that is how He planned it. Common folk like you and me take turns on the stage of life in front of the world's skeptical audience so that our friends, family, and all who fill the arena of our lives will see and hear the love and grace of Jesus Christ emerging from our lives.

I love Peter's reminder that we are "a people for his own possession, that [we] may proclaim the excellencies of him who called [us] out of darkness into his marvelous light" (1 Peter 2:9 ESV). You might think you're an unlikely source, but when you allow the Lord to flow through you, the watching world will stand up and take notice. —JOE STOWELL

The beauty of Jesus may come from the most unlikely sources.

MY LORD

READ: John 20:19–29

Thomas said to him, "My Lord and my God!" JOHN 20:28

ON THE DAY OF His resurrection, Jesus appeared to His disciples and showed them His hands and feet. We are told that at first they could not believe for joy—it appeared too wonderful to be true (Luke 24:40–41). Thomas was not with the disciples, but he also had trouble believing until he saw for himself. When Jesus appeared to Thomas and told him to put his fingers in the nail holes and his hand in His side, Thomas cried, "My Lord and my God!" (John 20:28).

Later, as Paul told the Philippians of his own suffering, he also declared Jesus as Lord. He testified that he had come to the place where he considered all his experiences as loss "because of the surpassing worth of knowing Christ Jesus my Lord" (Philippians 3:8).

You and I have never seen Jesus calm a storm or raise someone from the dead. We haven't sat at His feet on a Galilean hillside and heard Him teach. But through eyes of faith we have been spiritually healed by His death on our behalf. Thus we can join Thomas and Paul and countless others in acknowledging Jesus as our Lord.

Jesus said, "Blessed are those who have not seen and yet have believed" (John 20:29). When we believe, we too can call Jesus, "My Lord and my God!" —DAVID EGNER

Though we cannot see Him with our eyes, we can believe with our heart—He is Lord!

OUR DEPENDENCY

READ: 1 John 2:24–3:3

*"'For in him we live and move and have
our being.' As some of your own poets have said,
'We are his offspring.'"* ACTS 17:28

WHILE ENJOYING THE ARRIVAL of a new great-niece, I was reminded of how much work it is to take care of a newborn baby. They are needy little creations who want feeding, changing, holding, feeding, changing, holding, feeding, changing, holding. Totally unable to care for themselves, they depend on those older and wiser people surrounding them.

We're dependent children too—reliant on our Father in heaven. What do we need from Him that we can't provide for ourselves? "In Him we live and move and have our being" (Acts 17:28). He supplies our very breath. He also meets our needs "according to the riches of his glory in Christ Jesus" (Philippians 4:19).

We need our Father for peace in our troubles (John 16:33), love (1 John 3:1), and help in time of need (Psalms 46:1; Hebrews 4:16). He gives victory in temptation (1 Corinthians 10:13), forgiveness (1 John 1:9), purpose (Jeremiah 29:11), and eternal life (John 10:28). Without Him, we "can do nothing" (John 15:5). And from Him, "we have all received grace" (John 1:16).

Let's not think of ourselves as totally independent—because we're not. The Lord sustains us day by day. In many ways, we're as needy as a newborn baby. —ANNE CETAS

---

*Depending on God isn't weakness; it's
acknowledging His strength.*

KEEPING THE WONDER

READ: 2 Peter 1:2–11

If you possess these qualities in increasing measure, they will keep you from being ineffective and unproductive in your knowledge of our Lord Jesus Christ. 2 PETER 1:8

ON A RECENT TRIP, my wife was seated near a mother with a young boy on his first flight. As the plane took off, he exclaimed, "Mom, look how high we are! And everything's getting smaller!" A few minutes later he shouted, "Are those clouds down there? What are they doing under us?" As time passed, other passengers read, dozed, and lowered their window shades to watch the in-flight video. This boy, however, remained glued to the window, absorbed in the wonder of all he was seeing.

For "experienced travelers" in the Christian life, there can be great danger in losing the wonder. The Scriptures that once thrilled us may become more familiar and academic. We may fall into the lethargy of praying with our minds but not our hearts.

Peter urged the early followers of Christ to continue growing in their faith, virtue, knowledge, self-control, perseverance, godliness, mutual affection, and love (2 Peter 1:5–7). He said, "If you possess these qualities in increasing measure, they will keep you from being ineffective and unproductive in your knowledge of our Lord Jesus Christ" (v. 8). Without them we become blind and forget the marvel of being cleansed from our sins (v. 9).

May God grant us all grace to keep growing in the wonder of knowing Him. —DAVID MCCASLAND

Continual growing in Christ comes from a deepening knowledge of Him.

JOYFUL REUNION

READ: 2 Timothy 4:1–8

He who testifies to these things says, "Yes, I am coming soon." Amen. Come, Lord Jesus. REVELATION 22:20

SOME YEARS AGO WHEN our children were still small, I flew home after a ten-day ministry trip. In those days people were allowed to visit the airport boarding area to greet incoming passengers. When my flight landed, I came out of the jet-bridge and was greeted by our little ones—so happy to see me that they were screaming and crying. I looked at my wife, whose eyes were teary. I couldn't speak. Strangers in the gate area also teared up as our children hugged my legs and cried their greetings. It was a wonderful moment.

The memory of the intensity of that greeting serves as a gentle rebuke to the priorities of my own heart. The apostle John, eagerly desiring Jesus's return, wrote, "He who testifies to these things says, 'Yes, I am coming soon.' Amen. Come, Lord Jesus" (Revelation 22:20). In another passage, Paul even spoke of a crown awaiting those who have "longed for his appearing" (2 Timothy 4:8). Yet sometimes I don't feel as eager for Christ's return as my children were for mine.

Jesus is worthy of the very best of our love and devotion—and nothing on earth should compare to the thought of seeing Him face-to-face. May our love for our Savior deepen as we anticipate our joyful reunion with Him.   —BILL CROWDER

Those who belong to Christ should be longing to see Him.

TALKING ABOUT JESUS

READ: 1 Corinthians 15:51–57

Jesus said to her, "I am the resurrection and the life. The one who believes in me will live, even though they die." JOHN 11:25

PASTOR ELOY PACHECO SAID at a funeral for a believer that Jesus is the only lasting source of comfort. Afterward a woman came up to him and said, "You preachers are all alike. All you talk about is Jesus, Jesus, Jesus!"

"That's true," he replied kindly. "What comfort do you have to offer the grieving family?"

She was speechless for a few moments, and then she said, "You're right. At least you have Jesus."

Sooner or later someone dear to us will die, and we'll want to be comforted. A hug, a kind deed, shared tears, and the presence of a friend may ease sorrow's pain just a bit. But these gestures won't answer our most urgent questions: What's beyond the grave? Where is the person now? Will we be reunited in heaven? How can I have the assurance of eternal life?

For the answers to those questions, we must look to Jesus Christ. He is the One who defeated sin and death by dying on the cross for us and rising from the grave (1 Corinthians 15:1–28, 57). Because He lives, all who put their faith in Him will live forever with Him (John 11:25).

When a believer in Christ dies, we who are left behind can find comfort and confidence in Him. So, let's keep talking about Jesus.

—DENNIS DEHAAN

In life and in death, our only hope is Jesus.

WHEN JESUS COMES TO SUPPER

READ: Revelation 3:14–22

"Behold! I stand at the door and knock. If anyone hears My voice and opens the door, I will come in to him and dine with him, and he with Me." REVELATION 3:20 (NKJV)

REVELATION 3:20 PRESENTS THE Savior standing outside the church at Laodicea. He offers fellowship to anyone who will let Him in. In this passage, as is often true elsewhere in the Bible, a meal signifies fellowship. Our Lord desires fellowship with us!

Early twentieth-century pastor Walter B. Hanson told of an acquaintance in the English countryside where he grew up. She was an old saint known as Granny Pood. Hanson was walking along the road one day when he met Granny. They chatted and he asked, "Where are you going?" She told him she was on her way to visit another woman who was old and poor and that she would probably stay to have tea with her. Because he knew the other woman, Hanson said impulsively, "Well, I do not think you will find much tea there." Upon hearing that, Granny reached under her shawl and brought out a little paper package and replied, "I am taking the tea with me."

That's what our Lord does when we open our hearts fully to Him. He brings His provisions with Him—the infinite resources of His own person. The One who comes to dwell within us brings grace and strength for every need. He says, "I will come in to him and dine with him, and he with Me" (Revelation 3:20 NKJV). How can we remain lukewarm in our love for Jesus when He longs to come and dine with us?   —PAUL VAN GORDER

Christ does not want patronage, but fellowship.

OUR UNFAILING FRIEND

READ: John 15:9–17

*The scripture was fulfilled that says, "Abraham believed
God, and it was credited to him as righteousness,"
and he was called God's friend.* JAMES 2:23

AS A YOUNG MAN, Joseph Scriven had been engaged to a woman
he deeply loved. But tragedy struck the night before their wedding
when the boat she was in capsized and she drowned. In the hope
of forgetting the shock, which he never did, Joseph left his home
in Ireland and went to Canada.

There he taught school and served as a tutor. He chose to live
very simply, spending his money and strength in generously pro-
viding for destitute people. At times he even gave away his own
clothing. He was considered an eccentric by some, yet all he tried
to do was obey God's Word as best he could understand it.

In his loneliness, Scriven needed a steadfast friend. Having
found that friend in Jesus Christ, he wrote these simple words,
which movingly express his experience:

*What a friend we have in Jesus, / All our sins and griefs to
bear! / What a privilege to carry / Everything to God in prayer!*

Even if we have been blessed with deeply enriching friendships,
we all need Joseph Scriven's Friend. But before we can know Jesus
as our Friend, we must know Him as our Savior. Then, through all
of our changing circumstances, He will be the one we can depend
on—our unfailing Friend. —VERNON GROUNDS

*Christ's friendship prevails even
when human friendship fails.*

OUR CONSTANT COMPANION

READ: Acts 23:1–13

"[Teach] them to obey everything I have commanded you.
And surely I am with you always, to the very
end of the age." MATTHEW 28:20

AS THEY KNOCKED ON the door of Ed Claesson's room in a home for the elderly, Clair and Frances Hess heard Ed talking to someone. Frances whispered, "Clair, he has a visitor."

After Ed said, "Come in," they went into his room, but they didn't see anyone with him. When they said they had heard him talking to somebody, the stately ninety-eight-year-old Swede smiled and said, "Oh, I was just talking to Jesus. I asked Him why it is taking Him so long to call me Home."

Jesus Christ was in the room with Ed. Although bodily in heaven, Jesus is present in spirit with all of His people just as He promised (Matthew 28:20).

When the apostle Paul was facing serious charges and threats on his life, "the Lord stood by him and said, 'Be of good cheer, Paul'" (Acts 23:11 NKJV). And later, from a dungeon just before his execution, Paul recalled, "At my first defense no one came to my support. . . . But the Lord stood at my side and gave me strength . . . . The Lord will rescue me from every evil attack" (2 Timothy 4:16–18).

Paul sensed the nearness of Christ while he was a prisoner in a soldiers' barracks and later in life as he sat in a cold, damp dungeon. We too can know that the Lord is always with us. He is our constant companion.   —HERB VANDER LUGT

Jesus is only a prayer away.

TWO DAUGHTERS

READ: Luke 8:40–42, 49–56

While Jesus was still speaking, someone came from the house of Jairus, the synagogue leader. "Your daughter is dead," he said. *"Don't bother the teacher anymore."* LUKE 8:49

I HAD NEVER THOUGHT much about Jairus before. Oh, I had heard the story about this synagogue ruler, and I knew he had begged Jesus to come to his house and heal his dying daughter. But I never understood the depth of his sorrow. I never understood how his heart must have shattered in pain when a messenger came to him and announced, "Your daughter is dead."

No, I never comprehended his grief and anguish—until I heard those same words from a police officer who came to our house on June 6, 2002.

Jairus's daughter was twelve, and she died from an illness. Our daughter was seventeen, and it was an auto accident that broke our family's heart.

Jairus's daughter was restored to life by Jesus's touch. My daughter Melissa—though we ache to know she wasn't healed physically—was healed spiritually by Jesus's sacrifice of love when she trusted Him as Savior early in her life. Now our comfort comes from knowing that her eternal existence with the Lord has already begun.

Two daughters. The same Jesus. Two different results. His loving and compassionate touch is a miracle that can bring peace to grieving hearts—like Jairus's, like mine, like yours.

—DAVE BRANON

In every desert of trial, God has an oasis of comfort.

LINCOLN'S TEST

READ: Luke 24:13–27

"Did not the Messiah have to suffer these things and then enter his glory?" LUKE 24:26

ABRAHAM LINCOLN WAS A backwoodsman who rose from humble beginnings to the heights of political power. During the dark days of the US Civil War, he served as a compassionate and resolute president. Depression and mental pain were his frequent companions. Yet the terrible emotional suffering he endured drove him to receive Jesus Christ by faith.

Lincoln told a crowd in his hometown in Illinois: "When I left Springfield, I asked the people to pray for me; I was not a Christian. When I buried my son, the severest trial of my life, I was not a Christian. But when I saw the graves of thousands of our soldiers, I then and there consecrated myself to Christ. I do love Jesus." Life's most painful tragedies can bring us to a deeper understanding of the Savior.

When two men walked the road to Emmaus, they were dumbfounded by the senseless murder of Jesus of Nazareth. Then a stranger joined them and gave scriptural insight about the suffering Messiah (Luke 24:26–27). The stranger was Jesus himself, and His ministry to them brought comfort.

Heartache has a way of pointing us to the Lord Jesus, who has shared in our sufferings and can bring meaning to seemingly senseless pain. —DENNIS FISHER

Suffering can teach us what we can't learn in any other way.

THE MUTUAL FRIEND

READ: John 16:19–28

*"The Father himself loves you because you have loved me
and have believed that I came from God." JOHN 16:27*

I MET MY WIFE through a mutual acquaintance. I probably wouldn't have had the courage to approach her on my own. But a person we both knew made it easy by introducing us to each other. As a result, our first date was almost prearranged. By the time I asked her out, I already knew she would accept because our common friend had served as a go-between.

Christ fulfills that kind of role between sinners and a holy God. Through His redemptive work on the cross, Jesus has removed the barrier that would have kept us from ever being introduced to or accepted by the Father (Hebrews 7:25–27). Christ is the One who shows us that any friend of His is also a friend of the Father.

Jesus assured His disciples of this comforting truth when He told them He would soon be leaving them. He wanted them, and all who believe in Him, to know that because of their relationship to Him they could in His name go to God with their requests (John 16:23–24). Our Lord also made it clear that any request that is consistent with His character will be answered by the Father because He loves all who love the Son (vv. 26–27).

Because Jesus is our Friend, we can also be a friend of God.

—MART DEHAAN

*Christ bridges the gap between
the infinite God and finite man.*

LIVING UP TO THE NAME

READ: Ephesians 2:1–10

*God, who is rich in mercy, made us alive with Christ
even when we were dead in transgressions—it is by
grace you have been saved.* EPHESIANS 2:4–5

A NEW CHRISTIAN WAS reading through the Gospels. After she
finished, she told a friend she wanted to read a book on church history. When her friend asked why, the woman replied, "I'm curious.
I've been wondering when Christians started to become so unlike
Christ."

We can understand why this new convert was perplexed. There
is often disparity between the life of Christ and the lives of many
who bear His name. In fact, some believers are even imitating the
world instead of trying to live like Jesus.

Almost 2,000 years have passed since followers of Jesus were
first called Christians (Acts 11:26). Today, we who have placed our
trust in the Savior still bear that name and march under the same
banner as those early believers.

The Bible says that we are God's "handiwork, created in Christ
Jesus to do good works, which God prepared in advance for us to do"
(Ephesian 2:10). When we call ourselves Christians, we are saying to
the world that Christ is our Savior and that we are following Him.

Christians have a glorious name. It is a great privilege to be identified with Christ—and a great obligation to live up to His name!
—RICHARD DEHAAN

*When you walk with Christ,
you'll be out of step with the world.*

THE WONDROUS CROSS

READ: John 19:14–30

Carrying his own cross, he went out to the place of the Skull (which in Aramaic is called Golgotha). There they crucified him, and with him two others—one on each side and Jesus in the middle. JOHN 19:17–18

MAHATMA GANDHI ASKED SOME missionaries who visited him during one of his numerous fasts to sing a hymn for him. "Which hymn?" they asked. "The one that expresses all that is deepest in your faith," he replied. They thought for a moment and then with full hearts sang these words written by Isaac Watts:

> *When I survey the wondrous cross / On which the Prince of glory died, / My richest gain I count but loss / And pour contempt on all my pride.*

When George Briggs was governor of Massachusetts, three of his friends visited the Holy Land. While they were there, they climbed Golgotha's slope and cut from the hilltop a stick to be used as a cane. On their return they presented it to the governor, saying, "We want you to know that when we stood on Calvary, we thought of you." He accepted the gift with gratitude and then remarked, "I appreciate your consideration of me, gentlemen, but I am still more thankful for Another who thought of me there!"

Yes, Jesus thought of you and me when hanging there in agony. A life of gratitude would be our appropriate response. With Isaac Watts we can say, "Love so amazing, so divine, demands my soul, my life, my all!" —HENRY BOSCH

The cross reveals God's heart for the lost.

WHEN FRIENDS FAIL YOU

READ: Job 42

"My prayer is not for them alone. I pray also for those who will believe in me through their message." JOHN 17:20

WITH FRIENDS LIKE HIS, Job didn't need enemies. His three would-be comforters failed miserably in their efforts to ease his pain. Instead of bringing sympathy, they delivered accusations that only compounded his anguish.

Yet Job was able to emerge triumphantly from his cave of pain and confusion. A significant step toward that victory was his willingness to pray for the very friends who had criticized and accused him. God honored his prayers, and Job had the delight of seeing his friends turn to God for forgiveness (Job 42:7–10).

Jesus also prayed for His friends (John 17:6–19) despite their frequent failings. With the agony of the cross approaching, Jesus prayed for Peter even though He knew Peter would deny Him within hours (Luke 22:31–34).

Jesus prayed for you and me too (John 17:20–26). His work of prayer, which began before His death and resurrection, continues to this day. Although we sometimes act more like His enemies than His friends, Jesus is in the Father's presence interceding for us (Romans 8:34; Hebrews 7:25).

Following Christ's example, we are to pray for our friends and acquaintances—even when they hurt us. Is there someone you can pray for today?   —HADDON ROBINSON

To love more, pray more.

A PLEASANT DIVERSION

READ: Romans 11:33–12:2

Do not conform to the pattern of this world, but be transformed by the renewing of your mind. Then you will be able to test and approve what God's will is— his good, pleasing and perfect will. ROMANS 12:2

A FRIEND WAS LOOKING for a church to join and told me she had found just what she was looking for: "I like this church because I don't have to change my lifestyle of partying. It doesn't make me feel guilty or require anything of me. I feel good about myself when I'm there."

Her story makes me wonder how many people are in that type of situation. Their "Christianity" is what author W. Waldo Beach calls "a pleasant weekend diversion."

But is that the kind of life Jesus calls us to? Beach says, "No amount of air-conditioning and pew-cushioning in the suburban church can cover over the hard truth that . . . discipleship is costly; that, for the faithful, there is always a cross to be carried. No one can understand Christianity to its depths who comes to it to enjoy it as a pleasant weekend diversion."

Being a Christian means that we know Jesus personally. We have received Him by faith as our Savior from sin, and we present ourselves to Him. We deny our will and choose His instead. He transforms our thinking, our values, and our priorities to reflect what is acceptable to God (Romans 12:1–2).

Is your religion just a pleasant weekend diversion? That's no substitute for a vital relationship with Jesus!   —ANNE CETAS

Discipleship demands discipline.

THE CHILDREN'S FRIEND

READ: Matthew 19:13–15

*Jesus said, "Let the little children come to me, and
do not hinder them, for the kingdom of heaven
belongs to such as these."* MATTHEW 19:14

IT WAS IN THE mid-1800s that the great storyteller Hans Christian Andersen first published his delightful stories. The lessons and encouragement contained in his tales of "The Ugly Duckling," "The Little Mermaid," and "The Emperor's New Clothes" are still considered a great gift to children everywhere.

I'm reminded, however, that Jesus Christ is the greatest friend of children the world has ever known. No one has done more for them than Jesus.

When Jesus's disciples reprimanded people for bringing little ones to Him, the Lord said, "Let the little children come to me, and do not hinder them, for the kingdom of heaven belongs to such as these" (Matthew 19:14).

Jesus valued children as persons of worth. After His triumphal entry into Jerusalem, the Lord accepted the praise of children and reminded those who criticized them that God has ordained praise even "from the lips of children and infants" (Matthew 21:16; Psalm 8:2).

Companionship with the Savior is the privilege of everyone who trusts Him with the simple faith of a child. His loving arms and tender heart are ready to embrace every child who accepts Him. He willingly receives all who open their hearts to Him. He is the children's Friend. —DAVID MCCASLAND

*The Creator hides secrets from sages, yet
He can be known by children.*

IN THE FACE OF FEAR

READ: Matthew 14:22–33

*Jesus immediately said to them: "Take courage!
It is I. Don't be afraid."* MATTHEW 14:27

I'LL NEVER FORGET MY childhood fears that developed after my bedroom lights were turned off. My early experience of fear-driven insomnia reminds me that when trouble arrives on the doorstep of life, fear is not our friend. It disables us from moving forward and causes us to shrink from doing what is right—unless we have our eyes fixed on Jesus.

When the disciples faced the raging seas that were threatening to sweep them overboard, Jesus, walking on the water, assured them, "It is I. Don't be afraid" (Matthew 14:27). And to His followers who were fearfully locked away in a room after His crucifixion, Jesus appeared and asked, "Why are you troubled, and why do doubts rise in your minds?" (Luke 24:38). Recognizing the inevitability of trials, He said, "In this world you will have trouble. But take heart! I have overcome the world" (John 16:33). The point is clear. Trusting in His presence and power is the antidote to fear.

As the familiar hymn says, "Turn your eyes upon Jesus, look full in His wonderful face. And the things of earth will grow strangely dim in the light of His glory and grace." We can rest peacefully in the knowledge that God is with us. —JOE STOWELL

*Trust the presence and power of Jesus
in the midst of life's storms.*

DECLARING DEPENDENCE

READ: John 5:16–23

*"I am the vine; you are the branches. If you remain
in me and I in you, you will bear much fruit; apart
from me you can do nothing."* JOHN 15:5

LAURA'S MOM WAS BATTLING cancer. One morning Laura and a friend prayed for her. Her friend, who had been disabled for years by cerebral palsy, prayed: "Lord, you do everything for me. Please do everything for Laura's mother."

Laura was deeply moved by her friend's "declaration of dependence" on God. Reflecting on the moment, she said, "How often do I acknowledge my need for God in everything? It's something I should do every day!"

During His days on earth, Jesus demonstrated continual dependence on His heavenly Father. One might think that because Jesus is God in a human body, He would have the best of all reasons to be self-sufficient. But when the religious authorities asked Him to give a reason for "working" on a legally ordained day of rest because He healed someone on the Sabbath, He responded, "Very truly I tell you, the Son can do nothing by himself; he can do only what he sees his Father doing" (John 5:19). Jesus declared His dependence as well!

Jesus's reliance on the Father sets the ultimate example of what it means to live in relationship with God. Every moment we draw breath is a gift from God, and He wants our lives to be filled with His strength. When we live to love and serve Him through our moment-by-moment prayer and reliance on His Word, we are declaring our dependence on Him. —JAMES BANKS

*Prayerlessness is our declaration of independence
from God. —Daniel Henderson*

AWAKENED BY A CLOSE FRIEND

READ: John 14:1–7

"And if I go and prepare a place for you, I will
come back and take you to be with me that you
also may be where I am." JOHN 14:3

A FEW YEARS AGO, I had some tests to screen for cancer, and I was nervous about the outcome. My anxiety was magnified as I thought about the fact that while the medical personnel were well-trained and extremely competent, they were also strangers who had no relationship with me.

After awakening from the anesthesia, however, I heard the beautiful sound of my wife's voice: "It's great, Honey. They didn't find anything." I looked up at her smiling face and was comforted. I needed the assurance of someone who loved me.

A similar assurance lies ahead for all who have trusted Jesus. Believers can be comforted in knowing that when they wake up in heaven, One who loves them greatly—Jesus—will be there.

The Book of Common Prayer expresses this Christian hope: "After my awakening, [my Redeemer] will raise me up; and in my body I shall see God. I myself shall see, and eyes behold Him who is my friend and not a stranger."

Do you have trouble facing mortality? Jesus promised to be there when we slip from this world into the next. He said, "Where I am [heaven], there you may be also" (John 14:3 NKJV). What a comfort for believers to know that after death we will be awakened by a close Friend!   —DENNIS FISHER

To see Jesus will be heaven's greatest joy.

A BAD DREAM

READ: John 6:15–21

*Have no fear of sudden disaster or of the ruin that
overtakes the wicked.* PROVERBS 3:25

ALL OF US HAVE had bad dreams. Perhaps we were falling from a high building, fleeing from a hideous creature, or standing before an audience and forgetting our speech.

My wife had a nightmare recently. She dreamed she was in a small room when two men appeared out of the mist. Fear overwhelmed her. Just as the men were about to grab her, she said, "Let me tell you about Jesus." Immediately she was awakened by the sound of her own voice. The name "Jesus" had freed her from fear.

We read in John 6 that Jesus's disciples were afraid when in the dimness of nightfall they saw a strange figure walking on the stormy Sea of Galilee. But the mysterious figure was not part of a bad dream—He was real. Matthew reports that they "cried out in fear" (14:26). Then the disciples heard a familiar voice: "It is I; do not be afraid" (John 6:20). It was Jesus. Their fears were calmed, as was the sea.

The Savior speaks the same assurance to us today amid the many fears along our Christian journey. Solomon said, "The name of the LORD is a fortified tower; the righteous run to it and are safe" (Proverbs 18:10).

Fears will come, but we are assured that Jesus is always a light in the darkness. —DENNIS DEHAAN

―――――

*You need not fear the darkness if you are
walking with the Light of the World.*

MENTION THE NAME

READ: Acts 4:5–20

"Don't you believe that I am in the Father, and that the Father is in me? The words I say to you I do not speak on my own authority. Rather, it is the Father, living in me, who is doing his work." JOHN 14:10

A CHURCH GROUP INVITED a speaker to address their meeting. "Talk about God," the group leader told him, "but leave out Jesus."

"Why?" the man asked, taken aback.

"Well," the leader explained, "some of our prominent members feel uncomfortable with Jesus. Just use God and we'll be fine." Accepting such instructions was a problem for the speaker who said later, "Without Jesus, I have no message."

Something similar was asked of followers of Jesus in the days of the early church. Local religious leaders conferred together to warn the disciples not to speak about Jesus (Acts 4:17). But the disciples knew better. "We cannot help speaking about what we have seen and heard," they said (v. 20).

To claim to believe in God and not in His Son Jesus Christ is a contradiction in terms. In John 10:30, Jesus clearly describes the unique relationship between himself and God: "I and the Father are one"—thus establishing His deity. That is why He could say, "You believe in God; believe also in me" (John 14:1). Paul knew that Jesus is the very nature of God and equal with God (Philippians 2:6).

We need not shy away from the name Jesus, for "salvation is found in no one else, for there is no other name under heaven given to mankind by which we must be saved" (Acts 4:12).

—LAWRENCE DARMANI

The name of Jesus is at the heart of our faith and our hope.

THE HIGHEST PLACE

READ: Colossians 1:15–23

*He is before all things, and in him all things
hold together.* COLOSSIANS 1:17

MY HUSBAND INVITED A friend to church. After the service his friend said, "I liked the songs and the atmosphere, but I don't get it. Why do you give Jesus such a high place of honor?" My husband then explained to him that Christianity is a relationship with Christ. Without Him, Christianity would be meaningless. It's because of what Jesus has done in our lives that we meet together and praise Him.

Who is Jesus and what has He done? The apostle Paul answered this question in Colossians 1. No one has seen God, but Jesus came to reflect and reveal Him (v. 15). Jesus, as the Son of God, came to die for us and free us from sin. Sin has separated us from God's holiness, so peace could be made only through someone perfect. That was Jesus (vv. 14, 20). In other words, Jesus has given us what no one else could—access to God and eternal life (John 17:3).

Why does He deserve such a place of honor? He conquered death. He won our hearts by His love and sacrifice. He gives us new strength every day. He is everything to us!

We give Him the glory because He deserves it. We lift Him up because that is His rightful place. Let's give Him the highest place in our hearts.   —KEILA OCHOA

Jesus is the center of our worship.

I JUST SAW JESUS

READ: 2 Corinthians 4:1–10

*We always carry around in our body the death
of Jesus, so that the life of Jesus may also be
revealed in our body.* 2 CORINTHIANS 4:10

YEARS AGO I LOST my job in my chosen profession due to circumstances beyond my control. So I took on two lesser-paying jobs in order to try to make ends meet. Yet it still was very difficult to earn enough to pay my monthly expenses.

Then I reconnected with Joel and Dave, two friends from my past. Joel had become the pastor of a growing church in the suburbs. Dave had become an overseas missionary, but he was visiting in the US at the time. Both of them, recognizing my predicament, gave me money to help pay the rent. I was deeply moved. As I thought of my friends' actions, I said to myself: "I have just seen Jesus Christ!"

Just as I saw Jesus in my friends, sometimes others can see Him in us. Paul speaks of "Christ in you, the hope of glory" (Colossians 1:27). He confessed: "I have been crucified with Christ and I no longer live, but Christ lives in me" (Galatians 2:20). And he also understood that different circumstances can be opportunities for "the life of Jesus [to] be revealed in our body" (2 Corinthians 4:10).

Do you know someone struggling with physical or financial burdens? Why not let the indwelling Christ express His love through you by meeting that person's need?   —DENNIS FISHER

---

*When we take a step toward others in need, we may
be helping them take a step toward Jesus.*

"THAT'S JESUS!"

READ: Isaiah 53:4–12

He was pierced for our transgressions, he was crushed for our iniquities; the punishment that brought us peace was on him, and by his wounds we are healed. ISAIAH 53:5

AS A JEWISH KID growing up in New York, Michael Brown had no interest in spiritual things. His life revolved around being a drummer for a band, and he got mixed up with drugs. But then some friends invited him to church, where he found the love and prayers of the people to be irresistible. After a short spiritual struggle, Michael trusted Jesus as Savior.

This was a monumental change for a wayward Jewish teen. One day he told his dad he had heard about Old Testament texts describing Jesus. His dad, incredulous, asked, "Where?" When Michael opened his Bible, it fell to Isaiah 53. They read it, and Michael exclaimed, "That's Him! That's Jesus!"

Indeed, it is Jesus. Through the help of Christians and the guidance of the Holy Spirit, Brown (today a Bible scholar and an author) came to recognize the Messiah of Isaiah 53. He experienced the salvation that changes lives, forgives sin, and gives abundant life to all who trust the "Man of sorrows" (v. 3 NKJV). Jesus is the One who was "pierced for our transgressions" and who died for us on the cross (v. 5).

The Bible reveals Jesus, who alone has the power to change lives.
—DAVE BRANON

The Spirit of God uses the Word of God to change hearts.

LIBERATING TRUTH

READ: Ephesians 1:3–10

To the praise of his glorious grace, which he has freely given us in the One he loves. EPHESIANS 1:6

A MISSIONARY HAD BEEN disparaging herself. She was unhappy with her life in general, but she was especially displeased with what she felt was her low level of spiritual growth.

One morning she looked searchingly at herself in the mirror. Then, very slowly, she said, "God, I thank you that I am myself and can never be anybody else."

That was her moment of liberating self-acceptance. She realized that by God's design she was an absolutely unique person, a Christ-redeemed human being who could never be replaced or duplicated.

Do you condemn yourself because you aren't as spiritual as you think you ought to be? Do you see yourself as a second-rate disciple, lacking the gifts and graces possessed by fellow believers who seem to be models of prayer, witness, and service? We can rise above the mood of self-rejection and enjoy grateful self-acceptance when we put our lives into the nail-pierced hands of Jesus. "In him we have redemption through his blood, [and] the forgiveness of sins" (Ephesians 1:7). We are accepted and chosen by Him (vv. 4–6).

If the Lord has accepted us, surely we can accept ourselves! That's the liberating truth. —VERNON GROUNDS

Accepting Jesus's free gift of salvation frees us to accept ourselves.

SEEK AND SAVE

READ: Luke 19:1–10

"The Son of Man came to seek and to save the lost." LUKE 19:10

LACHLAN MACQUARIE, GOVERNOR OF New South Wales, Australia from 1810–1821, had a way of making everyone feel included in the new colony. When the "exclusives" (free settlers, civil servants, and military officers) shunned the society of the "emancipists" (transported convicts given conditional or absolute pardon), Governor Macquarie insisted that they be treated as social equals.

Jesus showed interest in Zacchaeus, a shunned tax collector in Jericho, and He included him in the recipients of His salvation plan (Luke 19:1–10). A marginalized and hated man because of his profession, Zacchaeus was desperate to see Jesus and climbed a tree to get a glimpse of Him. When Jesus passed by, He saw Zacchaeus's desire and told him to come down because he had a divine appointment at his house. Some complained that Jesus was spending time with a sinner, but His loving attention changed Zacchaeus's life. He repented and offered restitution for those he had defrauded. Salvation had come to his house.

Jesus's mission was simple: Diligently search for lost people, whatever their social standing, and offer them God's salvation plan. As followers of Christ, we too have that as our mission.

—MARVIN WILLIAMS

Those of us who have discovered salvation need to search for any and all who need Jesus.

UNTIL YOU ARE FULL

READ: John 6:25–29

*Jesus declared, "I am the bread of life. Whoever comes
to me will never go hungry, and whoever believes
in me will never be thirsty."* JOHN 6:35

A FRIEND WHO LIVES in Singapore told me about an old Chinese
greeting. Instead of "How are you?" people would ask "Have you
eaten until you are full?" The greeting likely originated during a
time when food was scarce and many people did not know when
they would have their next meal. When food was available, it was
advisable to eat until they were full.

After Jesus miraculously fed 5,000 people with five loaves and
two small fish (John 6:1–13), the crowd followed Him, wanting
more (vv. 24–26). The Lord told them not to work for physical food
that spoils, but "for food that endures to eternal life, which the Son
of Man will give you . . . . I am the bread of life. Whoever comes
to me will never hunger, and whoever believes in me will never be
thirsty" (vv. 27, 35).

As followers of Jesus, we should help those who lack adequate
physical nutrition. And with everyone, we can share the good news
that our hunger for inner peace, forgiveness, and hope can be satisfied by knowing Christ the Lord.

Jesus Christ, the Bread of Life, invites us to come to Him for
His feast for the soul, urging us to eat until we are full.

—DAVID MCCASLAND

———

There is a longing in every heart that only Jesus can satisfy.

THE GOOD LIFE

READ: Psalm 73:21–28

But as for me, it is good to be near God. I have made the Sovereign LORD my refuge; I will tell of all your deeds. PSALM 73:28

BEAUTY, WEALTH, POWER, LOVE, marriage, and pleasure are good things, but they're not the best. The best is loving God and taking in His love—bringing Him glory and making Him our friend for life. That leads to the best possible life because it gives us satisfaction and joy now (John 10:10), and it's what Christians are going to be doing forever.

That's why we should make time for God and rest in His love—the love that made you and me. It is the reason for our existence and the means by which we will make the most of our lives.

I like the way the psalmist put it: "it is good to be near God. I have made the Sovereign LORD my refuge; I will tell of all your deeds" (Psalm 73:28). In other words, the good life is drawing close to the One who loves us like no other.

And how can we "draw close" to Him? Here's a practice I began many years ago: Take a few minutes every morning to read some verses from the Gospels (Matthew, Mark, Luke, John) and note what Jesus said or did. After all, He came to show us what God is like (Hebrews 1:1–3). Put yourself in the story—in the place of the leper He healed with His loving touch, for example (Mark 1:40–45). Think about how much He loves you and then thank Him!

—DAVID ROPER

The wonder of it all—just to think that Jesus loves me!

THAT FIRST LOOK!

READ: Revelation 22:1–7

*They will see his face, and his name will be on
their foreheads.* REVELATION 22:4

IN THE LATE 1880S in England, a most unusual wedding took place. The bridegroom, William Montague Dyke, had been blinded when he was ten years old. As he was studying at Cambridge, he fell in love with the daughter of a British naval officer. Two weeks before they were to be married, Dyke had an operation on his eyes. On the wedding day, as the bride walked down the aisle with her father, William's father removed the bandages from his eyes. For the first time, he beheld his bride. With a surge of indescribable joy, he proclaimed, "You are more beautiful than I ever imagined."

There is a sense in which all of us as believers in Jesus Christ will someday have that kind of "aha" moment. When we read Revelation 22, one of the most thrilling portions in the entire Bible, we see that it describes the perfections of heaven. Among the things we will notice is this: "No longer will there be any curse" (v. 3). Also, the assurance that "his name shall be on their foreheads" (v. 4) reminds us of our complete identification with the Savior.

But here is the most important: We "will see his face!" (v. 4). Imagine opening our eyes for the first time and seeing our Savior face to face! That first look will be worth everything we've ever endured on this earth.   —HENRY BOSCH

———

*When in heaven we view the sunshine of Christ's
face, all earth's shadows will fall behind us.*

STRUGGLING WITH ADDICTION

READ: Hebrews 4:14–16

No temptation has overtaken you except what is common to mankind. And God is faithful; he will not let you be tempted beyond what you can bear. But when you are tempted, he will also provide a way out so that you can endure it. 1 CORINTHIANS 10:13

ERIC WAS STRUGGLING WITH an addiction, and he knew it. His friends and family members encouraged him to stop. He agreed that it would be best for his health and relationships, but he felt helpless. When others told him how they had quit their bad habits, he replied, "I'm happy for you, but I can't seem to stop! I want God to take the desire away right now."

Immediate deliverance may happen for some, but most face a daily battle. While we don't always understand why the temptation doesn't go away, we can turn to God on whatever path we find ourselves. We can learn to exchange our futile efforts to change for complete dependence on God.

Jesus was tempted also, just as we are, so He understands what we're feeling (Mark 1:13). He sympathizes with our struggles (Hebrews 4:15), and we can "approach God's throne of grace with confidence, so that we may receive mercy and find grace to help in our time of need" (v. 16). He also uses others, including trained professionals, to lean on along the way.

Whatever battles we may be facing today, we know this—God loves us and is faithful to come to our assistance. —ANNE CETAS

*We are not tempted because we are evil;
we are tempted because we are human.*

GROWING A SERVANT'S HEART

READ: Luke 22:24–30

"For who is greater, the one who is at the table or the one who serves? Is it not the one who is at the table? But I am among you as one who serves." LUKE 22:27

IT WAS A LONG day at work. But when I got home, it was time to start my "other" job—being a good dad. Greetings from my wife and kids soon became, "Dad, what's for dinner?" "Dad, can you get me some water?" "Dad, can we play soccer?"

I just wanted to sit down. And even though part of me really wanted to be a good dad, I didn't feel like serving my family's needs. That's when I saw it: a thank-you card my wife had received from someone at church. It pictured a bowl of water, a towel, and dirty sandals. Across the bottom were these words from Luke 22:27: "I am among you as one who serves."

That statement of Jesus's mission, to serve those He came to seek and save (Luke 19:10), was exactly what I needed. If Jesus was willing to do the dirtiest of jobs for His followers—like scrubbing His followers' no doubt filthy feet (John 13:1–17)—I could get my son a cup of water without grumbling about it. In that moment, I was reminded that my family's requests to serve them weren't merely an obligation, but an opportunity to reflect Jesus's servant heart and His love to them. When requests are made of us, they are chances to become more like the One who served His followers by laying down His life for us. —ADAM HOLZ

God's love for us empowers us to serve others.

I'M NOT LOOKING

READ: Romans 12:9–21

Love must be sincere. Hate what is evil;
cling to what is good. ROMANS 12:9

HAVE YOU EVER SEEN an IMAX film? I really enjoy walking into one of those huge auditoriums that have seven-story-tall, eighty-five-foot-wide screens, because when the lights go down, the ultimate travelogue begins. The IMAX film fills the screen, making you feel as if you are traveling in the space shuttle or careening through the Grand Canyon in a jet.

I recall that when our kids were still at home, our family saw an IMAX production at a large amusement park. At the end, to our surprise, we were subjected to a short advertisement for an IMAX rock concert by a group known for their immorality. As we left the auditorium, our daughter Melissa, a second-grader at the time, told us, "When they started playing that music, I shut my eyes and started singing 'Jesus Loves Me.'"

As careful parents who diligently try to keep wrong media influences from corrupting our children, my wife and I were proud of Melissa's response. Without being told, she recognized something that was not acceptable, and she knew how to counter it—by concentrating on Jesus. As adults, we should be as careful—and as wise.

Lord, help us to abhor and turn away from evil wherever it occurs. And help us to keep our thoughts on you as we "cling to what is good."
—DAVE BRANON

To escape temptation, flee to God.

AN ALL-TIME FRIEND

READ: John 15:9–17

*A friend loves at all times, and a brother is born
for a time of adversity.* PROVERBS 17:17

TEN-YEAR-OLD DEREK KRUISENGA HAD been stricken with cancer.
In a *Grand Rapids Press* article titled "Two Special Pals" was a letter to the *Press* by Derek's best friend, Josh Rettig. It read in part:

"My friend has cancer all over his body and has been fighting
it for a year and a half. The doctors say there is nothing they can
do. I would like to give him his dream. Let him meet one of his
favorite basketball stars."

Before Derek died, his wish came true. Because of Josh's letter,
Derek met Isiah Thomas, who was at that time an All-Star for the
NBA's Detroit Pistons.

God is a friend of sinners. He knows our heart's deepest desires
and highest hopes, and from eternity He had a plan to fulfill them.
In the Old Testament, God called Abraham "My friend" (Isaiah 41:8), revealing His purposes to him and promising to bring
them to pass. And in the New Testament, Jesus called His disciples
"friends" (John 15:15).

If you are trusting Jesus as Savior, you are assured of God's
friendship for time and eternity. He'll stay true to you through life's
severest trials and actually work in them so you can become like
Christ. You'll never find a better friend than that. He is an all-time
Friend. —DENNIS DEHAAN

Looking for a Friend? Jesus is looking for you.

TUNING IN

READ: John 10:1–10

When he has brought out all his own, he goes on ahead of them, and his sheep follow him because they know his voice. JOHN 10:4

I DON'T KNOW IF this is true in every marriage, but for some reason I have a tendency to tune out everything around me and concentrate on my own thoughts. This is especially frustrating to my wife, Martie, when she is talking to me about something important. When she notices the distant look in my eyes, she often says, "Have you heard anything I've said?"

Listening is an important part of any relationship, especially in our relationship with Christ. If we belong to Him, we have the privilege of communing with Him through His Word and the work of the Holy Spirit in our hearts. We know we are paying attention to the true Shepherd when His voice leads us to righteousness, love, grace, and all that is consistent with His character and will. As Jesus made clear when He identified himself as the "good Shepherd" in John 10, those who diligently listen to Him become devoted followers of Him (v. 4) who are becoming transformed into His likeness.

Just as listening attentively to your spouse or a friend communicates value and worth, paying close attention to the voice of Jesus is one way to affirm His importance in your life. So let's cast aside the distractions of life, tune in to His voice, and pray for the grace to do what He says.   —JOE STOWELL

Listening to Jesus is the first step to following Him.

THE NEXT CHAPTER

READ: Hebrews 12:1–11

Therefore, since we are surrounded by such a great cloud of witnesses, let us throw off everything that hinders and the sin that so easily entangles. And let us run with perseverance the race marked out for us, fixing our eyes on Jesus, the pioneer and perfecter of faith. For the joy set before him he endured the cross, scorning its shame, and sat down at the right hand of the throne of God. HEBREWS 12:1–2

STEVE WAS ALMOST FIVE when his father, missionary pilot Nate Saint, was killed in 1956, along with four other men, by the Waodani tribe in Ecuador. But as a result of the love and forgiveness demonstrated by the families of the martyred men, there is now a growing community of believers among the Waodani.

As an adult, Steve moved back to Ecuador and became friends with Mincaye, one of the men who killed his father. Steve's motto is: "Let God Write Your Story." He says, "You have a lot of people . . . who want to write their own story and have God be their editor when [it] goes wrong. I decided long ago to let God write my story." When Steve suffered a serious accident in 2012, he reassured his family: "Let's let God write this chapter too." His faith continues to carry him toward recovery.

The story continues to unfold for all followers of Jesus Christ. None of us knows how the next chapter of our life will read. But as we look to Jesus and "run with perseverance the race marked out for us," we can trust Him—the author and finisher of our faith (Hebrews 12:1–2). Jesus wrote the beginning of our story, and He'll write the next chapter and the ending as well.   —CINDY HESS KASPER

Let your life tell the story of Christ's love and mercy to the world around you.

KINDNESS GONE VIRAL

READ: Mark 10:13–16

When Jesus saw this, he was indignant. He said to them, "Let the little children come to me, and do not hinder them, for the kingdom of God belongs to such as these." MARK 10:14

NEWS OF A SIMPLE act of kindness on a New York subway has gone around the world. A young man, head covered by a hooded sweatshirt, fell asleep on the shoulder of an older passenger. When someone else offered to wake the young rider, the older man quietly said, "He must have had a long day. Let him sleep. We've all been there." Then he let the tired fellow rider sleep on his shoulder for the better part of the next hour, until the older man gently eased away to get up for his stop. In the meantime, another passenger snapped a photograph and posted it on social media, and it went viral.

The man's kindness seems to resonate with what we all long for—the kindness that reflects the heart of God. We see this gentleness in Jesus when His friends tried to protect Him from the noise and bother of little children. Instead, Jesus insisted on taking the little ones in His arms and blessing them (Mark 10:16). In the process, He invited all of us to trust Him like a little child (vv. 13–16).

Jesus lets us know that all of us are safe in His presence. Whether awake or asleep, we can lean on Him. When we're exhausted, He provides a safe place for us to rest. —MART DEHAAN

God is a safe resting place.

HOLD ON!

READ: Revelation 3:7–13

"I am coming soon. Hold on to what you have, so that no one will take your crown." REVELATION 3:11

A COWBOY FRIEND OF mine who grew up on a ranch in Texas has a number of colorful sayings. One of my favorites is this "It don't take much water to make good coffee." And when someone ropes a steer too big to handle or is in some kind of trouble, my friend will shout, "Hold everything you've got!" meaning "Help is on the way! Don't let go!"

In chapters two and three of the book of Revelation, we find letters to "the seven churches in the province of Asia" (1:4). These messages from God are filled with encouragement, rebuke, and challenge, and they speak to us today just as they did to the first-century recipients.

Twice in these letters we find the phrase, "Hold on to what you have." The Lord told the church at Thyatira, "Hold on to what you have until I come" (2:25). And to the church in Philadelphia He said, "I am coming soon. Hold on to what you have, so that no one will take your crown" (3:11). In the midst of great trials and opposition, these believers clung to God's promises and persevered in faith.

When our circumstances are harsh and sorrows outnumber joys, Jesus shouts to us, "Hold everything you've got! Help is on the way!" And with that promise, we can hold on in faith and rejoice.

—DAVID McCASLAND

The promise of Christ's return calls us to persevere in faith.

PRAISE IN THE DARK

READ: Matthew 26:17–30

*Through Jesus, therefore, let us continually offer
to God a sacrifice of praise—the fruit of lips that
openly profess his name.* HEBREWS 13:15

EVEN THOUGH MY FRIEND Mickey was losing his eyesight, he told me, "I'm going to keep praising God every day, because He's done so much for me."

Jesus gave Mickey, and us, the ultimate reason for such never-ending praise. The twenty-sixth chapter of Matthew tells us about how Jesus shared the Passover meal with His disciples the night before He went to the cross. Verse 30 shows us how they concluded the meal: "When they had sung a hymn, they went out to the Mount of Olives."

It wasn't just any hymn they sang that night—it was a hymn of praise. For millennia, Jews have sung a group of Psalms called "The Hallel" at Passover (*hallel* is the Hebrew word for "praise"). The last of these prayers and songs of praise, found in Psalms 113–118, honors the God who has become our salvation (118:21). It refers to a rejected stone that became a cornerstone (v. 22) and one who comes in the name of the Lord (v. 26). They may very well have sung, "The LORD has done it this very day; let us rejoice today and be glad" (v. 24).

As Jesus sang with His disciples on this Passover night, He was giving us the ultimate reason to lift our eyes above our immediate circumstances. He was leading us in praise of the never-ending love and faithfulness of our God. —JAMES BANKS

Praising God helps us recall His goodness that never ends.

FACE-TO-FACE

READ: Exodus 33:7–14

The LORD would speak to Moses face to face, as one speaks to a friend. Then Moses would return to the camp, but his young aide Joshua son of Nun did not leave the tent. EXODUS 33:11

ALTHOUGH THE WORLD IS connected electronically like never before, nothing beats time together in person. As we share and laugh together, we can often sense—almost unconsciously—the other person's emotions by watching their facial movements. Those who love each other, whether family or friends, like to share with each other face-to-face.

We see this kind of relationship between the Lord and Moses, the man God chose to lead His people. Moses grew in confidence over the years of following God, and he continued to follow Him despite the people's rebelliousness and idolatry. After the people worshiped a golden calf instead of the Lord (see Exodus 32), Moses set up a tent outside of the camp in which to meet God, while they had to watch from a distance (33:7–11). As the pillar of cloud signifying God's presence descended to the tent, Moses spoke on their behalf. The Lord promised that His Presence would go with them (v. 14).

Because of Jesus's death on the cross and His resurrection, we no longer need someone like Moses to speak with God for us. Instead, just as Jesus offered to His disciples, we can have friendship with God through Christ (John 15:15). We too can meet with Him, with the Lord speaking to us as one speaks to a friend.

—AMY BOUCHER PYE

We can speak to the Lord as a friend.

LEARNING TO KNOW GOD

READ: John 6:16–21

He said to them, "It is I; don't be afraid." JOHN 6:20

FOR AS LONG AS I can remember, I've wanted to be a mother. I dreamed about getting married, getting pregnant, and holding my baby in my arms for the first time. When I finally got married, my husband and I never even considered waiting to expand our family. But with each negative pregnancy test, we realized we were struggling with infertility. Months of doctors' visits, tests, and tears followed. We were in the middle of a storm. Infertility was a bitter pill to swallow, and it left me wondering about God's goodness and faithfulness.

When I reflect on our journey, I think about the story of the disciples caught in the storm on the sea in John 6. As they struggled against the waves in the dark of the storm, Jesus unexpectedly came to them walking on the stormy waves. He calmed them with His presence, saying, "It is I; don't be afraid" (v. 20).

Like the disciples, my husband and I had no idea what was coming in our storm, but we found comfort as we learned to know God more deeply as the One who is always faithful and true. Although we would not have the child we had dreamed of, we learned that in all our struggles we can experience the power of His calming presence. Because He is there powerfully working in our lives, we need not be anxious. —KAREN WOLFE

*We can experience God's powerful presence
even in the storms of our lives.*

AN ESCORT THROUGH THE VALLEY

READ: Psalm 23

"Where, O death, is your victory? Where, O death,
is your sting?" 1 CORINTHIANS 15:55

I'VE HEARD PEOPLE SAY, "I'm not afraid of death because I'm confident that I'm going to heaven; it's the dying process that scares me!" Yes, as Christians we look forward to heaven, but we may be afraid of dying. We need not be ashamed to admit that. It is natural to be afraid of the pain that comes with dying, of being separated from our loved ones, of possibly impoverishing our families, and of regret over missed earthly opportunities.

Why don't Christians need to be afraid of death? Because Jesus was raised from the grave, and we who are in Christ will also be raised. That is why in 1 Corinthians 15:56–57, Paul proclaimed: "The sting of death is sin, and the power of sin is the law. But thanks be to God! He gives us the victory through our Lord Jesus Christ."

The dying process itself is but an escort that ushers us into eternity with God. As we "walk through the darkest valley," we can have this confidence from God's Word: "You are with me; your rod and your staff, they comfort me" (Psalm 23:4). The picture here is of the Lord coming alongside us, giving comfort and direction as He escorts us through the dark valley to the "house of the LORD." There we will dwell with Him forever (v. 6).   —ALBERT LEE

Death is the last shadow before heaven's dawn.

A COLLECTOR'S HEAVEN

READ: Matthew 6:19–21

"Do not store up for yourselves treasures on earth, where moth and vermin destroy, and where thieves break in and steal. But store up for yourselves treasures in heaven, where moth and vermin do not destroy, and where thieves do not break in and steal." MATTHEW 6:19–20

PEOPLE LOVE TO COLLECT things—from baseball cards to stamps to coins. And while collecting can be a fun hobby, it is sobering to think that once we leave this earth, everything we own becomes part of someone else's collection. What value would it be to have collected much on earth but little or nothing for eternity?

Jesus had something to say about this. Speaking to His disciples, He said: "Store up for yourselves treasures in heaven, where moths and vermin do not destroy, and where thieves do not break in and steal" (Matthew 6:20).

Eternal treasures never lose their worth. They can never be spoiled or stolen. And just think—we can actually stockpile them! How? Through acts of service. Through leading others to Jesus. By being compassionate to those in need. By living according to the will and ways of Jesus. In the gospel of Mark, we read that the Lord tested the rich young ruler's heart when He asked him to sell all that he had, give it to the poor, and follow Him. The ruler's response revealed what he really valued (10:21–22).

It's easy to become enamored with earthside stuff, but when you make the choice to follow Jesus, He'll show you the joy of collecting eternal treasures. Nothing on earth can compare!

—JOE STOWELL

Hold tightly to what is eternal and loosely to what is temporal.

MAKING A DIFFERENCE

READ: Matthew 9:27–38

When he saw the crowds, he had compassion on them, because they were harassed and helpless, like sheep without a shepherd. MATTHEW 9:36

ELIZABETH'S STORY WAS MOVING, to say the least. Following a terribly humiliating experience in Massachusetts, she caught a bus to New Jersey to escape her embarrassment. Weeping uncontrollably, she hardly noticed that the bus had made a stop along the way. A passenger sitting behind her, a total stranger, began making his way off the bus when he suddenly stopped, turned, and walked back to Elizabeth. He saw her tears and handed her his Bible, saying that he thought she might need it. He was right. But not only did she need the Bible, she needed the Christ it speaks of. Elizabeth received Him as a result of this simple act of compassion by a stranger who gave a gift.

Jesus is our example of compassion. In Matthew 9, we read, "When he saw the crowds, he had compassion on them, because they were harassed and helpless, like sheep without a shepherd" (v. 36). Not only did our Lord notice the pain and hurt of broken people, but He also responded to it by challenging His followers to pray for the Father to send out workers to respond to the hurts and needs of this dying world (v. 38).

As we follow Christ's example, a heart of compassion for shepherdless people can compel us to make a difference in the lives of others. —BILL CROWDER

A world in despair needs Christians who care.

NOT INTERESTED IN RELIGION

READ: John 5:18, 37–47

"Jerusalem, Jerusalem, you who kill the prophets and stone those sent to you, how often I have longed to gather your children together, as a hen gathers her chicks under her wings, and you were not willing." MATTHEW 23:37

A RADIO AD FOR a church caught my attention: "Because you've heard about Christianity, you might not be interested in religion. Well, it might surprise you—Jesus wasn't interested in religion either. But He was big on relationship and teaching us to love one another." It continued, "You may not like everything about our church, but we offer authentic relationship, and we're learning to love God and each other. You're welcome to visit."

This church may have overstated things about Jesus and religion because Scripture does speak of "religion that God our Father accepts" in James 1:27 as helpful deeds toward others. But Jesus did have difficulties with religious people of His day. He said the Pharisees, guided by tradition and rules not by love for the Lord, "outwardly appear righteous to men, but inside [they] are full of hypocrisy and lawlessness" (Matthew 23:28 NKJV). They didn't have the love of God in their hearts (John 5:42). Jesus wanted relationship with them, but they "refuse to come to [Him]" (v. 40).

If being "religious" means following a set of rules so we can look good—instead of enjoying a relationship with the Savior—Jesus isn't interested. He offers forgiveness and love to all who want an intimate relationship with Him. —ANNE CETAS

There is a longing in every heart that only Jesus can satisfy.

A VOICE TO HEED

READ: John 10:1–6

The gatekeeper opens the gate for him, and the sheep listen to his voice. He calls his own sheep by name and leads them out. When he has brought out all his own, he goes on ahead of them, and his sheep follow him because they know his voice. JOHN 10:3–4

A FATHER WHO HAD been out of town for a few days wanted to see if his young daughter remembered him as he came home. After quietly entering the house, he hid so he could see her but she couldn't see him. Then he called softly, "Peggy."

Dropping her toys, she glanced around the room but soon went back to her play. Again, the father repeated her name. Joyously, she turned and stretched out her arms in the direction of the sound. She knew he was there, for she recognized his voice!

In John 10, people are compared to sheep that readily respond to the voice of their leader. Jesus the Great Shepherd calls His own by name. As we heed His voice through the Spirit-inspired Word of God, we will enjoy His fellowship and experience the security and peace of His perfect guidance. Sheep are unable to find their way by themselves. They must depend on the care and protection of the shepherd. Each herder has his own unique call, which he utters from time to time to help direct his flock. As the animals follow him, they avoid the dangers around them and find the nourishing green pastures!

Listen for the voice of the Good Shepherd. He's there, and He wants to lead, protect, and guide you. Only as we listen to Him and follow His guidance will we be safe and fruitful.

—HENRY BOSCH

The more we obey the voice of our Guide, the better the guidance.

YOU MATTER TO JESUS

*"I am the good shepherd; I know my sheep and
my sheep know me."* John 10:14

In this computer age, it's easy to begin feeling like a number
instead of a person. We are identified by our social security number
rather than by our name. Sometimes we get junk mail addressed
to "Resident." We get random phone call solicitations meant for
whoever answers the phone. Such impersonal methods may cause
some people to conclude, "No one cares for me."

But that's not true. Jesus cares. In fact, He knows everyone by
name.

We never need to feel like the young student who felt slighted
when Edward VII, the King of England from 1901 to 1910, was
visiting a city to lay the cornerstone for a new hospital. Thousands
of schoolchildren were present to sing for him. Following the ceremony, the King walked past the excited youngsters. After he was
gone, a teacher saw one of her students crying. She asked her, "Why
are you crying? Did you not see the King?" "Yes," the young girl
sobbed, "but the King did not see me."

King Edward couldn't have taken notice of each child in that
throng. Jesus, however, gives individual attention to each of us. He is
the Good Shepherd who "calls his own sheep by name" (John 10:3).

Think of it—Jesus knows who you are! You matter to Him. As
you worship Him, tell Him you love Him. Then, as you fellowship
with other believers, help them realize that they matter to Jesus.

—Paul Van Gorder

*You may be a number computers can trace, but Christ
knows your need, your name, and your face.*

CONSIDER THE POOR

READ: Matthew 25:31–40

The righteous considers the cause of the poor.
PROVERBS 29:7 (NKJV)

THE YEAR WAS 1780, and Robert Raikes had a burden for the poor, illiterate children in his London neighborhood. He noticed that nothing was being done to help these children, so he set out to make a difference.

He hired some women to set up schools for them on Sunday. Using the Bible as their textbook, the teachers taught the poorest children of London to read and introduced them to the wisdom of the Bible. Soon about 100 children were attending these classes and enjoying lunch in a safe, clean environment. These "Sunday schools," as they were soon called, eventually touched the lives of thousands of boys and girls. By 1831, Sunday schools in Great Britain reached more than a million children—all because one man understood this truth: "The righteous considers the cause of the poor" (Proverbs 29:7 NKJV).

It's no secret that Jesus cares greatly for those who struggle. In Matthew 25, He suggests that followers of Christ show a readiness for the Lord's return by helping the hungry to get food, helping the thirsty to get a drink, helping the homeless to find a home, helping the naked to get clothes, and helping the sick or imprisoned to receive comfort (vv. 35–36).

As we bear witness that Christ is in our hearts, we honor our compassionate Savior by considering those on God's heart.

—DAVE BRANON

Open your heart to God to learn compassion,
and open your hand to give help.

TRUST HIM FULLY

READ: Matthew 14:22–33

*Immediately Jesus reached out his hand
and caught him. "You of little faith," he said,
"why did you doubt?"* MATTHEW 14:31

WHEN THE *WASP*, ONE of America's great naval vessels in World War II, caught fire and began to sink, the sailors were ordered to abandon ship and swim away from the vessel immediately. They jumped overboard, but instead of trusting their well-tested life jackets for safety, many clung to the sides of the ship in fear. When the vessel plunged beneath the surface, these sailors were sucked down with it.

Peter's situation was somewhat different. Yet he too began to sink because of fear. When he saw his Master walking on the water, he obeyed Christ's invitation to step out of the boat and come to Him. At first, he was supernaturally held up. But then he became preoccupied with his perilous circumstances—the howling wind and turbulent waves. Fear gripped his heart, and he began to sink.

We as Christians make similar blunders in our relationship with Jesus. We tend to forget His instructions. Then when trials come, instead of relying on His promises we cling to false securities as those frightened sailors did. Or like Peter, we look at our frightening circumstances and push the panic button.

No matter what happens, let's keep our eyes on Jesus. We will find Him completely reliable. We need never be afraid to trust Him fully. —HERB VANDER LUGT

You start going down when you stop looking up.

LISTEN TO THE CHILDREN

READ: Matthew 21:1–17

*"Do you hear what these children are saying?" they
asked him. "Yes," replied Jesus, "have you never read,
"'From the lips of children and infants you, Lord,
have called forth your praise'?"* MATTHEW 21:16

THE RELIGIOUS LEADERS WERE wrong about Jesus that first Palm
Sunday. They couldn't have been more off-base if they had tried.
True, they knew a lot of theology, but they were dead wrong about
Jesus.

The children, however, were right. They were the ones in the
temple who shouted, "Hosanna to the Son of David!" (Matthew
21:15). They believed that the Person riding that unbroken colt was
the promised Son of David. They fulfilled the prophecy of Psalm
8:2 by giving praise to the Lamb who was about to die for the sins
of the world.

On that first Palm Sunday, it was the children who responded
with wholehearted joy, even though they may not have fully understood Jesus's mission to redeem mankind.

Yes, children can teach us a vital lesson about faith. In their
openness and innocence, it is easy for them to trust the One whose
pure character touches a responsive chord in their tender hearts.

As adults, we think we know so much. We try to be so mature,
so correct, so religious. I wonder if we would even recognize the
Savior if He walked among us, working the kind of miracles He
performed long ago.

Lord, give us the faith of little children.   —DAVID EGNER

———

Children are so transparent you can see right through them.

YOU CAN BELIEVE IT

READ: Acts 1:1–11

*After his suffering, he presented himself to them and
gave many convincing proofs that he was alive. He
appeared to them over a period of forty days and
spoke about the kingdom of God.* ACTS 1:3

IN 1957, LIEUTENANT DAVID STEEVES walked out of the California
Sierras fifty-four days after his Air Force trainer jet had disappeared.
He related an unbelievable tale of how he had lived in a snowy
wilderness after parachuting from his disabled plane. By the time
he showed up alive, he had already been declared officially dead.
When further search failed to turn up the wreckage, a hoax was
suspected, and Steeves was forced to resign under a cloud of doubt.
His story was confirmed, however, more than twenty years later
when a troop of Boy Scouts discovered parts of his plane.

Another "survival story" from centuries ago is still controversial.
A man by the name of Jesus Christ walked out of the wilderness
making claims a lot of people found difficult to believe. He was later
executed and pronounced dead. But three days later, He showed
up alive. And there have been skeptics ever since.

But consider the facts of Christ's life, death, and resurrection.
His integrity is well-founded. Prophets foretold His coming. Miracles supported His deity. Eyewitnesses verified His resurrection.
And today the Holy Spirit confirms that Jesus is alive to anyone
who is seeking to know the truth. Yes, you can believe it! Do you?

—MART DEHAAN

*The resurrection is a fact of history that
demands a response of faith.*

THE RELEASE OF FEAR

READ: Mark 6:45–53

*They all saw him and were terrified. Immediately
he spoke to them and said, "Take courage! It is I.
Don't be afraid."* MARK 6:50

OUR BODIES REACT TO our feelings of dread and fear. A weight in the pit of our stomachs, along with our hearts pounding as we gulp for breath, signal our sense of anxiety. Our physical nature keeps us from ignoring these feelings of unease.

The disciples felt shockwaves of fear one night after Jesus had performed the miracle of feeding more than five thousand people. The Lord had sent them ahead to Bethsaida so He could be alone to pray. During the night, they were rowing against the wind when suddenly they saw Him walking on the water. Thinking He was a ghost, they were terrified (Mark 6:49–50).

But Jesus reassured them, telling them not to be afraid and to take courage. As He entered their vessel, the wind died down and they made it to the shore. I imagine that their feelings of dread calmed as they embraced the peace He bestowed.

When we're feeling breathless with anxiety, we can rest assured in Jesus's power. Whether He calms our waves or strengthens us to face them, He will give us the gift of His peace that "transcends all understanding" (Philippians 4:7). And as He releases us from our fears, our spirits and our bodies can return to a state of rest.

—AMY BOUCHER PYE

The Lord releases us from fear.

MAKING FRIENDS

READ: Mark 2:13–17

While Jesus was having dinner at Levi's house, many tax collectors and sinners were eating with him and his disciples, for there were many who followed him. MARK 2:15

A LETTER FROM A friend described the adjustments that his son and daughter-in-law were facing as young missionaries in a country long resistant to the gospel of Christ. "After some rough early going," he wrote, "they are getting used to not having modern conveniences and are falling in love with the people."

A photo showed the couple's two-year-old-son Wesley and a waiter in a restaurant, both grinning widely as they shared a moment of friendship. My friend commented, "Ever smiling, Wesley makes friends wherever he goes." That got me to thinking. Making friends and loving people is the key to sharing the gospel wherever we are, because that's what Jesus did.

Some religious leaders were surprised when Jesus openly associated with people they considered undesirable. They said to His disciples, "Why does he eat with tax collectors and sinners?" (Mark 2:16). Yet Jesus was known as the friend of sinners. He said, "I have not come to call the righteous, but sinners" (v. 17).

A loving heart and a friendly smile go a long way toward communicating the love of Christ to the people we meet each day. May they say of us, as they did of little Wesley, "Ever smiling, he makes friends wherever he goes." —DAVID MCCASLAND

Loving the lost is the first step in leading them to Christ.

FRIEND OR FOE?

Rᴇᴀᴅ: John 15:9–15

"You are my friends if you do what I command." Jᴏʜɴ 15:14

Dɪᴄᴋ Sʜᴇᴘᴘᴀʀᴅ sᴇʀᴠᴇᴅ ᴀs a chaplain in the British army during World War I. One night he was lying in the dense blackness of no man's land when he heard footsteps approaching. Unable to see who it might be, he was tempted to cry out, "Friend or foe?"

Years later, on another dark night back in his homeland, Dick remembered that experience as he gazed up into the sky and wondered about the God of the universe. Again he felt like calling out, "Friend or foe?"

Often in the blackness of some bewildering trial, unable to discern God's purposes, we are tempted to question His goodness. Some even wonder whether there is a God; and if there is, whether He cares for us.

We who believe the Bible know that the almighty, eternal Creator has revealed himself as a loving Father, and that He infinitely cares for us. And through His Son, He has shown himself to be a Friend of sinners (Matthew 11:19). When in faith anyone accepts the sin-atoning sacrifice of Jesus, that person receives the promise that he will never be forsaken by God (Hebrews 13:5). What a privilege to know in our darkest moment that when we cry out, "Friend or foe?" Jesus answers, "I am your ever-present Friend!"

—Vᴇʀɴᴏɴ Gʀᴏᴜɴᴅs

If Christ is your friend, you need not fear.

TRUE PROSPERITY

READ: Luke 5:1–11

When Simon Peter saw this, he fell at Jesus' knees and said, "Go away from me, Lord; I am a sinful man!" LUKE 5:8

IMAGINE HAVING A FINANCIAL advisor whose stock market predictions were 100 percent accurate. Wall Street would soon put you on easy street. Or suppose your livelihood was fishing and you had a friend who could always lead you to just the right spot at just the right time. Every day you could have a moneymaking catch.

I wonder, did the appeal of such prosperity flash across the minds of the four seasoned fishermen who took Jesus's advice? After working all night with no success, they let down their nets at His command, and the catch nearly sank two boats (Luke 5:6–7).

Many people today seem to be drawn to Jesus by those who proclaim that God wants them healthy and wealthy. Without question, Jesus showed concern for the sick and the poor. It is not wrong to make health and material needs the objects of our prayers, for our heavenly Father cares deeply about us (Matthew 7:7–11). But His greatest concern and delight is not to "fill our nets with fish." He wants to fill our hearts with His love so we will become fishers of men. And He can do that only when we recognize, as Peter did (Luke 5:8), how spiritually needy we are. The richest people are those who have experienced the love of Christ and want to share it with others. That's true prosperity!   —DENNIS DEHAAN

No one is so poor as he who has nothing but money.

THREE NEEDS

READ: 1 John 4:7–21

So we know and rely on the love God has for us. God is love. Whoever lives in love lives in God, and God in them. 1 JOHN 4:16

I'VE HEARD IT SAID that there are three things a person needs to be happy:

1. Something to do—meaningful work or helping others.
2. Someone to love—someone to whom we can give of ourselves, such as a spouse, a child, or a friend.
3. Something to look forward to—a vacation, a visit from a loved one, improved health, the realization of a dream.

Those things may bring some temporary happiness. But for lasting fulfillment, they can all be found in a relationship with Jesus, God's Son.

Something to do. As believers, we have been given gifts from the Holy Spirit to serve our Savior by serving others in God's family (Romans 12:1–16). We are also called to spread the gospel around the world (Matthew 28:19–20).

Someone to love. We love God because He first loved us (1 John 4:19). And we love others, "for love comes from God" (v. 7).

Something to look forward to. One day we'll be welcomed into God's presence forever, where we will enjoy a perfect place prepared especially for us (John 14:2–3; Revelation 21:3–4). We'll see Jesus and be like Him (1 John 3:2).

For lasting fulfillment, Jesus Christ truly is everything we need.

—ANNE CETAS

Where there's hope, there's happiness.

THE LAMB IS MY SHEPHERD

READ: Psalm 23

"For the Lamb at the center of the throne will be their shepherd; 'he will lead them to springs of living water.' 'And God will wipe away every tear from their eyes.'" REVELATION 7:17

THE WRITERS OF THE Old and New Testaments used many different metaphors for the Lord Jesus Christ. These word pictures vividly describe the marvelous aspects of Jesus's life and ministry.

While visiting a friend, hymn writer Albert Simpson Reitz saw the following motto hanging on a wall: "The Lamb Is My Shepherd." *How foolish*, he thought. Then he realized that a smudge on his glasses had distorted the second word of the motto. Actually it read: "The Lord Is My Shepherd."

His mistake started him thinking. He remembered that the Scriptures present Jesus both as the Good Shepherd and as the Lamb of God. Reitz said to his friend, "I've just seen the glorious gospel of our Lord in a new light. I'm reminded that the apostle John on the island of Patmos saw a vision, assuring him that the resurrected 'Lamb who is in the midst of the throne' will guide His people even when they get to heaven. Misreading that motto on your wall has given me a rich blessing. It could actually read, 'The Lamb Is My Shepherd.'"

It's reassuring to know that our Shepherd will guide us safely through this life, and that He will continue to feed and lead us throughout eternity. —HENRY BOSCH

---

*The Lamb who died to save us is
the Shepherd who lives to lead us.*

A PLACE TO STAND

READ: 1 Corinthians 3:10–15

For no one can lay any foundation other than the one already laid, which is Jesus Christ. 1 CORINTHIANS 3:11

WHILE TAKING A BREAK during a ministry trip, we were snorkeling in the Caribbean Sea. The boat that had taken us to the deep water for better sites had gone back to shore, and I began to feel panicky about being in the open water. Finding it hard to control my breathing, I asked my son-in-law Todd and a friend, Dave Velzen, for help. They held my arms while I searched for an outcropping of coral close enough to the surface for me to stand on. Once I had a place to stand, even though surrounded by deep waters, I was okay.

Are you feeling a bit panicky about events in your life? Maybe it seems as if you are surrounded by the open waters of relationship problems, or money woes, or simply an inability to put your life in order. Perhaps you feel as if you are drowning in a sea of trials and trouble.

May I suggest two things? First, find a fellow Christian or two who can come beside you and hold you up (see Ecclesiastes 4:10), pray for you, talk with you, and remind you that you are not alone. Then rest your feet on the only solid foundation in life: Jesus Christ (1 Corinthians 3:11).

Life's troubles are too tough to take on alone. Get some help and find in Jesus a place to stand. —DAVE BRANON

———

Build your life on the solid foundation—Jesus Christ.

NO REGRETS

READ: 1 Peter 4:12–19

*For the Son of Man is going to come with his angels in
the glory of his Father, then he will repay each person
according to what he has done.* MATTHEW 16:27 (ESV)

A LITTLE GIRL WHO needed surgery was terrified. As an encouragement, her parents promised to give her something she had wanted for a long time—a kitten. The operation went well, but as the anesthesia was wearing off the youngster was heard mumbling to herself, "This sure is a lousy way to get a cat!"

Christians who endure hardship in serving the Lord will never feel that way when they look back on their trials. It's true that "everyone who wants to live a godly life in Christ Jesus will be persecuted" (2 Timothy 3:12). Jesus said to His disciples, "If anyone desires to come after Me, let him deny himself, and take up his cross, and follow Me" (Matthew 16:24 NKJV). He also assured them that when He returns to earth, "He will reward each according to his works" (v. 27 NKJV).

Paul said our sufferings for Christ aren't worthy to be compared "with the glory that will be revealed in us" (Romans 8:18). And Peter told us, "Rejoice inasmuch as you participate in the sufferings of Christ, so that you may be overjoyed when his glory is revealed" (1 Peter 4:13).

Believers who endure hardship for Christ count it a privilege to be identified with their Savior. Suffering for Him brings a sure reward—with no regrets. —RICHARD DEHAAN

Serving the Lord is an investment with eternal dividends.

IN THE NEIGHBORHOOD

READ: John 1:1–14

The Word became flesh and made his dwelling among us. We have seen his glory, the glory of the one and only Son, who came from the Father, full of grace and truth. JOHN 1:14

IT WAS THE BUZZ of our neighborhood. A famous professional football player had moved in just two houses down from where we lived. We had seen him on television and read about his great skills on the field, but we never thought he would choose to reside in our neighborhood. Initially, our expectations were that we would welcome him into the neighborhood and we would all become great friends. But his life was obviously far too busy for any of us to get to know him personally.

Imagine this: Jesus—the Lord of the universe and Creator of all things—chose to dwell among us! He left heaven and came to this earth. As John says, "We have seen his glory, the glory of the one and only Son, who came from the Father" (John 1:14). Jesus chose to become intimately involved with all who will come to Him. And, even more significant, for those of us who have received His redeeming love, the Holy Spirit has now set up residence in our hearts to comfort, counsel, convict, lead, and teach us.

When you think of the Babe in the manger, remember how special it is that He not only moved into our "neighborhood," but that He also did it so He could bless us with the intimate privileges of His residence within us. —JOE STOWELL

Take advantage of the gift of God's presence.

LEAVING A LEGACY

READ: Deuteronomy 6:4–9

Impress them on your children. Talk about them when you sit at home and when you walk along the road, when you lie down and when you get up. DEUTERONOMY 6:7

RECENTLY MY GRANDSON ALEX accompanied me as I ran errands. Unexpectedly, he asked, "So, Grandpa, how did you receive Christ as your Savior?" Touched, I told him about my childhood conversion. Alex was still interested, so I described how his great-grandfather had come to faith. This included a brief overview of how he survived World War II, his initial resistance to the gospel, and how his life changed after becoming a Christian.

Later I was reminded of our conversation when I read a Bible passage that spoke of faith being passed down through the generations. In Deuteronomy, Moses instructed the Israelites to take to heart God's truths and share them with the next generation as a way of life: "These words which I command you today shall be in your heart. You shall teach them diligently to your children, and shall talk of them when you sit in your house, when you walk by the way, when you lie down, and when you rise up" (6:6–7).

Biblical parenting is not a guarantee of having godly offspring. But when we see spiritual interest in the next generation, we can cultivate vital conversations about God's Word. This can be one of a parent's, or a grandparent's, greatest legacies. —DENNIS FISHER

---

*The richest legacy a parent can leave
a child is a godly example.*

HEART OF JOY

READ: John 15:1–11

"I have told you this so that my joy may be in you and that your joy may be complete." JOHN 15:11

WHILE WAITING IN THE gate area of Singapore's Changi Airport to board my flight, I noticed a young family—mom, dad, and son. The area was crowded, and they were looking for a place to sit. Suddenly, the little boy began loudly singing, "Joy to the World." He was about six years old, so I was pretty impressed that he knew all the words.

What captured my attention even more was the look on the boy's face—his beaming smile matched the words he was singing as he proclaimed to everyone at the gate the joy of the Christ who has come.

This joy is not limited to exuberant children nor should it be confined to the Christmas season. The overflowing joy of knowing Christ's presence in our lives was one of the themes of Jesus's final teaching with His disciples the night before He died on the cross. He told them of His extravagant love for them—that He loved them as the Father loved Him (John 15:9). After sharing what this eternal relationship looks like, Jesus said, "I have told you this so that my joy may be in you and that your joy may be complete" (v. 11).

What a promise! Through Jesus Christ our hearts can be filled with joy—real joy!   —BILL CROWDER

———

In every season of life we can know joy in Christ.

COME TO ME

READ: John 10:1–18

*"When he has brought out all his own, he goes
on ahead of them, and his sheep follow him
because they know his voice."* JOHN 10:4

AFTER A HIJACKED PLANE slammed into the Pentagon on September 11, 2001, many people inside the building were trapped by a cloud of thick, blinding smoke. Police officer Isaac Hoopi ran into the blackness, searching for survivors, and he heard people calling for help. He began shouting back, over and over: "Head toward my voice! Head toward my voice!"

Six people, who had lost all sense of direction in a smoke-filled hallway, heard the officer's shouts and followed. Hoopi's voice led them out of the building to safety.

"Head toward My voice!" That's also the invitation of Jesus to each of us when we are in danger or when we have lost our way. Jesus described the true spiritual shepherd of the sheep as one who "goes on ahead of them, and his sheep follow him because they know his voice" (John 10:4).

Are we listening for Jesus's voice during our times of prayer and Bible reading? When we're in difficult circumstances, are we walking toward Him instead of groping in the dark?

Jesus is "the good shepherd" (v. 11). Whatever our need for guidance or protection, He calls us to heed His voice and follow Him.

—DAVID MCCASLAND

*You don't need to know where you're going
if you're following the Shepherd.*

THE ASCENSION

READ: Acts 1:12–11

*"My Father's house has many rooms; if that were not so, would I
have told you that I am going there to prepare a place for you? And
if I go and prepare a place for you, I will come back and take you
to be with me that you also may be where I am."* JOHN 14:2–3

THE REPEATED APPEARANCES OF Jesus after His death and resurrection brought His followers so much joy that they must have wanted the visits to continue indefinitely. But on the fortieth day after His resurrection, having given His disciples final instructions, Jesus slowly ascended and a cloud hid Him from view.

Jesus could have vanished instantly, as He had done previously (Luke 24:31). But He chose to ascend visibly to impress on His followers that this was the end of His visits—at least for now. His bodily presence would soon be replaced by "another advocate," the Holy Spirit promised in John 14:16. Jesus's ascension marked the dawn of a new era.

In His glorified human body, the Lord Jesus ascended, entered heaven, sat down at the right hand of God, sent the Holy Spirit (John 14:16–18; Acts 2:33), and now intercedes for us (Romans 8:34; Hebrews 7:25). He permeates the whole universe with His spiritual presence and power (Colossians 1:15–23; Ephesians 4:10).

An ancient writing says that Jesus ascended bodily into heaven "our entrance to secure, and our abode to prepare." That's true. But it's also true that as God, He is always spiritually present with us and will be "to the end of the age" (Matthew 28:20). What a wonderful Savior we have!   —HERB VANDER LUGT

Jesus went away so the Holy Spirit could come to stay.

JESUS'S PRAYER PATTERN

READ: Luke 15:12–16

Jesus often withdrew to lonely places and prayed. LUKE 5:16

COMMUNICATION IS VITAL TO any relationship: parent and child, husband and wife, employer and employee, coach and athlete. And most important—God and those who love Him.

During His time on earth, Jesus showed us the importance of communication. The Gospels tell us of nearly twenty occasions when He prayed to His heavenly Father. He prayed in different circumstances: at His baptism (Luke 3:21), during brief rests from ministry (Luke 6:12), before raising Lazarus (John 11:41). And He prayed for different things: for guidance (Luke 6:12–13), to express His desire to do His Father's will (Matthew 26:39), to give thanks for food (John 6:11).

Jesus was a prayer warrior. Here was God himself in the person of the Son—the One in whom all the power of the universe dwelt. Yet He turned to God the Father in prayer. As hard as that may be to understand, its lesson for us is easy to grasp: If Jesus needed to communicate with God to accomplish His mission, how much more do we need to pray!

Think of what you have to face today. If it is your habit to ask, "What would Jesus do?" you can be sure from His example that He would pray first. Let's make that our pattern too.

—DAVE BRANON

Pray first!

GIVING IN TO JESUS

READ: James 4:6–10

*Count yourselves dead to sin but alive to
God in Christ Jesus.* ROMANS 6:11

THEY CALL IT "THE Devil's Footprint." It's a foot-shaped impression in the granite on a hill beside a church in Ipswich, Massachusetts. According to local legend, the "footprint" happened one fall day in 1740 when the evangelist George Whitefield preached so powerfully that the devil leaped from the church steeple, landing on the rock on his way out of town.

Though it's only a legend, the story calls to mind an encouraging truth from God's Word. James 4:7 reminds us, "Submit yourselves, then, to God. Resist the devil, and he will flee from you."

God has given us the strength we need to stand against our adversary and the temptations in our lives. The Bible tells us that "sin shall no longer be your master" (Romans 6:14) because of God's loving grace to us through Jesus Christ. As we run to Jesus when temptation comes, He enables us to stand in His strength. Nothing we face in this life can overcome Him, because He has "overcome the world" (John 16:33).

As we submit ourselves to our Savior, yielding our wills to Him in the moment and walking in obedience to God's Word, He is helping us. When we give in to Him instead of giving in to temptation, He is able to fight our battles. In Him we can overcome.

—JAMES BANKS

*The prayer of the feeblest saint . . . is a terror
to Satan. —Oswald Chambers*

SCATTERED FRUIT

READ: John 13:3–15

*Follow my example, as I follow the example
of Christ.* 1 CORINTHIANS 11:1

THE STORY IS TOLD of a Christian serving in the armed forces who
was home on furlough. He was rushing to catch his train when he
ran into a fruit stand on the station platform, knocking most of the
piled-up apples to the ground.

The young boy who operated the stand tried to pick up his
scattered fruit but was having difficulty. The apologetic serviceman
put down his luggage and started collecting the apples. He polished
each one with his handkerchief and put it back on the counter. So
impressed was the boy that he asked gratefully, "Soldier, are you
Jesus?" With a smile the soldier replied, "No, but I'm trying to be
like Him."

Sometimes, as we hurry about our own responsibilities, we
become too busy to care about other people. But we must remember that Jesus urges us to show kindness and concern for our fellow
travelers. He set the example for us in John 13 by being a servant.
We need to take the time to be helpful also.

Would anyone ask of us, "Are you Jesus?" And could we honestly
respond, "No, I'm not Jesus, but I'm trying to be like Him"? Christlike kindness can open the door for a heart-touching testimony.

—VERNON GROUNDS

Nothing is more attractive than being like Jesus.

WHO'S ON MY GUEST LIST?

READ: Luke 14:7–14

"But when you give a banquet, invite the poor, the crippled, the lame, the blind, and you will be blessed. Although they cannot repay you, you will be repaid at the resurrection of the righteous." LUKE 14:13–14

I LOVE HOSTING FESTIVE dinners. Sometimes I'll say: "Tonia, we haven't had anyone over for dinner in a while. Who do you think we should invite?" We go through our proposed guest list and suggest friends we have never invited or have not invited in a while. And it seems like this list is normally comprised of people who look and sound and live like we do, and who can reciprocate. But if we were to ask Jesus whom we should have over for dinner, He would give us a totally different guest list.

One day a prominent Pharisee invited Jesus into his home, probably for table fellowship, but possibly to watch Him closely so he could trap Him. While there, Jesus healed a man and taught the host a significant lesson: When creating your guest list for a dinner party, you should not be exclusive—inviting friends, relatives, rich neighbors, and those who can pay you back. Instead, you should be inclusive—inviting the poor, the crippled, the lame, and the blind. Although such people would not be able to pay the host back, Jesus assured him that he would be blessed and that God would reward him (Luke 14:12–14).

Just as Jesus loves the less fortunate, He invites us to love them by opening up our hearts and homes. —MARVIN WILLIAMS

Opening our hearts and homes blesses both us and others.

JUST LIKE JESUS

READ: 1 John 2:1–6

When they saw the courage of Peter and John and realized that they were unschooled, ordinary men, they were astonished and they took note that these men had been with Jesus. ACTS 4:13

A CHRISTIAN MAGAZINE ONCE carried an article about a senior executive of a large bank in New York City. It told how he had risen to a place of prominence and influence. At first he served as an office boy. Then one day the president of the company called him aside and said, "I want you to come into my office and work with me each day." The young man replied, "But what could I do to help you, sir? I don't know anything about finances."

"Never mind that. You will learn faster what I want to teach you if you just stay by my side and keep your eyes and ears open."

"That was the most significant experience of my life," said the executive. "Being with that wise man made me just like him. I began to do things the way he did, and that accounts for what I am today."

In a far deeper sense, we can be transformed by having a close fellowship with the Lord Jesus. John told us that if we say we are abiding in Christ, we ought to live just as He lived (1 John 2:6). Through meditation, prayer, and obedience to Him, we will gradually take on those qualities that characterize the Savior.

And that happens when we reflect a desire to be like Him.

—HENRY BOSCH

Christianity is not just Christ in you, but Christ living His life through you.

HIS SACRIFICE—AND OURS

READ: Hebrews 9:23–28

*Grace and peace to you from God our Father and the
Lord Jesus Christ, who gave himself for our sins to
rescue us from the present evil age, according to the
will of our God and Father.* GALATIANS 1:3–4

IN THESE DAYS WHEN so many people are insisting on their personal
rights, the biblical concept of self-sacrifice may seem old-fashioned
and ludicrous. Oh, people may give so they can get something
back, but many think it's foolish to give only to help someone else
without hope of return.

A great number of people have given sacrificially, though. Cana-
dian author William D. Matheson tells of a veteran who walked
through the streets of his hometown with an empty sleeve. When
a passerby commented on the loss of his arm, the veteran replied,
"I didn't lose it. I gave it."

That describes what Jesus did for us. He didn't lose His life on
the cross. He gave it. As Galatians 1:4 says, He "gave himself for
our sins." He paid the penalty so that all who believe on Him would
experience forgiveness of sin and have eternal life. In fulfillment of
the Old Testament picture of the sacrifice of the lamb, He yielded
His life for us.

Following Christ's example, we are to give ourselves unselfishly
to His service and help others. That makes sense, though it may
seem absurd to many. Our sacrifices will glorify the Lord and make
an impact for Christ on our selfish world.   —DAVID EGNER

*Christ's sacrifice of himself for us motivates
us to sacrifice ourselves for others.*

LEARNING TO WALK

READ: Colossians 2:1–7

As you therefore have received Christ Jesus the Lord,
so walk in Him. COLOSSIANS 2:6 (NKJV)

WALKING IS JUST ONE step away from falling. That's why venturing out on two unsteady legs can be frightening to a very young child. Yet children keep at it until walking becomes second nature.

This is similar to learning to "walk" as a Christian. We put our faith into practice one step at a time. Pastor and author F. B. Meyer explains, "We received Jesus into our hearts by faith. . . . In the same manner we must live always and everywhere, receiving from Him, by faith, grace upon grace, and allowing what He works in to work out in all manner of godliness, tenderness, and Christlikeness. This practice of looking to Jesus for grace in every circumstance of life tends to become more and more habitual."

Paul urged believers to live by faith so they would become firmly established in their walk with Christ (Colossians 2:6–7). We do that by focusing our thoughts on Him: what He has done, what He is doing now, and what He will do for us. We take a risk by depending completely on Him, obeying His commands, and putting His teaching into practice.

Walking with Christ may sometimes be frightening, but it is the only way to make progress in our spiritual development. Are you walking with Him today? —DENNIS DEHAAN

You cannot run the race until you learn to walk.

THE LONGING

Read: Luke 2:25–32

It had been revealed to him by the Holy Spirit that he would not die before he had seen the Lord's Messiah. Luke 2:26

LOOK AT THE PEOPLE around you: the shoppers walking the malls, the enthusiastic fans at football and basketball games, fellow employees in the workplace. Do you think they've found happiness?

As people rush through life—hurrying from paycheck to payment and from job to home and then doing it all over again—many of them feel empty inside. They long for something to make their existence more meaningful and fulfilling.

Unlike Simeon, whom we read about in Luke 2, many people don't know what will bring happiness. The Holy Spirit had told Simeon that he would not die until he had seen the promised Messiah. When that extraordinary day came and Simeon came to the temple to meet Jesus, peace and contentment were guaranteed.

All around us are people who could have that same peace and contentment if they could just meet Jesus. As we see the crowds each day, we should be reminded to pray that the Holy Spirit would touch their hearts and make them want to see Jesus. They may be rushing around, but in their hearts they have a void waiting to be filled by the Messiah, the Lord Jesus.   —DAVE BRANON

There is a longing in every heart that only Jesus can satisfy.

PEACE, BE STILL

READ: Mark 4:35–41

*[Jesus] got up, rebuked the wind and said to the
waves, "Quiet! Be still!" Then the wind died down
and it was completely calm.* MARK 4:39

MY FRIEND ELOUISE HAS a wonderful way of putting life into clever
perspectives. Once when I asked her, "How are you today?" I expected
the usual "fine" response. Instead, she said, "I've got to wake Him
up!" When I asked what she meant, she kiddingly exclaimed, "Don't
you know your Bible?" Then she explained: "When the disciples faced
trouble, they ran to wake up Jesus. I'm going to run to Him too!"

What do we do when we are stuck in a troubling situation with
nowhere to run? Maybe, like the disciples who were stuck in a life-
threatening storm, we run to Jesus (Mark 4:35–41). Sometimes,
however, we may try to bail ourselves out of trouble by seeking
revenge, slandering the one who has caused our problem, or just
cowering fearfully in the corner as we sink into despair.

We need to learn from the disciples who fled to Jesus as their
only hope. He may not bail us out immediately, but remembering
that He is in our boat makes a difference! Thankfully, He is always
with us in the storms of life, saying things like "Peace, be still!"
(v. 39 NKJV). So, look for Him in your storm and let Him fill you
with the peace that comes from knowing He is near.

—JOE STOWELL

*Make Jesus your first option when
the storms of life threaten you.*

LIKE A LITTLE CHILD

READ: Matthew 18:1–5; 19:13–14

*And he said: "Truly I tell you, unless you change
and become like little children, you will never enter
the kingdom of heaven."* MATTHEW 18:3

ONE EVENING MANY YEARS ago, after saying a goodnight prayer with our two-year-old daughter, my wife was surprised by a question. "Mommy, where is Jesus?"

Luann replied, "Jesus is in heaven and He's everywhere, right here with us. And He can be in your heart if you ask Him to come in."

"I want Jesus to be in my heart."

"One of these days you can ask Him."

"I want to ask Him to be in my heart now."

So our little girl said, "Jesus, please come into my heart and be with me." And that started her faith journey with Him.

When Jesus's disciples asked Him who was the greatest in the kingdom of heaven, He called a little child to come and join them (Matthew 18:1–2). "Unless you change and become like little children," Jesus said, "you will never enter the kingdom of heaven. . . . And whoever welcomes one such child in my name welcomes me" (vv. 3–5).

Through the eyes of Jesus we can see a trusting child as our example of faith. And we are told to welcome all who open their hearts to Him. "Let the little children come to me," Jesus said, "and do not hinder them, for the kingdom of heaven belongs to such as these" (19:14). —DAVID MCCASLAND

Our faith in Jesus is to be like that of a trusting child.

IMITATE ME

READ: 1 Corinthians 4:9–17

Imitate me, just as I also imitate Christ.
1 CORINTHIANS 11:1 (NKJV)

ANDREW MARTON RECALLS THE first time he met his future brother-in-law Peter Jennings, who was a top foreign news correspondent in 1977. He said he was so nervous that he acted like "a jittery fan in the presence of a journalistic hero whose personal wattage could light up Manhattan."

Andrew looked up to Peter and tried to emulate him. He became a journalist too and approached his assignments the way Peter did— "he dove in and worked harder than everybody else." Andrew tried to walk like Peter, to dress like him, and to have the same "aura."

We all tend to follow the patterns of others. The Corinthians did too. But they shifted their focus away from Christ and onto individual leaders. Rather than emulating the Christlike qualities of these leaders, they let their allegiances lead to various divisions and contentions in the church (1 Corinthians 1:10–13). The apostle Paul recognized their error, so he sent Timothy to remind them of his teachings and the importance of walking in obedience to the Lord (4:16–17).

We are to imitate Christ (1 Peter 1:15–16). It can also be helpful to have mentors who imitate Him. Those who walk in step with Christ provide a model for us to emulate. But our ultimate example is Jesus himself. —ANNE CETAS

Imitate those who imitate Christ.

GRACE, MERCY, AND PEACE

READ: 2 Timothy 1:1–10

*Praise the LORD, my soul; all my inmost being, praise his
holy name. . . . who redeems your life from the pit and
crowns you with love and compassion.* PSALM 103:1, 4

THE WORDS *GRACE* AND *peace* are found in all of Paul's greetings
in his New Testament letters to the churches. And in his letters to
Timothy and Titus, he also includes *mercy*: "Grace, mercy, and
peace from God the Father and Christ Jesus our Lord" (2 Timothy
1:2). Let's examine each of these words.

Grace is what our holy God gives that we, as sinful people, don't
deserve. In Acts 17:25, we learn that "he himself gives everyone life
and breath and everything else." His gifts include our very next
breath. Even in our darkest hour, strength is given by God so that
we can endure.

Mercy is what God withholds that we do deserve. In Lamentations 3:22, we read, "Because of the LORD's great love we are not
consumed." Even when we're wayward, God gives time and help
for us to turn back to Him.

Peace is what God brings to His people. Jesus said: "Peace I
leave with you; my peace I give you. I do not give to you as the
world gives" (John 14:27). Even in the worst of times, we have inner
tranquility because our God is in control.

We can be encouraged that throughout our lives the Lord will
give us the grace, mercy, and peace we need to live for Him.

—ALBERT LEE

---

*God's grace is immeasurable, His mercy
inexhaustible, His peace inexpressible.*

GETTING BEYOND OURSELVES

READ: 2 Corinthians 3:7–18

*And we all, who with unveiled faces contemplate the
Lord's glory, are being transformed into his image
with ever-increasing glory, which comes from the
Lord, who is the Spirit.* 2 CORINTHIANS 3:18

I HAVE ONE OF those friends who seems to be better than I am at just about everything. He is smarter; he thinks more deeply; and he knows where to find better books to read. He is even a better golfer. Spending time with him challenges me to become a better, more thoughtful person. His standard of excellence spurs me on to greater things.

That highlights a spiritual principle: It's crucial for us to spend time in God's Word so we can connect with the person of Christ. Reading about the impact of Jesus's unconditional love for us compels me to love without demand. His mercy and His free distribution of grace to the most undeserving make me ashamed of my tendency to withhold forgiveness and seek revenge.

I find myself becoming a more thankful person when I realize that, despite my shameful fallenness, the Lord has clothed me in the beauty of His perfect righteousness. His amazing ways and unsurpassed wisdom motivate and transform me. It's hard to be content with my life as it is when in His presence I am drawn to become more like Him.

The apostle Paul calls us to the joy of beholding Christ. As we do so, we are "being transformed into his image with ever-increasing glory" (2 Corinthians 3:18).　　　　　—JOE STOWELL

Stay close to God and you will never be the same.

LONGING FOR RESCUE

READ: Matthew 1:18–25

"She will give birth to a son, and you are to give him the name Jesus, because he will save his people from their sins." MATTHEW 1:21

THE MOVIE *Man of Steel*, released in 2013, is a fresh imagining of the Superman story. Filled with breathtaking special effects and nonstop action, it drew crowds to movie theaters around the world. Some said that the film's appeal was rooted in its amazing technology. Others pointed to the enduring appeal of the "Superman mythology."

Amy Adams, the actress who plays Lois Lane in the movie, has a different view of Superman's appeal. She says it is about a basic human longing: "Who doesn't want to believe that there's one person who could come and save us from ourselves?"

That's a great question. And the answer is that someone has *already* come to save us from ourselves, and that someone is Jesus. Several announcements were made regarding the birth of Jesus. One of them was from the angel Gabriel to Joseph: "[Mary] will give birth to a son, and you are to give him the name Jesus, because he will save his people from their sins" (Matthew 1:21).

Jesus came—He did so to save us from our sin and from ourselves. His name means "the Lord saves"—and our salvation was His mission. The longing for rescue that fills the human heart ultimately is met by Jesus. —BILL CROWDER

Jesus's name and mission are the same—He came to save us.

WHO'S WATCHING YOU

READ: Psalm 34:15–22

*The eyes of the LORD are on the righteous, and his
ears are attentive to their cry.* PSALM 34:15

NO MATTER WHERE YOU go in the city of Rio de Janeiro, you can
see Jesus. Standing high above this Brazilian city and anchored to
a 2,310-foot-high mountain called Corcovado is a 100-foot-tall
sculpture called *Cristo Redentor* (Christ the Redeemer). With arms
spread wide, this massive figure is visible day and night from almost
anywhere in the sprawling city.

As comforting as this iconic concrete and soapstone sculpture
may be to all who can look up and see it, there is much greater
comfort from this reality: The real Jesus sees us. In Psalm 34, David
explained it like this: "The eyes of the LORD are on the righteous,
and his ears are attentive to their cry" (v. 15). He noted that when
the righteous call out for His help, "The LORD hears them; he
delivers them from all their troubles. The LORD is close to the brokenhearted and saves those who are crushed in spirit" (vv. 17–18).

Just who are the righteous? Those of us who place our trust in
Jesus Christ, who himself is our righteousness (1 Corinthians 1:30).
Our God oversees our lives, and He hears the cries of those who
trust Him. He is near to help in our greatest times of need.

Jesus has His eyes on you.   —DAVE BRANON

The Lord never lets us out of His sight.

NOT IN VAIN

READ: 1 Corinthians 15:50–58

Therefore, my dear brothers and sisters, stand firm. Let nothing move you. Always give yourselves fully to the work of the Lord, because you know that your labor in the Lord is not in vain. 1 CORINTHIANS 15:58

A FINANCIAL ADVISOR I know describes the reality of investing money by saying, "Hope for the best and be prepared for the worst." With almost every decision we make in life, there is uncertainty about the outcome. Yet there is one course we can follow where no matter what happens: we know that in the end it will not be a wasted effort.

The apostle Paul spent a year with the followers of Jesus in Corinth, a city known for its moral corruption. After he left, he urged them in a follow-up letter not to be discouraged or feel that their witness for Christ was of no value. He assured them that a day is coming when the Lord will return and even death will be swallowed up in victory (1 Corinthians 15:52–55).

Remaining true to Jesus may be difficult, discouraging, and even dangerous, but it is never pointless or wasted. As we walk with the Lord and witness to His presence and power, our lives are not in vain! We can be sure of that. —DAVID MCCASLAND

Our life and witness for Jesus Christ are not in vain.

THROUGH THE VALLEY

READ: Psalm 23

Even though I walk through the darkest valley,
I will fear no evil, for you are with me; your rod
and your staff, they comfort me. PSALM 23:4

HAE WOO (NOT HER real name) was imprisoned in a North Korean labor camp for crossing the border into China. The days and nights were torture, she said, with brutal guards, backbreaking work, and little sleep on an ice-cold floor with rats and lice. But God helped her daily, including showing her which prisoners to befriend and share her faith with.

After she was released from the camp and living in South Korea, Woo reflected on her time of imprisonment, saying that Psalm 23 summed up her experience. Although she'd been trapped in a dark valley, Jesus was her Shepherd who gave her peace: "Even though it felt as if I was literally in a valley full of the shadow of death, I wasn't afraid of anything. God comforted me every day." She experienced God's goodness and love as He reassured her that she was His beloved daughter. "I was in a terrible place, but I knew . . . I would experience God's goodness and love." And she knew she'd stay in the Lord's presence forever.

We can find encouragement in Woo's story. Despite her dire circumstances, she felt God's love and leading; and He sustained her and took away her fear. If we follow Jesus, He will lead us gently through our times of trouble. We need not fear, for "[we] will dwell in the house of the LORD forever" (23:6).

—AMY BOUCHER PYE

The darkest valley is made bearable
by the One who is the Light.

LEARNING FROM LEANDRA

READ: John 15:1–8

"I am the vine; you are the branches. If you remain in me and I in you, you will bear much fruit; apart from me you can do nothing." JOHN 15:5

THREE-YEAR-OLD LEANDRA HAD BRIGHT brown eyes and a very good mind. One day I was babysitting her, and she was watching her brother Max play games on my computer. Suddenly she announced that she was going to get a snack. "I do it myself!" she said emphatically.

"I'll help you," I said, and began to follow her. She repeated firmly, "I do it myself!" I watched her walk down the stairs. She turned, saw me, and said, "You stay upstairs, Grandpa. Keep an eye on Max." I tried not to laugh. At the bottom of the stairs she turned back, put one hand on her hip, and said, "I mean it, Grandpa!" I backed out of sight and roared with laughter. Later I checked on her. She had opened the refrigerator, found some packaged pudding, and gotten "her" spoon, but she needed me to open the container for her.

I thought later that there's a lot of that spirit of independence in me. I too want to "do it myself" when it comes to growing and serving as a believer in Jesus Christ. Yet I need to realize that even though I may think I don't need His help, I really do. Without it, I am unable to produce the kind of spiritual fruit Jesus talked about in John 15.

We must remember the words of our Lord, who said, "Apart from me you can do nothing" (John 15:5).   —DAVID EGNER

———

You can depend on the Lord. Can the Lord depend on you?

JESUS'S VERY OWN PEACE

READ: Matthew 16:21–23

"Peace I leave with you; my peace I give you. I do not give to you as the world gives. Do not let your hearts be troubled and do not be afraid." JOHN 14:27

ON THE EVE OF the execution of Christian martyr Nicholas Ridley (1500–1555), his brother offered to stay with him in prison to be of comfort. Ridley declined, saying that he planned to sleep as soundly as usual. Because he knew the peace of Jesus, he could rest in his Lord.

The next morning, Ridley told a fellow Christian who was also being executed, "Be of good heart, brother, for God will either assuage the fury of the flame, or else strengthen us to abide it." Then they knelt and prayed by the stake and, after a brief conversation, were burned to death for their faith.

Jesus had given Nicholas Ridley His peace (John 14:27). But what kind of peace did Jesus have? In Matthew 16:21–23, we see His peace in His determination to go to Jerusalem even though He knew He would suffer and die (see Luke 9:51). Peter rebuked Him, but Jesus trusted His Father and went to the cross. His purpose for living was to die.

Amy Carmichael said, "The peace of Jesus stood every sort of test, every strain, and it never broke. It is this, His very own peace, which He says 'I give.'"

No matter how big or small our trials may be, we can trust Jesus to give us His very own peace in the midst of them.

—ANNE CETAS

When Jesus rules the heart, peace reigns.

WE ALL NEED JESUS

READ: Luke 18:18–27

As for you, you were dead in your transgressions and sins. EPHESIANS 2:1

A CHRISTIAN COUPLE TOLD their sons to be kind to the boys next door but not to become close companions with them. They explained that these boys could get them in trouble because of their dirty talk, their fighting, and their disrespectful attitude.

When the father of those boys learned this, he was angry. "You think your kids are too good for mine," he said one day to the other father. "No," the believer quietly replied. "My kids have so many bad traits that they need all the encouragement they can get in the right direction. In fact, we too are sinners who need forgiveness. That's why we believe in Jesus Christ. We're not better than you or your boys."

Even the best among us, young or old, think and act in sinful ways. We need the forgiveness that comes through faith in Jesus Christ, and we need Him to help us live a life that pleases God.

The rich young ruler in Luke 18 was outwardly religious and morally upright. But Jesus showed him his basic inner selfishness (vv. 22–23). He too needed forgiveness. He too needed a new birth and the gift of the Holy Spirit.

Let's not deceive ourselves. No matter how bad or how good we may be, we all need Jesus.   —HERB VANDER LUGT

No one is good enough to save himself; no one is so bad that God cannot save him.

THE UNFAILING SPRING

READ: John 4:7–14

*On the last and greatest day of the festival, Jesus
stood and said in a loud voice, "Let anyone who is
thirsty come to me and drink."* JOHN 7:37

JOSEPH CAMPBELL, A WELL-KNOWN authority on mythology, said that his friends were living "wasteland lives." He said they were "just baffled; they're wandering in the wasteland without any sense of where the water is—the Source that makes everything green."

That could also be said—and with deepest sorrow—about countless people today. They try one thing after another to quench the thirst of their souls. Many people even resort to an empty spirituality, which Campbell did so much to popularize. But as the prophet Jeremiah said, they've made for themselves "broken cisterns that cannot hold water" (Jeremiah 2:13).

Whatever Campbell himself may have believed, "the Source that makes everything green" is Jesus Christ, our blessed Savior. He is the One who gives "living water," which becomes "a spring of water welling up to eternal life" (John 4:10, 14).

If you have responded to the gospel and personally received Jesus Christ as your Savior from sin, you have "rivers of living water" in your soul (John 7:37–38). Now you can pray for the "baffled" people around you and offer the "living water" to those who are thirsty and wandering in a parched, Christless wasteland.

—VERNON GROUNDS

*Only Jesus, the Living Water,
can satisfy our thirst for God.*

I EXPECT JESUS

READ: Acts 27:9–15

*So keep up your courage, men, for I have faith in God
that it will happen just as he told me.* ACTS 27:25

A SUNDAY SCHOOL TEACHER gave every boy in his class a New
Testament and encouraged each of them to write his own name
inside the front cover.

Several weeks later, after repeatedly inviting the boys to receive
Christ as their Savior, he asked those who had done so to write these
words under his name: "I accept Jesus." One boy scribbled instead,
"I expect Jesus." When the teacher talked to him, he realized that
the boy knew what he had written after all. He had not only trusted
the Lord for salvation but expected Him to be with him at all times
and to do all He had promised.

That boy's statement presents a simple yet profound commentary on the true meaning of faith.

In Acts 27, we see the apostle Paul's expectant faith. He was a
prisoner being transported by ship to Rome when a violent storm
arose and threatened to destroy the vessel. During the night, an
angel of the Lord told Paul they would all survive (vv. 23–24). He
knew the word of the Lord could be trusted. In the midst of the
storm, he said, "I have faith in God that it will happen just as he
told me" (v. 25). And so it was.

It should be no surprise to us when God keeps His word. It's to
be expected!   —RICHARD DEHAAN

———

Attempt great things for God; expect great things from God.

IN THE DRIVER'S SEAT

Read: Matthew 5:13–16

*"In the same way, let your light shine before others,
that they may see your good deeds and glorify
your Father in heaven."* Matthew 5:16

I love the story of the stressed-out woman who was tailgating a man as they drove on a busy boulevard. When he slowed to a stop at a yellow light, the woman hit the horn, cussing and screaming in frustration and gesturing angrily. As she was still in mid-rant, she heard a tap on her window and looked up into the face of a police officer, who ordered her to exit the car with her hands up. He took her to the police station and placed her in a holding cell.

An hour later, the officer returned and said, "I'm sorry, Ma'am. This has been a big mistake. When I pulled up behind you, I noticed your 'What Would Jesus Do?' license plate holder and your 'Follow Me to Sunday School' bumper sticker. When I saw how you were acting, I assumed the car was stolen!"

Satan doesn't care so much if you're a Christian as long as you don't act like one. If he can get you to live by his signals, he can damage and disarm you every time and dishonor the name of Christ in the process.

Instead, Jesus calls believers to be "salt" and to "Let your light shine before others, that they may see your good deeds and glorify your Father in heaven" (Matthew 5:16).

With Jesus in the driver's seat of our lives, we can show off the love and glory of God.   —Joe Stowell

Don't let Satan manage the details of your life.

ORDINARY DAYS

READ: Luke 2:8–20

An angel of the Lord appeared to them, and the glory of the Lord shone around them, and they were terrified. LUKE 2:9

WRITER ANITA BRECHBILL OBSERVED in *God's Revivalist* magazine that "Most often the Word of the Lord comes to a soul in the ordinary duties of life." She cites the examples of Zacharias performing his duties as a priest and the shepherds watching their flocks. They were at work as usual with no idea that they were about to receive a message from God.

Luke describes the ordinary days when these men received their message from God: "Once when Zechariah's division was on duty and he was serving as priest before God, . . . an angel of the Lord appeared to him" (1:8, 11). Meanwhile, the shepherds were "living out in the fields nearby, keeping watch over their flock at night. An angel of the Lord appeared to them, and the glory of the Lord shone around them" (2:8–9).

In *My Utmost for His Highest*, Oswald Chambers said, "Jesus rarely comes where we expect Him; He appears where we least expect Him, and always in the most illogical situations. The only way a worker can keep true to God is by being ready for the Lord's surprise visits."

On this ordinary day, the Lord may have a word of encouragement, guidance, or instruction for us if we're listening and ready to obey. —DAVID MCCASLAND

God speaks to those who are quiet before Him.

MORE THAN LOAVES

READ: John 6:25–36

Jesus answered, "Very truly I tell you, you are looking for me, not because you saw the signs I performed but because you ate the loaves and had your fill." JOHN 6:26

SEVENTEENTH-CENTURY QUAKER LEADER ISAAC Pennington said, "The Lord has been teaching me to live upon Himself—not from anything received from Him, but upon the life itself." The people in John 6 wanted to live off Jesus, but not for the same reason. It was not because their hearts were loyal to Him, but because their hearts were loyal to what they thought He could provide for them—namely, food and deliverance from Roman oppression.

Jesus's provision of the loaves and fish was a confirmation in their minds of what He could do for them. Jesus knew that behind their interest in Him was their hope that He would become a different kind of king, so He withdrew from them (John 6:14–15). The next day they looked for Him and found Him, making their quest successful (vv. 22, 25–26). So they continued to follow Him because of what they thought He could provide. But Jesus turned the tables and identified himself as the Bread of Life (vv. 32–33). They wanted a better life from Him, but He told them He came to offer them eternal life (v. 40). Only those who believe in Jesus can find true fulfillment—now and forever.

Follow Jesus, not just because He can provide "the loaves," but because He can satisfy your deepest hunger—the quest for eternal fellowship with Him. —MARVIN WILLIAMS

You can experience complete fulfillment if your life is filled with Christ.

BEAUTIFUL

READ: Luke 7:36–50

"Leave her alone," said Jesus. "Why are you bothering her? She has done a beautiful thing to me." MARK 14:6

PICTURE TWO TEENAGE GIRLS. The first girl is strong and healthy. The other girl has never known the freedom of getting around on her own. From her wheelchair she faces not only the emotional challenges common to life but also a stream of physical pains and struggles.

But both girls are smiling cheerfully as they enjoy each other's company. Two beautiful teenagers—each seeing in the other the treasure of friendship.

Jesus devoted much of His time and attention to people like the girl in the wheelchair. People with lifelong disabilities or physical deformities as well as those who were looked down on by others for various reasons. In fact, Jesus let one of "those people" anoint Him with oil, to the disdain of the religious leaders (Luke 7:39). On another occasion, when a woman demonstrated her love with a similar act, Jesus told her critics, "Leave her alone . . . . She has done a beautiful thing to me" (Mark 14:6).

God values everyone equally; there are no distinctions in His eyes. In reality, we are all in desperate need of Christ's love and forgiveness. His love compelled Him to die on the cross for us.

May we see each person as Jesus did: made in God's image and worthy of His love. Let's treat everyone we meet with Christlike equality and learn to see beauty as He does.   —DAVE BRANON

Everyone we meet bears the image of God.

COPY THE PATTERN

READ: 1 John 2:1–6

*Whoever claims to live in him must
live as Jesus did.* 1 JOHN 2:6

IF WE WANT THE Lord Jesus to be glorified through the way we live, we must pattern ourselves after His life. The Bible says that He "went around doing good" (Acts 10:38), and that He remained "pure" even though He associated with sinners (Hebrews 7:26). We are to imitate Him in His holiness of life, His obedience to His Father's will, His self-denial, and His compassionate response to people. In word and action He humbly delighted to fulfill the purpose for which He was sent into the world.

Early twentieth-century writer Mitchell Bronk said that when he was a schoolboy he practiced penmanship in copybooks. He described the process like this: "A beautifully engraved pattern of the letters at the top of every page guided us, but each succeeding line we wrote became progressively less attractive. Then the school board purchased new books, designed so that the pattern line at the top could be pushed down the page. Because it was always directly before the pupil and covered what he had just written, the improvement in our penmanship was amazing."

Similarly, if we copy our perfect Pattern, the Lord Jesus Christ, we will increasingly walk "even as He walked" (1 John 2:6 NKJV). Let's imitate Christ. He is our perfect example. —HENRY BOSCH

Some of the most likable people are the most like Christ.

WHERE THE GOOD WAY IS

READ: Jeremiah 6:10–16

This is what the LORD says: . . . "Ask for the ancient paths, ask where the good way is, and walk in it, and you will find rest for your souls." JEREMIAH 6:16

WE WHO BELIEVE THAT God has absolute moral standards are viewed by some segments of society as intolerant simpletons. We are cautioned not to express our disapproval over certain immoral behavior.

Television commentator Andy Rooney once announced his revulsion at the perverse sexual conduct increasingly evident in our culture. But pressure from special interest groups that promote immoral lifestyles coerced him to apologize.

Our circumstances are amazingly similar to those Jeremiah confronted 2,600 years ago. The people had no shame. No perversion made them blush. Even the religious leaders were part of this deplorable situation!

Jeremiah, however, proclaimed God's anger and warned of imminent divine judgment. The prophet pleaded for a return to the "ancient paths, . . . where the good way is" (v. 16), the paths of renunciation of sin and obedience to God.

Jesus showed us the good way when He invited all who are "weary and burdened" to come to Him (Matthew 11:28). And He gave us the assurance that His "yoke is easy" and His "burden is light" (v. 30).

Lord, thank you for showing us the way that brings real happiness. Help us to walk in the good way. —HERB VANDER LUGT

You can't go crooked as long as you stay on the straight and narrow way.

LOOKING AHEAD

READ: Psalm 125

As the mountains surround Jerusalem, so the LORD surrounds his people both now and forevermore. PSALM 125:2

THE OTHER DAY I talked with a man who expressed his apprehension about the future. He is certain the stock market will crash. He thinks our country will be taken over by evil forces, and he fears that the church will be overrun with worldliness. And even though he professes faith in Jesus Christ, he is afraid that by some quirk or oversight he will end up in hell.

Psalm 125 reminds us that we do not need to fear the future. The psalmist praises God because He has promised to protect and preserve His people. As the mountains around Jerusalem will not be moved, the psalmist sang, so the Lord surrounds His people forever (vv. 1–2).

God promises to provide us with His grace. We are safe for all eternity because He said so. Jesus said that not one of His own will be snatched from His Father's hand (John 10:28). And Paul wrote that nothing can separate us from the love of God (Romans 8:38–39).

This does not mean we are free to go out and sin. Paul wrote emphatically about the inconsistency of practicing a sinful lifestyle when we have "died to sin" (Romans 6:1–4).

We who know the Lord and walk in His ways have every assurance that our future is as secure as the unchanging character of God.　　　　　　　　　　　　　　　　　　　—DAVID EGNER

You need not fear where you're going when you know God is going with you.

JOY LIST

READ: John 15:9–17

"I have told you this so that my joy may be in you and that your joy may be complete." JOHN 15:11

WRITER C. W. METCALF was working as a hospice volunteer when he met thirteen-year-old Chuck, who was terminally ill. One day Chuck gave Metcalf half a dozen sheets of paper with writing on both sides and said, "I want you to give this to my mom and dad after I die. It's a list of all the fun we had, all the times we laughed." Metcalf was amazed that this young boy on the verge of death was thinking about the well-being of others.

Metcalf delivered the list. Years later he decided to make a list of his own. Surprisingly, he found it difficult at first to compile his "joy list." But as he began looking each day for the moments of laughter, satisfaction, and joy, his list began to grow.

Any joy list that we compile will no doubt include many references to the presence and power of Jesus Christ. No matter what our circumstances, joy is His gracious gift to all who trust Him. Even as Jesus faced the cross, He looked beyond its agony to the glad result of His sacrifice. He told His disciples, "I have told you this so that my joy may be in you and that your joy may be complete" (John 15:11).

Why not begin your own joy list today. It can be a good reminder of the Lord's faithful love and the gladness of heart He brings.

—DAVID McCASLAND

To multiply your joy, count your blessings.

THROUGH THE EYES OF JESUS

READ: Matthew 9:35–38

*As he approached Jerusalem and saw the
city, he wept over it.* LUKE 19:41

ACTOR BRUCE MARCHIANO WANTED to see the world through the eyes of the character he was playing. So as he prepared for the role of Jesus in a presentation of Matthew's gospel, he prayed, "Lord, show me what it all looks like through your eyes."

That prayer was answered one day while Marchiano was filming the Lord's heartbroken denunciation of the unrepentant cities of Chorazin and Bethsaida (Matthew 11:20–22). The actor began to weep uncontrollably as he looked at the people around him. He said that he "saw people living their lives in ways that God didn't plan." He likened his reaction to what parents might feel if they saw their toddler walking into the street as a truck was coming. Marchiano realized that compassion is not just feeling sorry for people; it's a heartache so intense that it moves us to action.

As Jesus walked among people, He saw them as shepherdless sheep—spiritually ignorant, without hope, eternally lost. Moved with compassion, He taught them and used His supernatural power to meet their needs (Matthew 9:35).

Do we see people through the eyes of Jesus? Are we moved with compassion, not with just a passing twinge of pity but a profound reaction that motivates action?   —VERNON GROUNDS

Compassion is love in action.

THE ROCKS OF UNBELIEF

READ: Matthew 11:20–34

*The law of the LORD is perfect, refreshing the
soul. The statutes of the LORD are trustworthy,
making wise the simple.* PSALM 19:7

ROCKS. THAT'S ALL THAT'S left of the city of Chorazin. Just the rubble of a few buildings made of volcanic rock—yet this was once a thriving city on the Sea of Galilee.

Not far from Chorazin is another pile of rocks—the former city of Capernaum.

Same with Bethsaida. Once a bustling city where children played, men did business, and mothers ran households. Rocks. Nothing but rocks.

When Jesus walked the streets of those cities, He knew this would happen. In Matthew 11:21–23, He said, "Woe to you, Chorazin! Woe to you, Bethsaida! . . . And you, Capernaum, will you be lifted up to the heavens? No, you will go down to Hades."

In those cities, Jesus clearly showed himself to be the Son of God—the One who had almighty power and could perform miracles. But the people refused to listen to His message. As a result, Chorazin, Capernaum, and Bethsaida were cursed by God and reduced to heaps of rocks—monuments to unbelief.

The lesson for us today is clear. When Jesus speaks, we must take His words to heart. In fact, all of Scripture needs to be taken seriously. To disregard God's Word shows a heart of unbelief and will leave our lives in ruins. But to heed its life-giving instruction brings reward and blessing.   —DAVE BRANON

To ignore the Bible is to invite disaster.

DO UNTO OTHERS

READ: Matthew 7:7–12

*"So in everything, do to others what you would
have them do to you, for this sums up the Law
and the Prophets."* MATTHEW 7:12

IN MAY 2006, DAVID Sharp set off from base camp to make his
third attempt on Mount Everest. He actually reached the summit,
but on his way down he ran out of oxygen. As he lay on the side of
the mountain dying, forty climbers passed him by.

Some say that at such oxygen-deprived altitudes, rescues are too
perilous. But others say that climbers are too eager to reach the top
and too selfish to help those in trouble.

I wonder what would have happened if someone who passed
that stricken climber had said, "I will treat him the way I want
to be treated." In Matthew 7:12, the golden rule, Jesus gave His
disciples the secret to fulfilling the entire Old Testament relational
regulations—love others and live for their benefit. He said this in
the larger context of all the radical principles that He had taught
up to this point in His sermon (5:17–7:11).

As difficult as it is to live for the benefit of others, Jesus knew
His followers could consistently live out this ethic as they drew
strength from a righteousness that went beyond duty and outward
conformity to rules (5:20). It is a righteousness that can come only
from God himself.

If we are Jesus-followers, let's walk in His steps—loving others
and living for their benefit.   —MARVIN WILLIAMS

Love is the debt we owe one another.

IF YOU ARE WILLING

READ: Matthew 8:1–4

A man with leprosy came and knelt before him and said, "Lord, if you are willing, you can make me clean." MATTHEW 8:2

MOLLY WANTED HER DAD's help, but she was afraid to ask. She knew that when he was working on his computer, he didn't want to be interrupted. *He might get upset at me*, she thought, so she didn't ask him.

We need not have such fears when we come to Jesus. In Matthew 8:1–4, we read about a leper who didn't hesitate to interrupt Jesus with his needs. His disease made him desperate—he had been ostracized from society and was in emotional distress. Jesus was busy with "great multitudes," but the leper made his way through the crowd to talk with Jesus.

Matthew's gospel says that the leper came and "worshiped Him" (v. 2 NKJV). He approached Jesus in worship, with trust in His power, and with humility, acknowledging that the choice to help belonged to Jesus. He said, "Lord, if you are willing, you can make me clean" (v. 2). In compassion, Jesus touched him (leprosy had made him "untouchable" by the standards of Jewish law), and he was cleansed immediately.

Like the leper, we don't need to hesitate to approach Jesus with our desire for His help. As we go to Him in humility and worship, we can trust that He will make the best choices for us.

—ANNE CETAS

Let us come boldly to the throne of grace, that we may obtain mercy. —Hebrews 4:16 NKJV

FOUNDATION FOR LIFE

Read: Matthew 7:21–27

*"Therefore everyone who hears these words of mine
and puts them into practice is like a wise man who
built his house on the rock."* Matthew 7:24

Earthquakes are prevalent in the Pacific Rim region known as the "Ring of Fire." Ninety percent of the world's earthquakes and eighty-one percent of the world's largest earthquakes occur there. I learned that many buildings in the city of Hong Kong have been built on granite, which could help minimize damage in the event of an earthquake. The foundation of a building is especially important in earthquake-prone regions of the world.

Jesus Christ told His followers that a stable foundation is critical in building lives. He said, "Therefore everyone who hears these words of mine and puts them into practice is like a wise man who built his house on the rock. The rain came down, the streams rose, and the winds blew and beat against that house; yet it did not fall, because it had its foundation on the rock" (Matthew 7:24–25). The foundation of Jesus Christ is what will give us the stability our hearts and lives need now and into the future.

By allowing the Lord's wisdom to guide us in our relationships, decisions, and priorities, we find that He provides the most trustworthy foundation any life could be built upon.

—Bill Crowder

*Jesus is the best foundation upon
which to build a solid life.*

THE POWER OF EMPATHY

READ: Hebrews 2:14–18; 13:1–3

Continue to remember those in prison as if you were together with them in prison, and those who are mistreated as if you yourselves were suffering. HEBREWS 13:3

PUT ON THE R701 Age Suit and you immediately feel forty years older as you experience impaired vision, hearing loss, and reduced mobility. The Age Suit was designed to help caregivers better understand their patients. *Wall Street Journal* correspondent Geoffrey Fowler wore one and wrote, "The unforgettable, and at times distressing, experience shed light not just on aging, but also how virtual reality equipment can teach empathy and shape our perceptions of the world around us."

Empathy is the power to understand and share the feelings of another. During a time of severe persecution against the followers of Jesus, the writer of Hebrews urged fellow believers to "continue to remember those in prison as if you were together with them in prison, and those who are mistreated as if you yourselves were suffering" (13:3).

This is exactly what our Savior has done for us. Jesus was made like us, "fully human in every way . . . that he might make atonement for the sins of the people. Because he himself suffered when he was tempted, he is able to help those who are being tempted" (2:17–18).

Christ the Lord, who became like us, calls us to stand with others "as if [we] were together with them" (Hebrews 13:3) during their time of need.   —DAVID McCASLAND

Jesus calls us to stand with others as if we were in their place.

KEEP THE ROMANCE

READ: Jude 17–23

Keep yourselves in God's love as you wait for the mercy of our Lord Jesus Christ to bring you to eternal life. JUDE 21

THE GREAT AMERICAN STATESMAN and lawyer William Jennings Bryan (1860–1925) was having his portrait painted. The artist asked, "Why do you wear your hair over your ears?"

Bryan responded, "There is a romance connected with that. When I began courting Mrs. Bryan, she objected to the way my ears stood out. So, to please her, I let my hair grow to cover them."

"That was many years ago," the artist said. "Why don't you have your hair cut now?"

"Because," Bryan winked, "the romance is still going on."

Is the romance still going on in our relationship with Jesus? When we first came in faith to Christ, we experienced the joy of knowing our sins were forgiven and we were adopted into His family. Our hearts were full and overflowing with love for the Lord. We longed to please Him.

As time passed, however, the zeal of our first love may have begun to cool. That's why we need to take to heart the words of Jude in his brief letter. He wrote, "Keep yourselves in God's love" (v. 21). Jesus used similar terms when He said, "Remain in my love" (John 15:9). We nurture that love when we focus on pleasing Him instead of ourselves.

Keep the romance going. —DAVID EGNER

*To renew your love for Christ,
review His love for you.*

LIKE JESUS

READ: 1 John 2:5–11

*Whoever claims to live in him must
live as Jesus did.* 1 JOHN 2:6

DURING A CHILDREN'S CHURCH service, the teacher talked about the first of the Ten Commandments: "You shall have no other gods before me" (Exodus 20:3). She suggested some ways for the kids to keep this command. She said, "Nothing should come before God—not candy, not schoolwork, not video games." She told them that putting God first meant that time with Him reading the Bible and praying should come before anything else.

An older child in the group responded with a thought-provoking question. She asked if being a Christian was about keeping rules or if instead God wanted to be involved in all areas of our life.

Sometimes we make the mistake of viewing the Bible as a list of rules. Certainly obeying God (John 14:21) and spending time with Him is important, but not because we need to be rule-keepers. Jesus and the Father had a loving relationship. When we have a relationship with God, we desire to spend time with Him and obey Him so we can become more like Jesus. John said, "Whoever claims to live in him must live as Jesus did" (1 John 2:6). He's the example we can follow.

When we want to understand how to love or how to be humble or how to have faith or even how to set our priorities, we can look at Jesus and follow His heart. —ANNE CETAS

Jesus calls us to follow Him.

BRILLIANT THOUGHTS

READ: Luke 10:38–42

*"Take my yoke upon you and learn from me, for
I am gentle and humble in heart, and you will
find rest for your souls."* MATTHEW 11:29

A KIND FRIEND WHO knows my tastes and reading interests gave
me a fascinating book for my birthday. It's called *The Most Brilliant
Thoughts of All Time.* There's no question about the wit and wisdom
of the short sayings it contains. But are they the most brilliant
thoughts of all time?

The book doesn't contain a single quote from the Lord Jesus.
Yet when He lived on earth, even His critics were amazed at His
wisdom. They asked in dumbfounded wonder how He knew so
much (John 7:15).

As far as we know, Jesus did not have any formal education. He
wasn't the student of a prominent rabbi, like many of the teachers of
His day. Yet even the soldiers who were sent to arrest Him reported,
"No man ever spoke the way this man does!" (v. 46).

So if we are in search of brilliant thoughts, there are none better
than the words of Jesus Christ. Like Mary the sister of Lazarus,
we ought to sit at the feet of our Lord and learn from Him (Luke
10:39). Jesus said that choosing to hear His words is "what is better,
and it will not be taken away from her" (v. 42).

Let's respond to our Savior's invitation: "Take my yoke upon
you and learn from me" (Matthew 11:29). His words are the most
brilliant of all time.   —VERNON GROUNDS

*In the light of Christ's brilliance, the
world's wisdom is but a shadow.*

THE OLIVE PRESS

READ: Mark 14:32–39

*They went to a place called Gethsemane, and Jesus said
to his disciples, "Sit here while I pray."* MARK 14:32

IF YOU VISIT THE village of Capernaum beside the Sea of Galilee,
you will find an exhibit of ancient olive presses. Formed from basalt
rock, the olive press consists of two parts: a base and a grinding
wheel. The base is large, round, and has a trough carved out of
it. The olives were placed in this trough, and then the wheel, also
made from heavy stone, was rolled over the olives to extract the oil.

On the night before His death, Jesus went to the Mount of
Olives overlooking the city of Jerusalem. There, in the garden called
Gethsemane, He prayed to the Father, knowing what lay ahead of
Him.

The word *Gethsemane* means "place of the olive press"—and that
perfectly describes those first crushing hours of Christ's suffering
on our behalf. There, "in anguish, he prayed . . . and his sweat was
like drops of blood falling to the ground" (Luke 22:44).

Jesus the Son suffered and died to take away "the sin of the
world" (John 1:29) and restore our broken relationship with God
the Father. "Surely he took up our pain and bore our suffering
. . . . He was pierced for our transgressions, he was crushed for our
iniquities, the punishment that brought us peace was on him, and
by his wounds we are healed" (Isaiah 53:4–5).

Our hearts cry out in worship and gratitude.

—BILL CROWDER

---

*Gone my transgressions, and now I am free—all
because Jesus was wounded for me. —W. G. Ovens*

JESUS LOVES YOU

READ: 1 Timothy 1:12–15

Here is a trustworthy saying that deserves full acceptance:
Christ Jesus came into the world to save sinners—
of whom I am the worst. 1 TIMOTHY 1:15

A CHRISTIAN PRISON GUARD was assigned to duty on death row. He was so appalled at the crimes the prisoners had committed that at first he felt only contempt for them. It's not difficult to understand why. He told of one convict who joked about the fact that the eight-year-old girl he murdered looked him in the eye just as he was about to choke her and said, "Jesus loves you."

Gradually this Christian guard began to understand the full impact of the words spoken by that young girl. The Lord Jesus, who during His earthly ministry reached out to the most despised people in society, loves even men like that murderer and blasphemer. The guard also began to realize that he could not take credit for being different from these criminals. He saw that given the same circumstances he too could have been a death-row prisoner. His "I'm better than you" attitude evaporated. He still hates what they did, but now he loves them, desires their salvation, and prays for them.

Lord, deliver us from self-righteousness that leads us to despise people. Help us to see ourselves as Paul did: the chief of sinners. Enable us to love even the most unlovely person we know.

—HERB VANDER LUGT

———

The only difference between a sinner and
a saint is the grace of God.

TROUBLED TIMES

READ: John 16:25–33

"I have told you these things, so that in me you may have peace. In this world you will have trouble. But take heart! I have overcome the world." JOHN 16:33

IF YOU'VE NEVER HEARD of Murphy's Law, you've probably experienced it: "If anything can go wrong, it will."

Murphy's maxim reminds me of the principle Jesus shared with His disciples when He told them, "In this world you will have trouble" (John 16:33). In other words, we can count on it—sooner or later we will hit troubled times. It's not the way God originally intended life to be, but when the human race first succumbed to Satan's seduction in the garden, everything on this planet fell into the grip of sin. And the result has been disorder and dysfunction ever since.

The reality of trouble in life is obvious. It's the reality of peace that often eludes us. Interestingly, when Jesus warned His followers about trouble, in the same breath He also promised peace. He even told them to "take heart! I have overcome the world" (v. 33). The word *overcome* indicates a past event that has a continuing effect. Not only did Jesus conquer the fallen world through His death and resurrection but He also continues to provide victory—no matter how much trouble we may face.

So, although we can expect some trouble in this fallen world, the good news is that we can count on Jesus for peace in troubled times.

—JOE STOWELL

In the midst of troubles, peace can be found in Jesus.

THOMAS TIME

READ: John 20:24–28

Thomas said to him, "My Lord and my God!" JOHN 20:28

A YOUNG ADULT WAS struggling with his faith. After growing up in a home where he was loved and nurtured in a godly way, he allowed bad decisions and circumstances to turn him away from the Lord. Although as a child he had claimed to know Jesus, he now struggled with unbelief.

One day while talking to him I said, "I know that you walked with the Lord for a long time, but right now you're not so sure about Jesus and faith. Can I suggest to you that you are in the 'Thomas Time' of your life?"

He knew that Thomas was one of Jesus's twelve apostles and that he had trusted Christ openly for several years. I reminded this young man that after Jesus's death Thomas doubted that He had really risen from the tomb. But after eight days the Lord appeared to Thomas, showed him His scars, and told him to stop doubting and believe. Finally, ready to abandon his doubts, Thomas said, "My Lord and my God!" (John 20:24–28).

I told this young man, "Jesus patiently waited, and Thomas came back. I think you will too. I'm praying that someday you will again say to Jesus, 'My Lord and my God!'"

Could you be in a "Thomas Time"—finding it hard to feel close to Jesus, perhaps even doubting Him? Jesus is waiting for you. Reach out for His nail-scarred hand. —DAVE BRANON

A child of God is always welcomed home.

MARY & GOD

READ: Colossians 3:22–4:6

Whatever you do, work at it with all your heart, as working for the Lord, not for human masters. COLOSSIANS 3:23

HER BRIGHT SMILE AND cheerful voice seemed unusual for someone working at a discount store checkout counter early in the morning. I glanced at her nametag, then looked more closely to make sure I had read it correctly. It said: MARY-N-GOD. So I asked her if she and the Lord were doing this job together. "Oh, yes!" she said, beaming. "He works with me and walks with me and talks with me, and we share the most wonderful life together. I couldn't do it without Him."

Mary was a winsome representative of Christ and a vivid illustration of Colossians 3:23, "Whatever you do, work at it with all your heart, as working for the Lord." Although not in the limelight, Mary, through her attitude and actions, witnessed to hundreds of people every day. Mary's pulpit was a checkout counter, and her smile was the opening sentence in a powerful sermon about the difference Christ makes in a life. If someone asked, she was happy to tell that person more.

When I told my wife about Mary, she said, "I think she's one of those who seem to be last here on earth but will be first when they get to heaven." I had to agree.

You and I can also be effective witnesses if we know, love, and walk with Jesus the way Mary does.   —DAVID MCCASLAND

Often it's the joy behind our words that makes our testimony ring true.

ALWAYS WITH YOU

READ: Matthew 28:16–20

"Teaching them to observe all things that I have commanded you; and lo, I am with you always, even to the end of the age." MATTHEW 28:20 (NKJV)

A YOUNG CHINESE CHRISTIAN named Lo was given a New Testament, and he began to read it. When he discovered Matthew 28:20 and the words, "Lo, I am with you always," he was greatly excited because he took this verse as a personal promise to himself.

Although he misinterpreted the first word of that text for his own name, Lo didn't miss the impact of the verse. In fact, it became all the more real to him.

We who have received Christ as our Savior and are committed to serving Him may read our name into this promise as well. "Braylyn, Kurt, Katie, David, Mia, I am with you always!"

Christ gave the reassuring words of Matthew 28:20 to His disciples because He knew how lonely they would feel when the full burden of the task of spreading the gospel became theirs. He would no longer be present with them physically. They would no longer see His look of encouragement or hear His comforting voice. Knowing the weakness of human nature, He consoled them with the truth that He would still be with them in the person of His Holy Spirit, and He would assist them in preaching, teaching, living, and witnessing.

As you walk the Christian pathway, remember that Jesus is always with you. —HENRY BOSCH

When Christ sends us, He always goes with us.

EYES ONLY FOR HER

READ: Revelation 19:6–10

My dove in the clefts of the rock, in the hiding places on the mountainside, show me your face, let me hear your voice; for your voice is sweet, and your face is lovely. SONG OF SONGS 2:14

I WAS PRIVILEGED TO officiate at Steve's marriage to Karen. God himself had brought this couple together, and it was obvious that they were deeply in love.

When the wedding day finally arrived, all preparations had been made. The bridesmaids' dresses were ready, the flowers were in place, the rehearsal was complete. As the ceremony began, Steve and I walked in first. We stood at the front as the bridesmaids came down the aisle and took their places. The flower girls came next, dropping petals as they walked. They were cute as could be, and all eyes were on them—all except Steve's. Then I heard him sigh. Karen had stepped into his vision. He hadn't been concerned about the bridesmaids, or even the flower girls. He was watching for his bride. He had eyes only for her.

The church is Jesus Christ's fiancée—His betrothed. He loves her with a sacrificial, unending love. He died to redeem her. He is faithful, as the beloved in Song of Solomon was true to his love. And the day is nearing when Christ will return to earth to receive His bride unto himself. The joyous marriage supper of the Lamb will follow (Revelation 19:7–9).

As part of the church, we are the bride of Christ. He loves us. He has eyes for us only. Do we have eyes only for Him?

—DAVID EGNER

God loves every one of us as if there were but one of us to love. —*Augustine*

FRIENDSHIP WITH GOD

Read: John 15:13–15

*"I no longer call you servants, because a servant does
not know his master's business. Instead, I have called
you friends, for everything that I learned from my
Father I have made known to you."* John 15:15

PAGE THROUGH AN OLD-TIME hymnal and notice how often the
songwriters referred to the blessing of God's friendship. Stop and
think about what that really means.

Yes, it's a blessing to have human friends who enrich our lives.
A devoted friend, as Proverbs 17:17 tells us, "loves at all times,"
standing with us steadfastly through life's sunshine and storm.

Indeed, some of us know by our own experience that "there
is a friend who sticks closer than a brother" (Proverbs 18:24). We
identify with David and Jonathan when we read about the bond
between them (1 Samuel 18:1).

Friendship on a human level is wonderful, but what about friendship with God? It's an incredible blessing to have the Creator and
Sustainer of our universe as a friend. Although worshiped by countless heavenly hosts, He takes great joy in His relationship with us.

Are we neglecting the privilege of walking with God, the greatest of all friends? Today, with gratitude and awe, let's spend time
with Him in prayer and in reading His Word.

Remember that Jesus called His followers "friends" (John 15:15).
What an honor that we can enjoy that kind of friendship with our
Savior!   —VERNON GROUNDS

*When you spend time with God,
you invest in a forever friendship.*

BEARING GRAPES

READ: John 15:1–8

"Remain in me, as I also remain in you. No branch can bear fruit by itself; it must remain in the vine. Neither can you bear fruit unless you remain in me." JOHN 15:4

AS I READ a modern paraphrase of John 15:1–8, I began to reconsider my concept of what it means to be a fruitful Christian. Jesus said, "I am the Real Vine and my Father is the Farmer. He cuts off every branch of Me that doesn't bear grapes. And every branch that is grape-bearing He prunes back so it will bear even more" (MSG).

Grapes—they're the result of the life of the vine flowing through the branches. Often I have viewed fruitfulness in the Christian life as activities such as teaching Sunday school or leading a Bible study. These acts of service are good and worthwhile, but Jesus said that being fruitful is allowing His life to flow through me: "No branch can bear fruit by itself; it must remain in the vine. Neither can you bear fruit unless you remain in me" (v. 4). No one can bear "grapes" without being connected to Christ, the Vine. Fruitfulness is not primarily a matter of what I accomplish. It's the result of my being in close fellowship with Him.

Whenever you wonder if you're being a "fruitful" Christian, ask yourself, "Am I like Jesus? Is His life flowing through me in the ordinary activities and relationships of each day? Do the 'grapes' of my life point others to the Vine?"　　—DAVID MCCASLAND

Fruitfulness for Christ depends on fellowship with Christ.

MULTIPLY IT

READ: Revelation 22:1–5

*No longer will there be any curse. The throne of
God and of the Lamb will be in the city, and his
servants will serve him.* REVELATION 22:3

AMY HAD BATTLED CANCER for five years. Then the doctor told her
that the treatments were failing and she had just a few weeks to live.
Wanting some understanding and assurance about eternity, Amy
asked her pastor, "What will heaven be like?"

He asked her what she liked most about her life on earth. She
talked about walks and rainbows and caring friends and the laughter of children. "So, then, are you saying I will have all of that
there?" she asked longingly.

Amy's pastor replied, "I believe that your life there will be far
more beautiful and amazing than anything you ever loved or experienced here. Think about what's best here for you and multiply it
over and over and over. That's what I think heaven will be."

The Bible doesn't describe in detail what life in eternity will be
like, but it does tell us that being with Christ in heaven is "better by
far" than our present circumstance (Philippians 1:23). "No longer
will there be any curse. The throne of God and of the Lamb will
be in the city, and his servants will serve him" (Revelation 22:3).

Best of all, we will see the Lord Jesus face-to-face. Our deepest
yearnings will be fully satisfied in Him.   —ANNE CETAS

To be with Jesus forever is the sum of all happiness.

THE VISITOR

READ: Matthew 25:31–40

"I needed clothes and you clothed me, I was sick and you looked after me, I was in prison and you came to visit me." MATTHEW 25:36

A FRIEND ASKED A newly retired man what he was doing now that he was no longer working full-time. "I describe myself as a visitor," the man replied. "I go see people in our church and community who are in the hospital or care facilities, living alone, or just need someone to talk and pray with them. And I enjoy doing it!" My friend was impressed by this man's clear sense of purpose and his care for others.

A few days before Jesus was crucified, He told His followers a story that emphasized the importance of visiting people in need. "The King will say to those on his right, '. . . I needed clothes and you clothed me; I was sick and you looked after me; I was in prison and you came to visit me'" (Matthew 25:34, 36). When asked, "When did we see you sick or in prison and go to visit you?" The King will reply, "Truly I tell you, whatever you did for one of the least of these brothers and sisters of mine, you did for me" (vv. 39–40).

Our ministry of visiting has two beneficiaries—the person visited and Jesus himself. To go to a person with help and encouragement is direct service to our Lord.

Is there someone who would be encouraged by your visit today?
—DAVID MCCASLAND

*Compassion is understanding the troubles of others,
coupled with an urgent desire to help.*

HE CAME FOR YOU!

READ: Luke 4:14–21

*"The Spirit of the Lord is on me, because he has anointed
me to proclaim good news to the poor. He has sent me to
proclaim freedom for the prisoners and recovery of sight
for the blind, to set the oppressed free."* LUKE 4:18

IN HIS NOVELS *The Trial* and *The Castle*, Franz Kafka (1883–1924)
portrays life as a dehumanizing existence that turns people into
a sea of empty faces without identity or worth. Kafka said, "The
conveyer belt of life carries you on, no one knows where. One is
more of an object, a thing, than a living creature."

Early in His ministry, Jesus went to a synagogue in Nazareth,
stood up in front of the crowd, and read from Isaiah: "The Spirit
of the Lord is on me, because he has anointed me to proclaim good
news to the poor. He has sent me to proclaim freedom for the prisoners and recovery of sight for the blind, to set the oppressed free,
to proclaim the year of the Lord's favor" (Luke 4:18–19).

Then Christ sat down and declared, "Today this scripture is fulfilled in your hearing" (v. 21). Centuries earlier, the prophet Isaiah
had proclaimed these words (Isaiah 61:1–2). Now Jesus announced
that He was the fulfillment of that promise.

Notice who Jesus came to rescue—the poor, brokenhearted,
captive, blind, and oppressed. He came for people dehumanized
by sin and suffering, by brokenness and sorrow. He came for us!

—BILL CROWDER

*No matter how impersonal the world may seem, Jesus
loves each of us as if we were His only child.*

WE JUST HAVE TO TALK

READ: Exodus 33:1–11

The LORD would speak to Moses face to face, as one speaks to a friend. Then Moses would return to the camp, but his young aide Joshua son of Nun did not leave the tent. EXODUS 33:11

LISA AND SHERYL HAVE been friends since grade school. Even though their paths have taken them in different directions since those schoolgirl days in New Jersey, they have maintained their close friendship.

Sheryl is married, settled in the Midwest, and the mother of young children. Lisa is single and involved in mission work, most recently in Russia. "Every now and then we just have to talk," says Sheryl. So they pick up the phone to catch up on what's been happening and to share their hearts.

In Exodus 33:11, we read that "the LORD would speak to Moses . . . as one speaks to a friend." Moses enjoyed something far better than an occasional long-distance talk with the Lord. He had frequent, face-to-face conversations with Him. During those intimate talks, the Lord gave Moses instructions for leading the people of Israel.

Because of what Jesus Christ has done for us, and because the Holy Spirit now lives within all followers of Christ, we too can enjoy a special friendship and closeness with God. He speaks to us through His Word and by His Spirit, and we have the privilege of talking to Him in prayer.

If you are like me, as you go through your day you'll find yourself saying to God, "We just have to talk."   —DAVID EGNER

Prayer is meant to be an intimate conversation with God—our best friend.

THE HEAVEN FILE

READ: 1 Thessalonians 4:13–18

After that, we who are still alive and are left will be caught up together with them in the clouds to meet the Lord in the air. And so we will be with the Lord forever. 1 THESSALONIANS 4:17

MY WIFE LUANN HAS a folder she calls her "heaven file." It contains articles, obituaries, and photos, along with cards from the memorial services of family and friends. She keeps them, not as a sad reminder of people we have loved and lost, but in anticipation of our glad reunion with them in heaven.

Paul wrote of this wonderful expectation to the Christians in Thessalonica, so they would not grieve like people who have no hope. "For the Lord himself will come down from heaven, with a loud command . . . . and the dead in Christ will rise first. After that, we who are still alive and are left will be caught up together with them in the clouds to meet the Lord in the air. And so we will be with the Lord forever. Therefore encourage one another with these words" (1 Thessalonians 4:16–18).

This passage speaks of our future joy together in the presence of Jesus Christ our Savior. For now, we on earth have fellowship with the Lord, and we experience what hymn writer Samuel J. Stone called "mystic sweet communion with those whose rest is won."

Much about the future remains a mystery, but we can confidently look forward to being in the presence of Christ with all the saints who have gone ahead. —DAVID MCCASLAND

God's children never say goodbye for the last time.

NO GREATER LOVE

Read: Mark 12:28–34

*Greater love has no one than this: to lay down
one's life for one's friends.* John 15:13

You can't show a greater love for people than James Harrison demonstrated. And he did it for people he didn't even know.

Harrison, a member of the Ouachita Baptist University choir, was returning home from Europe with his fellow singers. As their plane was landing in Little Rock, Arkansas, it was hit by heavy rains and high winds. The jet skidded off the runway and hit a bank of lights, ripping open the fuselage.

As chaos reigned and flames broke out in the mangled plane, Harrison began to help others. Over and over, he pulled passengers to safety and ran back to the plane for more. On his last trip into the burning wreckage, he was overcome with smoke. He didn't make it out alive.

At his funeral, the choir director quoted John 15:13, "Greater love has no one than this: to lay down one's life for one's friends." Jesus was really speaking of His own death on our behalf, and the choir leader pointed out the value of this ultimate sacrifice.

We may never be called upon to make the kind of sacrifice James made during that horrible tragedy. Yet every day we have opportunities to set aside our comfort to love our neighbors (Mark 12:31). How much love do we show?   —Dave Branon

*In a world that "couldn't care less,"
Christians should care more.*

THUNDERSTORM THOUGHTS

READ: Matthew 8:23–27

Whatever you have learned or received or heard from me, or seen in me—put it into practice. And the God of peace will be with you. PHILIPPIANS 4:9

I LAUGH EVERY TIME I hear the radio commercial that has a woman shouting to her friend in conversation. She's trying to talk above the sounds of the thunderstorm in her own head. Ever since a storm damaged part of her home, that's all she hears because her insurance company isn't taking care of her claims.

I've heard thunderstorms in my head, and maybe you have too. It happens when a tragedy occurs—to us, to someone close to us, or to someone we hear about in the news. Our minds become a tempest of "what if" questions. We focus on all the possible bad outcomes. Our fear, worry, and trust in God fluctuate as we wait, we pray, we grieve, and we wonder what the Lord will do.

It's natural for us to be fearful in a storm (literal or figurative). The disciples had Jesus right there in the boat with them, yet they were afraid (Matthew 8:23–27). He used the calming of the storm as a lesson to show them who He was—a powerful God who also cares for them.

We wish that Jesus would always calm the storms of our life as He calmed the storm for the disciples that day. But we can find moments of peace when we're anchored to the truth that He's in the boat with us and He cares. —ANNE CETAS

To realize the worth of the anchor, we need to feel the stress of the storm.

FROM AWE TO ADORATION

Read: Revelation 1:9–18

I will give thanks to you, Lord, with all my heart;
I will tell of all your wonderful deeds. Psalm 9:1

What's the greatest activity we can spend time doing? Worshiping God! Worship is not repeating hasty, routine petitions or listening to mood-inducing music. Worship is the experience of being "lost in wonder, love, and praise," as Charles Wesley wrote. It's awe that inspires adoration.

My first sight of the Grand Canyon left me speechless. The friend who had driven me there appreciated my reaction and stood silent beside me. I gazed in awe at this magnificent spectacle and thought, *This is a glimpse of God's majesty.* But my awe, by itself, was not worship.

My reaction is different when I come face-to-face with Jesus in the Scriptures. Awe changes into adoration as I behold Him in all His beauty. What grips my soul? His unsullied purity: "Can any of you prove me guilty of sin?" (John 8:46). His unrivaled wisdom: "No one ever spoke the way this man does!" (John 7:46). His unbounded pity: "When he saw the crows, he had compassion on them" (Matthew 9:36). And His overwhelming majesty: "He was transfigured before them" (Matthew 17:2).

As I see Jesus in the Gospels, my awe changes to adoration. I bow in worship and exclaim with Thomas: "My Lord and my God!" (John 20:28).   —Vernon Grounds

---

True worship of Christ changes admiration into adoration.

LOOKALIKES

READ: 2 Corinthians 3:17–4:2

*And we all, who with unveiled faces contemplate the
Lord's glory, are being transformed into his image
with ever-increasing glory, which comes from the
Lord, who is the Spirit.* 2 CORINTHIANS 3:18

THEY SAY WE ALL have one: Doppelgangers some call them. Lookalikes. People unrelated to us who look very much like us.

Mine happens to be a star in the music field. When I attended one of his concerts, I got a lot of double takes from fellow fans during intermission. But alas, I am no James Taylor when it comes to singing and strumming a guitar. We just happen to look alike.

Who do you look like? As you ponder that question, reflect on 2 Corinthians 3:18, where Paul tells us that we "are being transformed into [the Lord's] image." As we seek to honor Jesus with our lives, one of our goals is to take on His image. Of course, this doesn't mean we have to grow a beard and wear sandals—it means that the Holy Spirit helps us demonstrate Christlike characteristics in how we live. For example, in attitude (humility), in character (loving), and in compassion (coming alongside the down and out), we are to look like Jesus and imitate Him.

As we "contemplate the Lord's glory" by fixing our eyes on Jesus, we can grow more and more like Him. What an amazing thing it would be if people could observe us and say, "I see Jesus in you"!
—DAVE BRANON

---

*Love is the family resemblance the world
should see in followers of Christ.*

THE END?

READ: 1 Corinthians 15:50–58

But thanks be to God! He gives us the victory through our Lord Jesus Christ. 1 CORINTHIANS 15:57

EVERYTHING IN THIS WORLD eventually comes to an end, which at times can be disheartening. It's the feeling you get when you read a book that's so good you don't want it to end. Or when you watch a movie that you wish would go on a little while longer.

But all things—good and bad—do come to "The End." In fact, life ultimately does come to the end—sometimes sooner than we expect. All of us who have stood by the casket of a loved one know the painful emptiness of a heart that wishes it wasn't over yet.

Thankfully, Jesus steps into the fray of terminal disappointments, and through His death and resurrection He interjects hope for us. In Him "the end" is a prelude to a death-free eternity, and words like "it's over" are replaced by a joy-filled "forever." Since our bodies are not an eternal reality, Paul assures us that "we will all be changed" (1 Corinthians 15:51), and he reminds us that because of Christ's conquering work we can confidently say, "Where, O Death, is your victory?" (v. 55).

So let not your heart be troubled. Our sorrow is real, but we can be filled with gratitude because God "gives us the victory through our Lord Jesus Christ" (v. 57). —JOE STOWELL

In Christ, the end is only the beginning.

PUT DOWN YOUR BURDENS

READ: Matthew 11:25–30

*"Come to me, all you who are weary and burdened,
and I will give you rest."* MATTHEW 11:28

A MAN DRIVING HIS pickup truck on a country road saw a woman carrying a heavy load, so he stopped and offered her a lift. The woman expressed her gratitude and climbed into the back of the truck.

A moment later, the man noticed a strange thing: the woman was still holding onto her heavy load despite sitting in the vehicle! Astonished, he pleaded, "Please, Madam, put down your load and take your rest. My truck can carry you and your stuff. Just relax."

What do we do with the load of fear, worry, and anxiety we often carry as we go through life's many challenges? Instead of relaxing in the Lord, I sometimes behave like that woman. Jesus said, "Come to me, all you who are weary and burdened, and I will give you rest" (Matthew 11:28), yet I've caught myself carrying burdens I should offload onto Jesus.

We put down our burdens when we bring them to the Lord in prayer. The apostle Peter says, "Cast all your anxiety on [Jesus] because he cares for you" (1 Peter 5:7). Because He cares for us, we can rest and relax as we learn to trust Him. Instead of carrying the burdens that weigh us down and weary us, we can give them to the Lord and let Him carry them.   —LAWRENCE DARMANI

———

Prayer is the place where burdens change shoulders.

JESUS OVER EVERYTHING

READ: Colossians 1:15–20

He is before all things, and in him all things hold together. COLOSSIANS 1:17

MY FRIEND'S SON DECIDED to wear a sports jersey over his school clothing one day. He wanted to show support for his favorite team that would be playing an important game later that night. Before leaving home, he put something on over his sports jersey—it was a chain with a pendant that read, "Jesus." His simple action illustrated a deeper truth: Jesus deserves first place over everything in our lives.

Jesus is above and over all. "He is before all things, and in him all things hold together" (Colossians 1:17). Jesus is supreme over all creation (vv. 15–16). He is "the head of the body, the church" (v. 18). Because of this, He should have first place in all things.

When we give Jesus the highest place of honor in each area of our lives, this truth becomes visible to those around us. At work, are we laboring first for God or only to please our employer? (3:23). How do God's standards show up in the way we treat others? (vv. 12–14). Do we put Him first as we live our lives and pursue our favorite pastimes?

When Jesus is our greatest influence in all of life, He will have His rightful place in our hearts.   —JENNIFER BENSON SCHULDT

Put Jesus first.

HE WATCHES ME

READ: Matthew 10:16–31

So don't be afraid; you are worth more than many sparrows. MATTHEW 10:31

ONE SUNDAY MORNING AT church, we sang "His Eye Is on the Sparrow" as a congregational hymn. It was a rare opportunity to give voice to a song usually performed by a soloist.

During the first chorus, I noticed a friend who was weeping so hard that he couldn't sing. Knowing a bit of what he had been through recently, I recognized his tears as ones of joy at realizing that, no matter what our situation, God sees, knows, and cares for us.

Jesus said, "Are not two sparrows sold for one penny? Yet not one of them will fall to the ground outside your Father's care. And even the very hairs of your head are all numbered. So don't be afraid; you are worth more than many sparrows" (Matthew 10:29–31). The Lord spoke these words to His twelve disciples as He sent them out to teach, heal, and bear witness of Him to "the lost sheep of Israel" (v. 6). He told them that even though they would face persecution for His sake, they should not be afraid, even of death (vv. 22–26).

When threatening circumstances press us, causing us to lose hope, we can find encouragement in the words of this song: "I sing because I'm happy, I sing because I'm free. For His eye is on the sparrow, and I know He watches me." We are under His watchful care. —DAVID McCASLAND

When you put your cares in God's hands,
He puts His peace in your heart.

IN HIS PRESENCE

READ: Revelation 5

Then I heard every creature in heaven and on earth and under the earth and on the sea, and all that is in them, saying: "To him who sits on the throne and to the Lamb be praise and honor and glory and power, for ever and ever!" REVELATION 5:13

AS THE BUS ROUNDED another bend in the Israeli road, I was not prepared for my reaction to what I would see. There stretching before us lay the Sea of Galilee. Its beauty sparkled in the bright sunlight, but my heart was not touched just by its natural grandeur. No, the tears of wonderment that clouded my vision came when I realized anew that I was in the land of Jesus's earthly life.

When I looked over that body of water, I was viewing the sea on which Jesus sailed. When I visited ruins of the city of Capernaum, I was walking exactly where He walked. When I came to the Mount of the Beatitudes, I was standing in the very place where Jesus gave His remarkable sermon.

My heart was renewed by these realizations. It was warmed with the realities of Jesus's life—and especially His sacrificial death. Although those experiences in Israel have no redeeming power, they made me think about something that will happen in the future. I was touched by this thought: If being in the place where Jesus walked has the power to quicken my heart, how overwhelming it will be to stand in His presence in heaven!

Imagine the absolute ecstasy of being where Jesus is—not just where He was. It will be astounding!   —DAVE BRANON

The greatest joy on earth is the sure prospect of heaven.

DON'T BOTHER ME

READ: Revelation 3:14–22

*"Behold, I stand at the door and knock. If anyone hears
my voice and opens the door, I will come in to him and eat
with him, and he with me."* REVELATION 3:20 (ESV)

AS A YOUNG MAN, C. S. Lewis abandoned his childhood faith in
God and declared his belief in no religion, saying they were all
myths created by man. Years later, after acknowledging Jesus as the
Son of God and his Savior, Lewis wrote of that time in his book
Surprised by Joy. He said:

"No word in my vocabulary expressed deeper hatred than the
word *interference.* But Christianity placed at the center what then
seemed to me a transcendental Interferer. There was no region even
in the innermost depth of one's soul which one could surround
with a barbed wire fence and guard with a notice 'No Admittance.'
And that was what I wanted; some area, however small, of which I
could say to all other beings, 'This is my business and mine only.'"

Every person has the right to say to God, "Leave me alone.
Don't bother me." But it is the Lord's right to pursue us with His
persistent mercy. To the self-satisfied church at Laodicea, the risen
Christ said: "Behold, I stand at the door and knock. If anyone hears
my voice and opens the door, I will come in to him and eat with
him, and he with me" (Revelation 3:20 ESV).

By His grace, the Lord keeps knocking, ready to fill our lives
with His love.   —DAVID MCCASLAND

God's love is persistent but never pushy.

OUR REPRESENTATIVE

READ: Hebrews 4:9–16

*Let us then approach God's throne of grace with
confidence, so that we may receive mercy and find grace
to help us in our time of need.* HEBREWS 4:16

IN A SMALL MIDWESTERN college a professor was asked to contact a wealthy man on behalf of the school. Special funds were needed for an expansion program, and the financier could afford a sizable contribution. Being a Christian, the professor prayed earnestly that God would guide him.

As he walked into the building where the man had his office, he was greeted by a young man he recognized as a former student. He recalled that he had befriended this fellow at a time when he needed guidance, but he had forgotten his background. When the former student learned of the professor's errand, he said, "Come right in. My father's in here." Entering the office, the son introduced the professor and said simply, "Dad, this is a friend of mine. He's all right. He's come in behalf of the college I attended." The father looked up at the visitor, reached for his checkbook, and said, "How much do you want?" Within minutes the professor had a generous contribution in his pocket.

Seated at God the Father's right hand is Jesus Christ, His Son, who lives to make intercession for us. Because Christ is our representative, we are encouraged to "approach God's throne of grace with confidence, so that we may receive mercy and find grace to help us in our time of need" (Hebrews 4:16).   —PAUL VAN GORDER

*Jesus came into the world to talk to men for God;
He is now in heaven talking to God for men.*

A NEW NORMAL

READ: Hebrews 4:9–16

For we do not have a high priest who is unable to empathize with our weaknesses, but we have one who has been tempted in every way, just as we are—yet he did not sin. HEBREWS 4:15

A PASTOR WHO WAS trained in trauma and grief counseling commented that the greatest challenge for people who are hurting is often not the immediate heartache of the loss. Instead, the biggest problem is adjusting to the different kind of life that follows. What once was normal may never be normal again. So the challenge for those offering help is to assist the sufferers as they establish a "new normal." It may be a new normal that no longer includes robust health, a treasured relationship, or a satisfying job. Or it may be living without a loved one who has been taken in death. The gravity of such losses forces us to live a different kind of life—no matter how unwelcome it may be.

When our "new normal" comes, it's easy to think no one understands how we feel. But that isn't true. Part of the reason Jesus came was to experience life among us, resulting in His present ministry: "For we do not have a high priest who is unable to empathize with our weaknesses, but we have one who has been tempted in every way, just as we are—yet he did not sin" (Hebrews 4:15).

Our Savior lived a perfect life, yet He also knew the pains of a broken world. He endured sorrow; He suffered agony. And He stands ready to encourage us when the dark moments of life force us to embrace a new normal. —BILL CROWDER

In our desert of grief, Jesus can provide an oasis of hope.

LEANING ON JESUS

READ: John 13:12–26

One of them, the disciple whom Jesus loved, was reclining next to him. JOHN 13:23

SOMETIMES WHEN I PUT my head on my pillow at night and pray, I imagine I'm leaning on Jesus. Whenever I do this, I remember something the Word of God tells us about the apostle John. John himself writes about how he was sitting beside Jesus at the Last Supper: "One of them, the disciple whom Jesus loved, was reclining next to him" (John 13:23).

John used the term "the disciple whom Jesus loved" as a way of referring to himself without mentioning his own name. He is also depicting a typical banquet setting in first-century Israel, where the table was much lower than those we use today, about knee height. Reclining without chairs on a mat or cushions was the natural position for those around the table. John was sitting so close to the Lord that when he turned to ask him a question, he was "leaning back against Jesus" (John 13:25), with his head on his chest.

John's closeness to Jesus in that moment provides a helpful illustration for our lives with Him today. We may not be able to touch Jesus physically, but we can entrust the weightiest circumstances of our lives to Him. He said, "Come to me, all you who are weary and burdened, and I will give you rest" (Matthew 11:28). How blessed we are to have a Savior we can trust to be faithful through every circumstance of our lives! Are you "leaning" on Him today?

—JAMES BANKS

Jesus alone gives the rest we need.

GENUINE FRIENDS

READ: John 15:9–17

"You are my friends if you do what I command." JOHN 15:14

NOT LONG AGO, EXPERTS who track the changing vocabulary of the English language chose *unfriend* as the *New Oxford American Dictionary* Word of the Year. They defined it as a verb, "to remove someone as a friend on a social networking website," such as Facebook. On that site, friends allow each other to access the personal information on their Facebook pages. They may never meet face-to-face or even exchange greetings online. In our world of fleeting cyber acquaintants, we are beginning to realize that having a true friend means more now than ever before.

When Jesus called His disciples "friends" (John 15:15), He spoke of a unique relationship involving mutual commitment. He was only hours from laying down His life (v. 13), and He asked them to show their friendship by keeping His commands (v. 14). Most astonishing, perhaps, is Jesus's statement: "I no longer call you servants, because a servant does not know his master's business. Instead, I have called you friends, for everything that I learned from my Father I have made known to you" (v. 15).

In a genuine friendship, one's faithfulness can shore another person's faith in times of discouragement or fear. That is what Jesus is to us—our always faithful, forever Friend.

—DAVID MCCASLAND

The dearest friend on earth is but a mere shadow compared to Jesus.

THE GIFT OF PRESENCE

READ: John 11:14–27

Many Jews had come to Martha and Mary to comfort them in the loss of their brother. JOHN 11:19

A NUMBER OF YEARS ago, when I was a recently hired human resource manager for a company, I attended the visitation and funeral of a longtime employee I had never met. The worker, a bricklayer, was loved by his coworkers, yet very few came to see his widow. I listened to someone trying to console her by saying that many people stay away because they are afraid of saying or doing the wrong thing and making the family more miserable.

In times of distress, however, people rarely remember what we say. What they most remember is that we were there. Familiar faces offer strength beyond description; they provide comfort for the deep feelings of loneliness setting in from the loss. This "gift of presence" is one we're all capable of offering, even if we're tongue-tied or uncomfortable.

Martha and Mary were surrounded by friends and mourners who comforted them when their brother Lazarus died (John 11:19). Then the One they most longed to see—Jesus—came and wept with them (vv. 33–35). The people responded, "See how he loved him!" (v. 36).

In loss of any kind, Jesus always gives His comforting presence, and we have the ability to give deeply of His compassion simply by the gift of our presence. —RANDY KILGORE

Often the best comfort is just being there.

BLESSED ARE THE MEEK

READ: Matthew 5:1–10

*Blessed are the meek, for they will
inherit the earth.* MATTHEW 5:5

ONE PROBLEM WITH THE English word *meek* is that it rhymes with *weak*, and people have linked the two words together for years. A popular dictionary offers a secondary definition of meek as "too submissive; easily imposed on; spineless; spiritless." This causes some people to question why Jesus would say, "Blessed are the meek, for they will inherit the earth" (Matthew 5:5).

Greek scholar W. E. Vine says that meekness in the Bible is an attitude toward God "in which we accept His dealings with us as good, and therefore without disputing or resisting." We see this in Jesus, who found His delight in doing the will of His Father.

Vine goes on to say that "the meekness manifested by the Lord and commended to the believer is the fruit of power. . . . The Lord was 'meek' because He had the infinite resources of God at His command." He could have called angels from heaven to prevent His crucifixion.

Jesus told His weary, burdened followers, "Take my yoke upon you, and learn of me, for I am meek . . . , and [you] will find rest unto your souls" (Matthew 11:29 KJV). He was the perfect model of meekness.

When we are tired and troubled, Jesus invites us to discover the peace of meekly trusting Him.   —DAVID MCCASLAND

---

*God has two dwellings, one in heaven and the
other in a meek and thankful heart.*

LOVED WELL

READ: Ephesians 3:14–21

And I pray that you, being rooted and established in love, may have power, together with all the Lord's holy people, to grasp how wide and long and high and deep is the love of Christ, and to know this love that surpasses knowledge—that you may be filled to the measure of all the fullness of God. EPHESIANS 3:17–19

WE WERE GATHERED WITH family for Thanksgiving dinner when someone asked if each person would share what he or she was thankful for. One by one we talked. Three-year-old Joshua was thankful for "music," and Nathan, aged four, for "horses." We were all silenced, though, when Stephen (who was soon to turn five) answered, "I'm thankful that Jesus loves me so well." In his simple faith, he understood and was grateful for the love of Jesus for him personally. He told us that Jesus showed His love by dying on a cross.

The apostle Paul wanted the believers in the church at Ephesus to understand how well God loved them, and that was his prayer: "To grasp how wide and long and high and deep is the love of Christ" (Ephesians 3:17–19). He prayed that they would be rooted and grounded in that love.

To ground ourselves in God's love, it would be helpful to review these verses frequently or even memorize them. We can also take a few minutes each day to thank the Lord for the specific ways He shows His love to us. This will help us to grow in our belief and be thankful—as Stephen is—that Jesus loves us "so well."

—ANNE CETAS

To renew your love for Christ, review Christ's love for you.

SHALLOW FRIENDLINESS

READ: John 15:9–17

One who has unreliable friends soon comes to ruin, but there is a friend who sticks closer than a brother. PROVERBS 18:24

RECENTLY I RECEIVED A phone call from a friendly-sounding person who told me she wanted to make my life easier. She called me by my first name and warmly asked how my day was going. Then she informed me that she could help me save thousands of dollars a year if I would simply refinance my home with a particular mortgage company. Once she understood that I really wasn't interested, her friendliness evaporated.

Such insincere friendliness is often just a culturally correct attitude that some people use to impress others or to get something from them.

Contrast that self-serving attitude with the genuine friendship Jesus showed us. He said, "Greater love has no one than this: to lay down one's life for one's friends" (John 15:13). Then He demonstrated self-sacrificing love for us by dying on the cross to forgive our sins.

When we trust Jesus as our Savior and learn to obey Him, we experience a deep friendship that gives reality and sincerity to the friendliness we show others.

Lord, help us to avoid the shallow friendliness that uses others to get what we want. Teach us instead to radiate the warmth of genuine Christlike friendliness to everyone we meet. —DAVID EGNER

**True friendliness can be a magnet
that draws people to Christ.**

THE FEET OF JUDAS

READ: John 13:1–20

*"I have set you an example that you should do
as I have done for you."* JOHN 13:15

WHEN WE READ THE story of Jesus washing the disciples' feet, we may think we understand why He was doing that for them. John, for instance, was a close friend. Then there were Peter and Andrew, who had been so faithful in following the Master.

Each of the disciples must have had something that endeared him to Jesus. But why did He wash the feet of Judas? Jesus knew that He was stooping down to serve the one who would soon stoop to perform history's worst act of treachery.

Jesus was performing the most menial of tasks for a person who treated the Creator of the universe as being someone worth no more than thirty pieces of silver. Knowingly, the One whose name is associated with giving life got His hands dirty to serve the one whose name would stand for betrayal and death for the rest of time.

Doesn't Jesus's example tell us something special about service? Doesn't it remind us that we are not called to serve only those who are like us, or even those who care for us? We are called to serve all people—the lovely and the unlovely, the friendly and the not-so-friendly.

When was the last time you "washed the feet" of someone like Judas? —DAVE BRANON

*It's difficult to stand on a pedestal and wash the
feet of those below.* —*Charles Colson*

THE MINISTRY OF MOURNING

READ: Acts 7:54–8:2

*Godly men buried Stephen and
mourned deeply for him.* ACTS 8:2

SEVERAL YEARS AGO, A few months after my sister Martha and her
husband, Jim, died in an accident, a friend invited me to a "Growing through Grief" workshop at our church. I reluctantly agreed
to attend the first session but had no intention of going back. To
my surprise, I discovered a caring community of people trying to
come to grips with a significant loss in their lives by seeking the help
of God and others. It drew me back week after week as I worked
toward acceptance and peace through the process of sharing our
grief together.

Like the sudden loss of a loved one or friend, the death of Stephen, a dynamic witness for Jesus, brought shock and sorrow to
those in the early church (Acts 7:57–60). In the face of persecution,
"Godly men buried Stephen and mourned deeply for him" (8:2).
These men of faith did two things together: They buried Stephen,
an act of finality and loss. And they mourned deeply for him, a
shared expression of their sorrow.

As followers of Jesus, we need not mourn our losses alone. In
sincerity and love we can reach out to others who are hurting, and
in humility we can accept the concern of those who stand beside us.

As we grieve together, we can grow in understanding and in
the peace that is ours through Jesus Christ, who knows our deepest
sorrow.   —DAVID MCCASLAND

*The ministry of mourning with others
helps bring healing to our hearts.*

TRULY AMAZING

READ: Romans 5:6–11

See what great love the Father has lavished on us, that we should be called children of God! And that is what we are! The reason the world does not know us is that it did not know him. 1 JOHN 3:1

I READ THESE WORDS on a young woman's personal website: "I just want to be loved—and he has to be amazing!"

Isn't that what we all want—to be loved, to feel cared for by someone? And so much the better if he or she is amazing!

The one who fits that description most fully is Jesus Christ. In a display of unprecedented love, He left His Father in heaven and came to earth as the baby we celebrate at Christmas (Luke 2). Then, after living a perfect life, He gave His life as an offering to God on the cross in our behalf (John 19:17–30). He took our place because we needed to be rescued from our sin and its death penalty. "While we were still sinners, Christ died for us" (Romans 5:8). Then three days later, the Father raised Jesus to life again (Matthew 28:1–8).

When we repent and receive Jesus's gift of amazing love, He becomes our Savior (John 1:12; Romans 5:9), Lord (John 13:14), Teacher (Matthew 23:8), and Friend (John 15:14). "See what great love the Father has lavished on us, that we should be called children of God!" (1 John 3:1).

Looking for someone to love you? Jesus loves us so much more than anyone else possibly could. And He is truly amazing!

—ANNE CETAS

The wonder of it all—just to think that Jesus loves me.

TIME FOR FRIENDSHIP

READ: John 15:12–17

*A friend loves at all times, and a brother is born
for a time of adversity.* PROVERBS 17:17

WE REALLY CAN'T MAKE more time. There are only twenty-four hours in a day, and no matter how frantically we try, it's impossible to stretch those twenty-four into twenty-five. So our problem isn't how to increase time but how wisely to use our daily allotment of those 1,440 minutes as they steadily tick away.

Stop, then, and think about this vital issue. Apart from eating, sleeping, doing necessary tasks, and working at income-earning jobs, how are we spending that precious commodity we call time? Whatever else we're doing, are we giving time to relationships?

Well-known author Les Parrott III points out that few things are more conducive to our well-being than investing time in friendships. Research shows, he reports, that "ignoring friendship not only diminishes your quality of life but could also be a health hazard." Parrott says that close friendships can reduce the risk of illness.

If investing time in strengthening our friendships is so essential to our well-being, what about our relationship with Jesus? He said to His disciples, "I no longer call you servants, . . . Instead, I have called you friends" (John 15:15).

If you have trusted Him as Savior, are you devoting time to deepen your relationship with the best of all friends?

—VERNON GROUNDS

*Time is a friend when you use it to strengthen
your friendship with Jesus!*

LONELY, BUT NOT ALONE

READ: John 16:25–33

"A time is coming and in fact has come when you will be scattered, each to your own home. You will leave me all alone. Yet I am not alone, for my Father is with me." JOHN 16:32

HER BRIEF NOTE TO me spoke volumes. "I am a handicapped person in a wheelchair," she wrote. "I am very lonely even though I know I'm never alone. God is always there. I don't have a lot of people to talk to."

Loneliness has been termed the most desolate word in the English language. It is no respecter of age, race, economic status, or intelligence. Albert Einstein said, "It is strange to be known so universally, and yet to be so lonely."

God made us for intimacy and companionship with others. Even before sin entered the world, He declared that it is not good for man to be alone (Genesis 2:18). That's why many people often feel so empty inside.

Jesus knew loneliness too. He surely must have felt it when His disciples deserted Him (Mark 14:50). The Father's presence more than compensated for this, however. He said, "I am not alone, for my Father is with me" (John 16:32). That intimacy with the Lord is available to all who put their trust in Him and His Word (14:16–23).

We can lessen our feelings of loneliness by reaching out to others. But even more important, we must reach out to the Lord. He is always with us, and He wants us to fellowship with Him throughout the day. —DENNIS DEHAAN

Those who know Jesus are never alone.

FELLOWSHIP WITH JESUS

READ: Philippians 3:7–14

What is more, I consider everything a loss because of
the surpassing worth of knowing Christ Jesus my Lord,
for whose sake I have lost all things. I consider them
garbage, that I may gain Christ. PHILIPPIANS 3:8

I'LL NEVER FORGET THE time I had the privilege of sitting next to Billy Graham at a dinner. I was honored but also somewhat nervous about what would be appropriate to say. I thought it would be an interesting conversation starter to ask what he loved most about his years of ministry. Then I awkwardly started to suggest possible answers. Was it knowing presidents, kings, and queens? Or preaching the gospel to millions of people around the world?

Before I had finished offering suggestions, Rev. Graham stopped me. Without hesitation he said, "It has been my fellowship with Jesus. To sense His presence, to glean His wisdom, to have Him guide and direct me—that has been my greatest joy." I was instantly convicted and challenged. Convicted because I'm not sure that his answer would have been my answer, and challenged because I wanted it to be.

That's what Paul had in mind when he counted his greatest achievements to be of no worth compared to the "surpassing worth of knowing Christ Jesus my Lord" (Philippians 3:8). Think of how rich life would be if Jesus and our fellowship with Him was our highest pursuit. —JOE STOWELL

To remain faithful where God has placed you,
give Christ first place in your heart.

HUMILITY AND GREATNESS

READ: Matthew 20:20–28

*Not so with you. Instead, whoever wants to become great
among you must be your servant.* MATTHEW 20:26

AS A SEVEN-YEAR-OLD, Richard Bernstein admired Jackie Robinson's athletic ability and courage as the first African-American man to play Major League Baseball in the modern era. A few years later, while working at a small-town golf course, Bernstein was astonished to find himself carrying the bag of his hero, Jackie Robinson. When rain postponed the game, Robinson held an umbrella over the two of them and shared his chocolate bar with the young caddy. Writing in *The International Herald Tribune*, Bernstein cited that humble act of kindness as a mark of greatness he has never forgotten.

True greatness is shown by humility, not pride. This was powerfully demonstrated and taught by Jesus Christ, who told His ambitious disciples: "Whoever wants to become great among you must be your servant, and whoever wants to be first must be your slave—just as the Son of Man did not come to be served, but to serve, and to give his life a ransom for many" (Matthew 20:26–28).

When God himself walked on earth as a man, He washed feet, welcomed children, and willingly gave His life to deliver us from the self-centered tyranny of sin. His example gives credence to His command.

The greatest Man ever showed humility we can all learn from.

—DAVID MCCASLAND

*We can do great things for the Lord if we are
willing to do little things for others.*

SPEAK UP

READ: Luke 22:54–56

*Then seizing him, they led him away and
took him into the house of the high priest.
Peter followed at a distance.* LUKE 22:54

WHEN I HEAR STORIES about young people who have been bullied,
I notice there are always at least two levels of hurt. The first and
most obvious comes from the mean-spirited nature of those actually
doing the bullying. That's terrible on its own. But there's another,
deeper hurt that may end up being even more damaging than the
first: The silence of everyone else.

It hurts the one being bullied because that person is stunned
that no one will help. That often makes bullies more brazen, leading them to intensify their meanness. Worse, it heightens the
embarrassment, false shame, and loneliness of the victim. So it is
imperative to speak up for others and speak out against the behavior
(see Proverbs 31:8).

Jesus knows precisely what it feels like to be bullied and to be
left to suffer completely alone. Without cause, He was arrested,
beaten, and mocked (Luke 22:63–65). Matthew 26:56 says that
"all the disciples deserted him and fled." Peter, one of His closest
friends, even denied three times that he knew Him (Luke 22:61).
While others may not understand fully, Jesus does.

When we see others being hurt, we can ask Him for the courage
to speak up.   —RANDY KILGORE

---

*The voice of a courageous Christian
is an echo of the voice of God.*

WELCOME HOME!

READ: Luke 15:11–24

*"So he got up and went to his father. But while he was
still a long way off, his father saw him and was filled
with compassion for him; he ran to his son, threw his
arms around him and kissed him."* LUKE 15:20

WHEN WE WERE GOING through a particularly challenging time
with our son, a friend pulled me aside after a church meeting. "I
want you to know that I pray for you and your son every day," he
said. Then he added: "I feel so guilty. I've never had to deal with
prodigal children. My kids pretty much played by the rules. But it
wasn't because of anything I did or didn't do. Kids," he shrugged,
"make their own choices."

I wanted to hug him. His compassion was a reminder of the
Father's understanding for my struggle with my son.

No one understands the struggle with prodigals better than
our heavenly Father. The story of the prodigal son in Luke 15 is
our story and God's. Jesus told it on behalf of all sinners who so
desperately need to come home to their Creator and discover the
warmth of a loving relationship with Him.

Jesus is God in the flesh seeing us in the distance and looking
on us with compassion. He is God running to us and throwing His
arms around us. He is heaven's kiss welcoming the repentant sinner
home (v. 20).

God hasn't just left the porch light on for us. He's out on the
front porch watching, waiting, calling us home.   —JAMES BANKS

---

*Our loved ones may spurn our appeals, reject our message,
oppose our arguments, despise our persons—but they are
helpless against our prayers. —J. Sidlow Baxter*

BEING CONSUMED

READ: Psalm 32

When I kept silent, my bones wasted away through my groaning all day long. PSALM 32:3

IN HIS BOOK *The Call*, Os Guinness describes a moment when Winston Churchill, on holiday with friends in the south of France, sat by the fireplace to warm himself on a cold night. Gazing at the fire, Churchill, who had been England's prime minister during one of her greatest hours of crisis, saw pine logs "crackling, hissing, and spitting as they burned. Suddenly, his familiar voice growled, 'I know why logs spit. I know what it is to be consumed.'"

Difficulties, despair, dangers, distress, and the results of our own wrongdoings can all feel consuming. Circumstances slowly drain our hearts of joy and peace. When David experienced the consuming consequences of his own sinful choices, he wrote, "When I kept silent, my bones wasted away through my groaning all day long. . . . My strength was sapped as in the heat of summer" (Psalm 32:3–4).

In such difficult times, where do we turn for help? For hope? Paul, whose experiences were filled with ministry burdens and brokenness, wrote, "We are hard pressed on every side, but not crushed; perplexed, but not in despair; persecuted, but not abandoned; struck down, but not destroyed" (2 Corinthians 4:8–9).

How does that work? As we rest in Jesus, the Good Shepherd restores our souls (Psalm 23:3) and strengthens us for the next step of our journey. He promises to walk that journey with us every step of the way (Hebrews 13:5).   —BILL CROWDER

Our Shepherd not only gives us strength and restores our hearts but He also walks through life with us.

EVERYTHING WE NEED

READ: 2 Peter 1:1–11

*His divine power has given us everything we need for
a godly life through our knowledge of him who called
us by his own glory and goodness.* 2 PETER 1:3

I OFTEN FEEL INADEQUATE for the tasks I face. Whether it's teaching Sunday school, advising a friend, or writing articles for this publication, the challenge often seems larger than my ability. Like Peter, I have a lot to learn.

The New Testament reveals Peter's shortcomings as he tried to follow the Lord. While walking on water to Jesus, Peter began to sink (Matthew 15:25–31). When Jesus was arrested, Peter swore he didn't know Him (Mark 14:66–72). But Peter's encounter with the risen Christ and the power of the Holy Spirit changed his life.

Peter came to understand that God's "divine power has given us everything we need for a godly life through our knowledge of him who called us by his own glory and goodness" (2 Peter 1:3). An amazing statement from a man who had many flaws!

"[God] has given us his very great and precious promises, so that through them you may participate in the divine nature, having escaped the corruption in the world caused by evil desires" (v. 4).

Our relationship with the Lord Jesus Christ is the source of the wisdom, patience, and power we need to honor God, help others, and meet the challenges of today. Through Him, we can overcome our hesitations and feelings of inadequacy.

In every situation, He has given us everything we need to serve and honor Him.   —DAVID MCCASLAND

---

*God promises to provide everything we
need to honor Him with our lives.*

THE ADVANCE TEAM

READ: John 14:1–14

*"My Father's house has many rooms; if that were
not so, would I have told you that I am going
there to prepare a place for you?"* JOHN 14:2

A FRIEND RECENTLY PREPARED to relocate to a city more than 1,000 miles from her current hometown. She and her husband divided the labor of moving to accommodate a short timeline. He secured new living arrangements, while she packed their belongings. I was astounded by her ability to move without previewing the area or participating in the house hunt, and I asked her how she could do so. She acknowledged the challenge but said she knew she could trust her husband because of his attention to her preferences and needs over their years together.

In the upper room, Jesus spoke with His disciples about His coming betrayal and death. The darkest hours of Jesus's earthly life, and that of the disciples as well, lay ahead. He comforted them with the assurance that He would prepare a place for them in heaven, just as my friend's husband prepared a new home for their family. When the disciples questioned Jesus, He pointed them to their mutual history and the miracles they had witnessed Him perform. Although they would grieve Jesus's death and absence, He reminded them He could be counted on to do as He had promised.

Even in the midst of our own dark hours, we can trust Him to lead us forward to a place of goodness. As we walk with Him, we too will learn to trust increasingly in His faithfulness.

—KIRSTEN HOLMBERG

We can trust God to lead us through difficult times.

WALK FOR YOUR HEALTH

READ: 1 John 1:5–2:6

But if we walk in the light, as he is in the light, we have fellowship with one another, and the blood of Jesus, his Son, purifies us from all sin. 1 JOHN 1:7

PHYSICAL EXERCISE MAY HELP us fight off colds and infection. The theory is that a good workout puts our body in a condition similar to what happens at the onset of a fever. That's not all bad. A fever is the body's way of fighting back when micro-intruders get into our system. Increased body temperature aids our white blood cell defense system while slowing down the action of bacteria and viruses. Exercise does the same thing. It releases chemicals into the blood that stimulate the brain to make our temperature rise.

The first two chapters of 1 John indicate that a regular practice of good spiritual exercise is beneficial to the health of our soul. To ward off sin, we must "walk in the light, as he is in the light" (1:7) and obey Jesus each day.

Disobedience, however, cools our spiritual temperature. Fellowship with God and other believers is neglected. Sin is neither confessed nor forsaken. If we have a lukewarm faith (Revelation 3:16), we are not taking advantage of the defense mechanisms necessary to fight spiritual infection.

The right exercise program is one of faith and obedience. It is essential to spiritual health. Walk with Jesus every day, and you'll truly be walking for your health. —MART DEHAAN

For a healthy heart, give your faith a workout.

GOD WAITING

READ: John 14:1–6

The Lord is not slow in keeping his promise, as some understand slowness. Instead he is patient with you, not wanting anyone to perish, but everyone to come to repentance. 2 PETER 3:9

DURING THE CHRISTMAS SEASON we wait. We wait in traffic. We wait in checkout lines to purchase gifts. We wait for family to arrive. We wait to gather around a table filled with our favorite foods. We wait to open presents lovingly chosen.

All of this waiting can be a reminder to Christians that Christmas is a celebration of waiting for something much more important than holiday traditions. Like the ancient Israelites, we too are waiting for Jesus. Although He already came as the long-awaited Messiah, He has not yet come as ruler over all the earth. So today we wait for Christ's second coming.

Christmas reminds us that God also waits . . . He waits for people to see His glory, to admit that they are lost without Him, to say yes to His love, to receive His forgiveness, to turn away from sin. While we wait for His second coming, He waits for repentance. What seems to us like God's slowness in coming is instead His patience in waiting (2 Peter 3:9).

The Lord is waiting to have a relationship with those He loves. He made the first move when He came as baby Jesus and the sacrificial Lamb. Now He waits for us to welcome Him into our lives as Savior and Lord. —JULIE ACKERMAN LINK

God patiently keeps His promises.

THE CRASH

READ: Micah 7:8–9, 18–20

Because I have sinned against him, I will bear the LORD's wrath,
until he pleads my case and upholds my cause. He will bring
me out into the light; I will see his righteousness. MICAH 7:9

FOR YEARS AFTER THE Great Depression, the stock market struggled to win back investors' confidence. Then, in 1952, Harry Markowitz suggested that investors spread their stock holdings over several companies and industries. He developed a theory for portfolio selection that helped investors in uncertain times. In 1990, Markowitz and two others won the Nobel Memorial Prize in Economic Sciences for their theory.

Like those jittery investors, we followers of Jesus may also find ourselves frozen in fear after a "crash" in our personal lives, unsure how to pick up the pieces and move on. We might even spend our remaining lives waiting for a "Markowitz moment," when one big idea or action can help us recover from a previous failure.

Jesus has already done that on our behalf. He covered our shame, and He set us free to fellowship with God and serve Him daily. Because He gave His life and rose from the dead, when we "have fallen," we can "rise" with Him, for He will "delight to show mercy" (Micah 7:8, 18).

The moment we put our faith in Jesus, our eternity with Him begins. He walks alongside us so He can change us into the people we long to be and were created to be.   —RANDY KILGORE

Look up from your failures, and you'll find
God standing ready to receive you.

BASIN OF LOVE

READ: John 13:1–17

*After that, he poured water into a basin and began
to wash his disciples' feet, drying them with the towel
that was wrapped around him.* JOHN 13:5

ONE DAY IN PHYSICS class many years ago, our teacher asked us to tell him—without turning around—what color the back wall of the classroom was. None of us could answer, for we hadn't noticed.

Sometimes we miss or overlook the "stuff" of life simply because we can't take it all in. And sometimes we don't see what's been there all along.

It was like that for me as I recently read again the account of Jesus washing His disciples' feet. The story is a familiar one, for it is often read during Passion Week. That our Savior and King would stoop to cleanse the feet of His disciples awes us. In Jesus's day, even Jewish servants were spared this task because it was seen as beneath them. But what I hadn't noticed before was that Jesus, who was both man and God, washed the feet of Judas. Even though He knew Judas would betray Him, as we see in John 13:11, Jesus still humbled himself and washed Judas's feet.

Love poured out in a basin of water—love that He shared even with the one who would betray Him. As we ponder the events of the week that led up to the celebration of Jesus's resurrection, may we too be given the gift of humility so we can extend Jesus's love to everyone we come in contact with.   —AMY BOUCHER PYE

*Because of love, Jesus humbled himself
and washed His disciples' feet.*

WASTED TIME?

READ: Matthew 20:29–34

*Jesus had compassion on them and touched
their eyes. Immediately they received their sight
and followed him.* MATTHEW 20:34

YOU HAVE A FULL day of activity lined up—washing, shopping, errands—when your neighbor calls and invites you over for coffee. You don't think she's a believer in Christ, and you've been praying for a chance to talk with her. You know she's been having a rough time. Do you go?

Or a friend asks if you will consider being a big brother to a teenager who desperately needs a father figure. It will take some precious hours out of your day. Do you do it? Is it worth your time?

Jesus often interrupted His schedule to minister to people He met along the way. In Matthew 20:29–34, we read that He stopped and healed two blind men who called for His help, ignoring the crowd that tried to keep the two quiet. On another occasion, Jesus rebuked His disciples for keeping little children away from Him (Luke 18:15–17).

Author Henri Nouwen mirrored this sense of service. For the last ten years of his life he ministered at a home for the seriously disabled, taking two hours every morning to bathe, shave, dress, and feed a profoundly disabled man.

Serving a man incapable of responding may seem inefficient to us. But when we look at the example Jesus set, we learn that love and service are never a waste of time! —DAVID EGNER

Serve God by serving others.

I'M READY

READ: Luke 12:22–40

"You also must be ready, because the Son of Man will come at an hour when you do not expect him." LUKE 12:40

A FRIEND OF MINE who has lived all her life in California goes to sleep every night with her shoes and a flashlight under the bed. When she was a child, her father required every family member to be ready to leave the house if an earthquake were to come during the night.

"During a tremor," my friend says, "windows shatter and electricity is lost. With shoes I can walk on broken glass and with a light I can find my way in the dark. I never go to bed without them. I'm ready."

When Jesus spoke to His followers about His return, He said, "You must be ready, because the Son of Man will come at an hour when you do not expect him" (Luke 12:40).

What does it mean for a Christian to be ready for Christ's return? Jesus said that instead of worrying about material things, we are to trust God's provision and make His kingdom our priority (vv. 22–31). Instead of fear that grasps, we are to demonstrate faith that gives (vv. 32–34). Like faithful servants, we should expect our Master at any time, because He will return at an unexpected hour (vv. 35–40).

Jesus promised to return and told us how to live as we wait for His coming. Our lives, more than our lips, are to say, "I'm ready!"
—DAVID MCCASLAND

Be ready for the last moment by being ready every moment.

GET TO KNOW JESUS

READ: 2 Peter 1:1–11

*But grow in the grace and knowledge of our Lord
and Savior Jesus Christ. To him be glory both
now and forever! Amen.* 2 PETER 3:18

OS GUINNESS, IN HIS book *The Call*, tells a story about Arthur
Burns, chairman of the US Federal Reserve Board during the 1970s.
Burns, who was Jewish, became part of a Bible study held at the
White House at that time. One day, those in the group listened in
surprise as Burns prayed, "O God, may the day come when all Jews
will come to know Jesus." But an even bigger surprise came when he
prayed for the time "when all Christians will come to know Jesus."

Burns hit on a profound truth we all need to wrestle with. Even
if we claim the name of Jesus Christ, it may not be evident to others
that we really know Him. Do we have a personal relationship with
Him? If so, are we striving, praying, and working to know Jesus
more intimately each day?

Peter, a man who knew Jesus well, said that "the knowledge of
God and of Jesus our Lord" will bring us multiplied "grace and peace"
(2 Peter 1:2). Knowing Jesus gives us "everything we need for a godly
life" (v. 3). And knowledge of Jesus will help us develop character
traits that show the world that we are connected to Him (vv. 5–8).

Can you and I honestly say, "I know Jesus better today than I
did yesterday"? —DAVE BRANON

*The better you know Jesus in your heart,
the more the world will see Jesus in your life.*

BEST FRIEND—FOREVER

READ: James 2:18–26

The scripture was fulfilled that says, "Abraham believed God, and it was credited to him as righteousness," and he was called God's friend. JAMES 2:23

ONE OF THE PIECES of wisdom I have come to appreciate is my dad's often-repeated statement, "Joe, good friends are one of life's greatest treasures." How true! With good friends, you are never alone. They're attentive to your needs and gladly share life's joys and burdens.

Before Jesus came to earth, only two individuals were called friends of God. The Lord spoke to Moses "as one speaks to a friend" (Exodus 33:11), and Abraham "was called God's friend" (James 2:23; see 2 Chronicles 20:7; Isaiah 41:8).

I am amazed that Jesus calls those of us who belong to Him friends: "I have called you friends, for everything that I learned from my Father I have made known to you" (John 15:15). And His friendship is so deep that He laid down His life for us. John says, "Greater love has no one than this: to lay down one's life for one's friends" (v. 13).

What a privilege and blessing to have Jesus as our friend! He is a friend who will never leave us or forsake us (Hebrews 13:5). He intercedes for us before the Father and supplies all our needs. He forgives all our sins, understands all our sorrows, and gives us sufficient grace in times of trouble. He is indeed our best friend!

—JOE STOWELL

What a friend we have in Jesus.

THE BLAME GAME

READ: Leviticus 16:5–22

*The next day John saw Jesus coming toward him
and said, "Look, the Lamb of God, who takes
away the sin of the world!"* JOHN 1:29

I'VE BEEN BLAMED FOR a lot of things, and rightly so. My sin, failure, and incompetence have caused grief, anxiety, and inconvenience for friends and family (and probably even for strangers). I've also been blamed for things that were not my fault, things I was powerless to change.

But I have stood on the other side of the fence hurling accusations at others. If they had just done something different, I tell myself, I would not be in the mess I'm in. Blame hurts. So whether guilty or not, we waste lots of time and mental energy trying to find someone else to carry it for us.

Jesus offers us a better way to deal with blame. Even though He was blameless, He took upon himself the sin of the world and carried it away (John 1:29). We often refer to Jesus as the sacrificial lamb, but He was also the final scapegoat for everything that is wrong with the world (Leviticus 16:10).

Once we acknowledge our sin and accept Christ's offer to take it away, we no longer have to carry the weight of our guilt. We can stop looking for someone to blame for what's wrong with us, and we can stop accepting blame from others trying to do the same.

Thanks to Jesus, we can stop playing the blame game.

—JULIE ACKERMAN LINK

Honesty about our sin brings forgiveness.

TIME FOR A CHECKUP

READ: 1 Corinthians 11:27–29

Everyone ought to examine themselves before they eat of the bread and drink from the cup. 1 CORINTHIANS 11:28

EVERY YEAR I HAVE a physical—that periodic visit to the doctor's office where I'm poked and prodded, screened and studied. It is something that can be easy to dread, and even to fear. We aren't sure what the tests will show or what the doctors will say. Still, we know that we need this evaluation to understand our physical well-being and what is needed as we move forward.

The same is true spiritually in the life of the Christ-follower. We need to pause from time to time and reflect on the condition of our hearts and lives.

One place for an important self-study is at the Lord's Table. Paul wrote to the Corinthians, some of whom were eating in an unworthy manner: "Let a man examine himself, and so let him eat of the bread and drink of the cup" (1 Corinthians 11:28 NKJV). In the remembrance of Christ's death for us, there can be a sobering clarity of thought and understanding, for as we consider the price Jesus paid for us, it is the best time to consider the condition of our heart and our relationships. Then, with honest understanding of our spiritual well-being, we can turn to Him for the grace we need to move forward in His name.

Is it time for your checkup?   —BILL CROWDER

Self-examination is one test from which no Christian is excused.

THE END OF SHAME

READ: Hebrews 12:1–2

*Fixing our eyes on Jesus, the pioneer and perfecter
of faith. For the joy set before him he endured the
cross, scorning its shame, and sat down at the right
hand of the throne of God.* HEBREWS 12:2

HAVE YOU EVER FELT ashamed? Perhaps you feel shame now. You
have lied or you have slandered a friend. Perhaps you have broken
a vow or betrayed a trust. You have sinned and you know it. You
are guilty and you feel ashamed.

When we sin, guilt and shame are the appropriate emotions to feel.
We need to confess to God and to those we have offended what we
have done and how wrong it was. We shouldn't shrug off sin or carry
it as a terrible secret. And we shouldn't explain it away as the result of
circumstances or the seduction of the devil. When we see our sin for
what it is and what it has done to others, we ought to be ashamed.

Guilt and shame can be good if they drive us to the Savior.
When Jesus carried our sin to the cross, He also carried our shame.
He "endured the cross, scorning its shame" (Hebrews 12:2). He
now sits enthroned in heaven, but it cost Him dearly. He hung on
a Roman execution rack, naked and humiliated. Jesus endured
shame—*our* shame.

When we give ourselves to Jesus, who triumphed over death
and experienced the shame caused by our sin, we will not only have
forgiveness for what we have done, but it will be the beginning of
the end of our shame.   —HADDON ROBINSON

---

*A judge may suspend a sentence, but only
God can remove our guilt.*

ONLY BY PRAYER

READ: Mark 9:14–29

*"'If you can'?" said Jesus. "Everything is possible
for one who believes."* MARK 9:23

MY FRIEND CALLED ME late one night during her cancer treatment.
Grieved by her uncontrollable sobs, I soon added my own tears and
a silent prayer. *What am I supposed to do, Lord?*

Her wails squeezed my heart. I couldn't stop her pain, fix her
situation, or find one intelligible word of encouragement. But I
knew who could help. As I wept with my friend, stumbling through
a prayer, I whispered repeatedly, "Jesus. Jesus. Jesus."

Her cries quieted to sniffs and whimpers, until her breathing
slowed. Her husband's voice startled me. "She's asleep," he said.
"We'll call tomorrow."

I hung up, weeping prayers into my pillow.

The gospel of Mark shares a story of another person who wanted
to help his loved one. A desperate father brought his suffering son
to Jesus (Mark 9:17). Doubt clung to his plea, as he reiterated the
impossibility of their circumstances (vv. 20–22) and acknowledged
his need for Jesus to empower his belief (v. 24). The father and son
experienced freedom, hope, and peace when Jesus stepped in and
took control (vv. 25–27).

When loved ones are hurting, it's natural to want to do the right
things and say the perfect words. But Christ is the only One who
can truly help us. When we call on the name of Jesus, He can enable
us to believe and rely on the power of His presence.

—XOCHITL DIXON

*The name of Jesus is the powerful prayer that
leads us into His mighty presence.*

OUR LORD'S RETURN

READ: 1 Thessalonians 5:1–22

He who testifies to these things says, "Yes, I am coming soon." Amen. Come, Lord Jesus. REVELATION 22:20

NEARLY 2,000 YEARS AGO Jesus said, "I am coming soon" (Revelation 22:20). Since then, some have wrongly tried to predict when He will return. Others have scoffed. Was Jesus wrong? Did something happen that He didn't foresee?

Of course not! We view time from the perspective of our own brief life span. But to the eternal God, "With the Lord a day is like a thousand years, and a thousand years are like a day" (2 Peter 3:8).

Jesus told His disciples that God had not given them specific information about "times or dates" (Acts 1:7). He wanted them—as He wants us—to live in an attitude of expectation. Paul echoed this when he spoke of Christ's return as "the blessed hope" (Titus 2:13).

But how do we live expectantly? Jesus instructed the disciples to be witnesses to all the world (Acts 1:8). Paul said, "be awake and sober" (1 Thessalonians 5:6) and love other believers (vv. 12–15). John urged us to walk in close fellowship with Jesus (1 John 2:28–3:3) and to purify ourselves so that we will "be confident and unashamed before him at his coming" (2:28).

The Lord's any-moment return is no cause for date setting but for watchful expectation. Let's serve Him in every aspect of our lives, and one day we'll hear Him say, "Well done, good and faithful servant" (Matthew 25:21).   —HERB VANDER LUGT

A watching Christian will be a working Christian.

SLOW DOWN

READ: Genesis 2:1–3

*By the seventh day God had finished the
work he had been doing; so on the seventh day
he rested from all his work.* GENESIS 2:2

WE LIVE IN an action-oriented world, and it seems that simplifying our lives has never been more complicated! Doesn't it seem that there's always work to do and no time for rest? Answer the following questions as honestly as you can to determine if you need to rest: Do I feel stressed when functioning in my normal day-to-day activities? Is it difficult to find joy? Do I get the kind of rest my body needs? Do I wake up tired?

In creation, God established a pattern of work and rest, which is a model for believers. For six days God worked to bring order to our world. But on the seventh day, after He had finished all His creative activity, He rested. God demonstrated that rest is appropriate and right.

Jesus showed us the importance of rest when He sat wearily beside a well after a long walk (John 4:6) and when He slept in the back of a boat with His head on a pillow (Mark 4:38). He also rested when He and His disciples got away from the crowds (Mark 6:31–32).

If the Lord rested from the work of creation and from His earthly ministry, we need to rest from our work as well. Our times of rest refresh us for times of service. Schedule some "slow down" time this week. —MARVIN WILLIAMS

All work and no play will take the joy of life away.

DEALING WITH DISTRACTION

READ: Matthew 13:14–22

The worries of this life . . . choke the word. MATTHEW 13:22

A RESTAURANT OWNER IN the village of Abu Ghosh, just outside Jerusalem, offered a fifty-percent discount for patrons who turned off their cell phones. Jawdat Ibrahim believes that smartphones have shifted the focus of meals from companionship and conversation to surfing, texting, and business calls. "Technology is very good," Ibrahim says. "But . . . when you are with your family and your friends, you can just wait for half an hour and enjoy the food and enjoy the company."

How easily we can be distracted by many things, whether in our relationship with others or with the Lord.

Jesus told His followers that spiritual distraction begins with hearts that have grown dull, ears that are hard of hearing, and eyes that are closed (Matthew 13:15). Using the illustration of a farmer scattering seed, Jesus compared the seed that fell among thorns to a person who hears God's Word but whose heart is focused on other things. "The worries of this life and the deceitfulness of wealth choke the word, making it unfruitful" (v. 22).

There is great value in having times throughout each day when we turn off the distractions of mind and heart and focus on the Lord. —DAVID MCCASLAND

Focusing on Christ puts everything else in perspective.

JESUS CRIED

READ: John 11:17–37

Jesus wept. JOHN 11:35

A FRIEND WHOSE YOUNG daughter was killed in a car accident told me: "I cried easily before Natalie's accident. . . . Now I am always crying. Sometimes the tears just slip out."

Anyone who has suffered such intense personal tragedy understands what she is talking about.

Is there anything wrong with crying? Do we have biblical evidence to suggest that it's okay to cry?

Jesus gives us the answer. Lazarus, a close friend of His, had died. When Jesus arrived at the home of Lazarus's sisters, they were surrounded by friends who had come to console them. Jesus saw Mary and Martha and their friends mourning, and He too was overcome. Sorrowing with them, "Jesus wept" (John 11:35).

Sadness, tears, and mourning are familiar territory for everyone on this earth—even for Jesus. His tears tell us that it's okay if our tears "just slip out." And they remind us that the reason tears of sorrow will be extinct in eternity is that "there will be no more death or mourning or crying or pain" (Revelation 21:4).

When God wipes out the effects of sin, He will wipe out the need for tears—one more reason to look forward to eternity.

—DAVE BRANON

Heaven—no pain, no night, no death, no tears.

PONDERING THE BIRTH OF CHRIST

READ: Luke 2:8–20

*And all who heard it were amazed at what the shepherds
said to them. But Mary treasured up all these things
and pondered them in her heart.* LUKE 2:18–19

NINETEENTH-CENTURY PREACHER Charles Spurgeon says of Jesus's
mother Mary after she had been visited by the angel: "She exercised
. . . her memory—she treasured 'all these things'; her affections—
she stowed them 'in her heart'; and her intellect—for she 'pondered
them.'"

As we, like Mary, contemplate Jesus, let's consider what Andrew
Murray, viewing Luke 2 in the light of Colossians 1, observed. He
said, "Jesus was born twice! His coming to Bethlehem was a birth
into a life of weakness. Later, however, as 'the firstborn from the
dead' (Colossians 1:18 KJV), He arose from the grave in the power
and glory of heaven and ascended to the throne."

And think of this: The shepherds were willing to leave their
sheep because they were interested in viewing "the Lamb of God,
who takes away the sin of the world" (John 1:29). The wise men,
having worshiped the young child Jesus, "returned to their own
country by another route" (Matthew 2:12). Similarly, after bowing
before Christ as Savior and Lord, we can no longer walk the broad
road we once walked but must go "another way" to journey home.

As did Mary, we should prayerfully ponder these and the many
other blessed truths surrounding Christ's birth, and then adore God
for our salvation. —HENRY BOSCH

First be thoughtful about Christ's birth—then be thankful!

JESUS KNOWS WHY

READ: Mark 8:22–26

When Jesus had finished saying these things, the crowds were amazed at his teaching. MATTHEW 7:28

I HAVE FRIENDS WHO have received partial healing but still struggle with painful aspects of their diseases. Other friends have been healed of an addiction but still struggle with feelings of inadequacy and self-loathing. And I wonder, *Why doesn't God heal them completely—once and for all?*

In Mark 8:22–26, we read the story of Jesus healing a blind man. Jesus first took the man away from the village. Then He spit on the man's eyes and "put his hands on him." The man said he now saw people who looked "like trees walking around." Then Jesus touched the man's eyes again, and this time he saw "everything clearly."

In His ministry, Jesus's words and actions often amazed and baffled the crowd and His followers (Matthew 7:28; Luke 8:10; 11:14) and even drove many of them away (John 6:60–66). No doubt this two-part miracle also caused confusion. Why not immediately heal this man?

We don't know why. But Jesus knew what the man—and the disciples who viewed his healing—needed in that moment. And He knows what we need today to draw us closer in our relationship with Him. Though we won't always understand, we can trust that God is working in our lives and the lives of our loved ones. And He will give us the strength, courage, and clarity we need to persevere in following Him.   —ALYSON KIEDA

Open our eyes, Lord. We want to see Jesus. —Robert Cull

GOD MANIFESTED IN THE FLESH

READ: 2 Corinthians 4:1–18

For God, who said, "Let light shine out of darkness," made his light shine in our hearts to give us the light of the knowledge of God's glory displayed in the face of Christ. 2 CORINTHIANS 4:6

A LITTLE BOY WHO was frightened as night approached called for his mother. She told him not to be afraid in the dark because "God is here with you." "Yes, I know," responded the child, "but I want someone with a face!" He was expressing a deep longing of the human heart. It is hard to conceive of God as infinite Spirit, but it is easy to picture the Lord Jesus Christ when we pray or reflect upon Him. The desire of the youngster who wanted "someone with a face" was realized when the Baby Jesus was born in Bethlehem's manger.

Some people were privileged to behold the glory of God in the face of the little Babe at Bethlehem. For instance, the shepherds returned from visiting Him "glorifying and praising God for all the things they had heard and seen . . ." (Luke 2:20). The aged Simeon held the eight-day-old Infant in his arms and said, "Lord, . . . you may now dismiss your servant in peace. For my eyes have seen your salvation" (Luke 2:29–30).

We who know Jesus should earnestly pray that many sin-blinded eyes may be opened by the Holy Spirit to see that Jesus is indeed God in human form! —HERB VANDER LUGT

The fool said in his heart, "There is no God,"
but the wise men found Him in a manger!

CHRISTMAS REST

READ: Matthew 11:28–12:8

*"Come to me, all you who are weary and burdened,
and I will give you rest."* MATTHEW 11:28

As A BOY I delivered newspapers in order to earn money. Since it was a morning newspaper, I was required to get up at 3 o'clock every morning, seven days a week, in order to have all 140 of my papers delivered to their appropriate homes by 6 a.m.

But one day each year was different. We would deliver the Christmas morning newspaper on Christmas Eve—meaning that Christmas was the only morning of the year I could sleep in and rest like a normal person.

Over the years, I came to appreciate Christmas for many reasons, but one that was special in those days was that, unlike any other day of the year, it was a day of rest.

At that time, I didn't fully understand the meaning of the true rest that Christmas brings. Christ came so that all who labor under the weight of a law that can never be fulfilled might find rest through the forgiveness Christ offers. Jesus said, "Come to me, all you who are weary and burdened, and I will give you rest" (Matthew 11:28). In a world that is too much for us to bear alone, Christ has come to bring us into a relationship with Him and give us rest.

—BILL CROWDER

Our soul finds rest when it rests in God.

IS JESUS STILL HERE?

READ: Romans 8:31–39

*For I am convinced that neither death nor life, neither
angels nor demons, neither the present nor the future, nor
any powers, neither height nor depth, nor anything else
in all creation, will be able to separate us from the love of
God that is in Christ Jesus our Lord.* ROMANS 8:38–39

TED ROBERTSON'S HOME IN Colorado was one of more than 500
destroyed by the Black Forest Fire in June 2013. When he was
allowed to return and sift through the ash and rubble, he was hop-
ing to find a precious family heirloom made by his wife—a tiny
ceramic figurine of baby Jesus about the size of a postage stamp. As
he searched the charred remains of their home, he kept wondering,
"Is the baby Jesus still here?"

When our lives are rocked by disappointment and loss, we may
wonder if Jesus is still here with us. The Bible's answer is a resound-
ing Yes! "Neither death nor life, neither angels nor demons, neither
the present nor the future, nor any powers . . . will be able to separate
us from the love of God that is in Christ Jesus our Lord" (Romans
8:38–39).

In a corner of what used to be his garage, Ted Robertson discovered the burned remnants of a nativity scene, and there he found
the baby Jesus figurine undamaged by the flames. He told KRDO
NewsChannel 13, "[We've] gone from apprehension to hope . . .
that we're going to recover some parts of our life that we thought
were lost."

Is Jesus still here? He is indeed, and that is the everlasting wonder of Christmas. —DAVID MCCASLAND

If you know Jesus, you'll never walk alone.

SOMEONE TO CELEBRATE

READ: Matthew 2:1–12

*Come, let us bow down in worship, let us kneel
before the LORD our Maker.* PSALM 95:6

MANY MANGER SCENES DEPICT the wise men, or magi, visiting Jesus in Bethlehem at the same time as the shepherds. But according to the gospel of Matthew, the only place in Scripture where their story is found, the magi showed up later. Jesus was no longer in the manger in a stable at the inn, but in a house. Matthew 2:11 tells us, "On coming to the house, they saw the child with his mother Mary, and they bowed down and worshiped him. Then they opened their treasures and presented him with gifts of gold, frankincense and myrrh."

Realizing that the magi's visit happened later than we may think provides a helpful reminder as we begin a new year. Jesus is always worthy of worship. When the holidays are past and we head back to life's everyday routines, we still have Someone to celebrate.

Jesus Christ is Immanuel, "God with us" (Matthew 1:23), in every season. He has promised to be with us "always" (28:20). Because He is always with us, we can worship Him in our hearts every day and trust that He will show himself faithful in the years to come. Just as the magi sought Him, may we seek Him too and worship Him wherever we are.   —JAMES BANKS

When we find Christ we offer our worship.

A WIDOW'S CHOICE

READ: Psalm 34:15–22

The LORD is close to the brokenhearted and saves those who are crushed in spirit. PSALM 34:18

WHEN A GOOD FRIEND suddenly lost her husband to a heart attack, we grieved with her. As a counselor, she had comforted many others. Now, after forty years of marriage, she faced the unwelcome prospect of returning to an empty house at the end of each day.

In the midst of her grief, our friend leaned on the One who "is close to the brokenhearted." As God walked with her through her pain, she told us she would choose to "wear the label widow proudly," because she felt it was the label God had given her.

All grief is personal, and others may grieve differently than she does. Her response doesn't diminish her grief or make her home less empty. Yet it reminds us that even in the midst of our worst sorrows, our sovereign and loving God can be trusted.

Our heavenly Father suffered a profound separation of His own. As Jesus hung on the cross He cried out, "My God, my God, why have you forsaken me?" (Matthew 27:46). Yet He endured the pain and separation of crucifixion out of his love for us!

He understands! And because "the LORD is close to the brokenhearted" (Psalm 34:18), we find the comfort we need. He is near.

—DAVE BRANON

God shares in our sorrow.

FRIENDSHIP WITH JESUS

READ: John 15:9–17

"You are my friends if you do what I command." JOHN 15:14

JOSEPH SCRIVEN (1820–1886), WRITER of the much-loved hymn "What a Friend We Have in Jesus," knew the pain of heartache and loneliness. His bride-to-be drowned the evening before their wedding. Later, a second fiancée died, and again his hopes for marriage were dashed. Yet Christ's friendship sustained him.

Anyone can have that same friendship. Many years ago, I came to know John, a recovering addict who at the lowest point in his life met Jesus. He sensed that the Lord was asking him, "Do you want a friend forever?" As John wept over his broken condition, he sobbed, "Yes," and Christ came into his life.

Recently John told me that he urgently needs a liver transplant. "You know, John," I said, "cynical people might say, 'Some friend Jesus has turned out to be, considering your condition.'" John replied, "But I'm not saying that." Then he added, "I certainly don't want to leave my family. But however it goes, Jesus remains my friend."

In John 15:14, Jesus said that we are His friends, suggesting that this is a two-way relationship. But He added one important condition: We must walk obediently with Him. Only then can we testify, "Whatever happens, Jesus remains my friend."

—JOANIE YODER

There is no truer friend than Jesus.

A LIGHT IN THE DARKNESS

READ: Luke 2:25–33

*When Jesus spoke again to the people, he said, "I am the
light of the world. Whoever follows me will never walk in
darkness, but will have the light of life."* JOHN 8:12

AN ARTIST WAS PAINTING a winter scene. Snow blanketed the
ground and the pine trees. Night was falling, and the landscape
was enveloped in semi-darkness. A log cabin was barely visible in
the shadows. The whole scene was one of gloom.

Then the artist used some yellow tints to put the cheerful glow
of a lamp in one of the cabin windows. That lone light, its golden
rays reflecting on the snow, completely transformed the impression
given by the painting. In contrast to the cold darkness of the surrounding forest, that light in the window created a warm feeling
of love and security.

What happened on that canvas is a striking portrayal of one of
the most dramatic events in all of history. When Jesus was born in
Bethlehem's stable, a light was placed in this sin-darkened world.
The apostle John testified, "In him was life, and the life was the
light of all mankind" (John 1:4).

As we continue to think about the birth of the Lord Jesus, let's
be mindful of how much brighter this world is because He came
into it. Jesus declared, "I am the light of the world. Whoever follows me will never walk in darkness, but will have the light of life"
(John 8:12).

How has Jesus brightened your life?   —RICHARD DEHAAN

Without the Light of Jesus, we would be in the dark about God.

OUR DAILY BREAD WRITERS

JAMES BANKS Pastor of Peace Church in Durham, North Carolina, Dr. James Banks has written several books for Discovery House, including *Praying the Prayers of the Bible* and *Prayers for Prodigals*.

HENRY BOSCH (1914–1995) Henry G. Bosch was the first managing editor of *Our Daily Bread* and one of its first writers. Throughout his life, he battled illness but turned his weaknesses into spiritual encouragement for others through his devotional writing.

MONICA BRANDS Monica has a master of theological studies from Calvin Seminary in Grand Rapids. She has worked with children with special needs. Monica grew up in Minnesota in a family with eight children. She began writing for *Our Daily Bread* in 2017.

DAVE BRANON An editor with Discovery House, Dave has been involved with *Our Daily Bread* since the 1980s. He earned his master of arts degree in English from Western Michigan University. Dave has written nearly twenty books, including *Beyond the Valley* and *Living the Psalms Life*, both Discovery House publications.

ANNE CETAS After becoming a Christian in her late teens, Anne was introduced to *Our Daily Bread* right away and began reading it. Now she reads it for a living as senior content editor of *Our Daily Bread*. Anne began writing articles for *ODB* in 2004.

POH FANG CHIA Like Anne Cetas, Poh Fang trusted Jesus Christ as Savior as a teenager. She is the director of content development and a part of the Chinese editorial review committee serving in the Our Daily Bread Ministries Singapore office.

BILL CROWDER A former pastor who is now vice president of ministry content for Our Daily Bread Ministries, Bill travels extensively as a Bible conference teacher, sharing God's truths with fellow believers in Malaysia and Singapore and other places where ODB Ministries has international offices. His Discovery House books include *Seeing the Heart of Christ* and *Let's Talk*.

LAWRENCE DARMANI A noted novelist and publisher in Ghana, Lawrence is editor of *Step* magazine and CEO of Step Publishers. He and his family live in Accra, Ghana. His book *Grief Child* earned him the Commonwealth Writers' Prize as best first book by a writer in Africa.

DENNIS DEHAAN (1932–2014) When Henry Bosch retired, Dennis became the second managing editor of *Our Daily Bread*. A former pastor, he loved preaching and teaching the Word of God. Dennis went to be with the Lord in 2014.

KURT DEHAAN (1953–2003) Kurt was a vital part of the ministry founded by his grandfather Dr. M. R. DeHaan in 1938. Kurt faithfully led *Our Daily Bread* as the managing editor for many years, and often wrote for other ministry publications until his sudden death in 2003. Kurt died of a heart attack while jogging. He and his wife Mary (who died in 2014) had four children: Katie, Anna, Claire, and Nathan.

MART DEHAAN The former president of Our Daily Bread Ministries, Mart followed in the footsteps of his grandfather M. R. and his dad Richard in that capacity. Mart, who has long been associated with *Day of Discovery* as host of the program from Israel, is now senior content advisor for Our Daily Bread Ministries and cohost of *Discover the Word*.

RICHARD DEHAAN (1923–2002) Son of the founder of Our Daily Bread Ministries, Dr. M. R. DeHaan, Richard was responsible for the ministry's entrance into television. Under his leadership, *Day of Discovery* television made its debut in 1968.

XOCHITL DIXON Xochitl (soh-cheel) equips and encourages readers to embrace God's grace and grow deeper in their personal relationships with Christ and others. Her first book is *Waiting for God: Trusting Daily in God's Plan and Pace*. Serving as an author, speaker, and blogger at xedixon.com, she enjoys singing, reading, motherhood, and being married to her best friend, Dr. W. Alan Dixon Sr.

DAVID EGNER A retired Our Daily Bread Ministries editor and longtime *Our Daily Bread* writer, David was also a college professor during his working career. In fact, he was a writing instructor for both Anne Cetas and Julie Ackerman Link at Cornerstone University.

DENNIS FISHER For many years, Dennis was senior research editor at Our Daily Bread Ministries, using his theological training to guarantee biblical accuracy. He is also an expert in C. S. Lewis studies. He and his wife, Janet, a former university professor, have retired to Northern California.

VERNON GROUNDS (1914–2010) A longtime college president (Denver Seminary) and board member for Our Daily Bread Ministries, Vernon's life story was told in the Discovery House book *Transformed by Love*. Dr. Grounds died in 2010 at the age of 96.

TIM GUSTAFSON Tim writes for *Our Daily Bread* and serves as an editor for Discovery Series. As the son of missionaries to Ghana, Tim has an unusual perspective on life in the West. He and his wife, Leisa, are the parents of one daughter and seven sons.

C. P. HIA Hia Chek Phang and his wife, Lin Choo, reside in the island nation of Singapore in Southeast Asia. C. P. came to faith in Jesus Christ at the age of thirteen. During his early years as a believer, he was privileged to learn from excellent Bible teachers who instilled in him a love for God's Word. He is special assistant to the president of Our Daily Bread Ministries, and he helps with translating resources for the ministry. He and his wife have a son, daughter-in-law, grandson, and granddaughter.

KIRSTEN HOLMBERG Kirsten has been a part of the *Our Daily Bread* writing team since March 2017. She lives in the northwest part of the United States, and in addition to her writing, she has a ministry of speaking to various church, business, and community groups. She is the author of *Advent with the Word: Approaching Christmas through the Inspired Language of God*.

ADAM HOLZ Adam's first *Our Daily Bread* articles appeared in January 2018. His main job is as senior associate editor of Focus on the Family's media review website, *Plugged In*. He has written a Bible study called *Beating Busyness*. He and his wife, Jennifer, have three children.

ARTHUR JACKSON Having grown up in Kansas City, Arthur returned home after spending nearly three decades in pastoral ministry in Chicago. He began writing for *Our Daily Bread* in 2017. He serves as director of two ministries—one that cares for pastors and one that seeks to plant churches worldwide. He and his wife, Shirley, have five grandsons.

CINDY HESS KASPER An editor for the Our Daily Bread Ministries publication *Our Daily Journey* until her retirement in 2018, Cindy began writing for *Our Daily Bread* in 2006. She and her husband, Tom, have three children and seven grandchildren.

ALYSON KIEDA Most of Alyson's professional career has been wrapped up in editing. She has been an editor at Our Daily Bread Ministries for more than ten years. Her first article in *Our Daily Bread* was published in 2014.

RANDY KILGORE Randy spent most of his twenty-plus years in business as a senior human resource manager before returning to seminary. Since finishing his master of divinity in 2000, he has served as a writer and workplace chaplain. A collection of those devotionals appears in his Discovery House book *Made to Matter: Devotions for Working Christians*. Randy and his wife, Cheryl, and their two children live in Massachusetts.

ALBERT LEE Albert Lee was director of international ministries for Our Daily Bread Ministries for many years. Albert's passion, vision, and energy expanded the work of the ministry around the world. Albert grew up in Singapore and took a variety of courses from Singapore Bible College, as well as serving with Singapore Youth for Christ from 1971–1999. Albert appreciates art and collects paintings. He and his wife, Catherine, have two children.

JULIE ACKERMAN LINK (1950–2015) A book editor by profession, Julie began writing for *Our Daily Bread* in 2000. Her books *Above All, Love* and *100 Prayers Inspired by the Psalms* are available through Discovery House. Julie lost her long battle with cancer in April 2015.

DAVID MCCASLAND Living in Colorado, David enjoys the beauty of God's grandeur as displayed in the Rocky Mountains. An accomplished biographer, David has written several books, including the award-winning *Oswald Chambers: Abandoned to God* and *Eric Liddell: Pure Gold.*

KEILA OCHOA In addition to her work with *Our Daily Bread*, Keila assists with Media Associates International, a group that trains writers around the world to write about faith. She and her husband have two children.

AMY PETERSON Amy Peterson has a BA in English Literature from Texas A&M and an MA in Intercultural Studies from Wheaton College. Amy taught English as a Second Language for two years in Southeast Asia before returning stateside to teach. She is the author of the book *Dangerous Territory: My Misguided Quest to Save the World.*

AMY BOUCHER PYE Amy is a writer, editor, and speaker. The author of *Finding Myself in Britain: Our Search for Faith, Home, and True Identity*, she runs the Woman Alive book club in the UK and enjoys life with her family in their English vicarage.

PATRICIA RAYBON A former magazine editor and associate professor of journalism, Patricia began writing for *Our Daily Bread* in October 2018. She has written several books, including *My First White Friend* and *I Told the Mountain to Move*. She and her husband, Dan, live in Colorado.

HADDON ROBINSON (1931–2017) Haddon, a renowned expert on preaching, served many years as a seminary professor. He wrote numerous books and hundreds of magazine articles. For a number of years he was a panelist on Our Daily Bread Ministries' radio program *Discover the Word*. Dr. Robinson went home to his eternal reward on July 22, 2017.

DAVID ROPER David Roper lives in Idaho, where he takes advantage of the natural beauty of his state. He has been writing for *Our Daily Bread* since 2000, and he has published several successful books with Discovery House, including *Out of the Ordinary* and *Teach Us to Number Our Days*.

LISA SAMRA Lisa calls Grand Rapids home after growing up and attending both college (University of Texas) and seminary (Dallas Theological Seminary) in the Lone Star State. A journalism major in college, she continues her love of writing through *Our Daily Bread*. She and her husband, Jim, who pastors the church founded by Dr. M. R. DeHaan, have four children.

JENNIFER BENSON SCHULDT Chicagoan Jennifer Schuldt writes from the perspective of a mom of a growing family. She has written for *Our Daily Bread* since 2010.

JULIE SCHWAB Julie plans to use her recently earned master of arts degree from Liberty University to continue her love of writing about God's Word and life in Christ. Julie's first *Our Daily Bread* articles appeared in the publication in 2017 when she was an intern at Our Daily Bread Ministries from Cornerstone University.

JOE STOWELL As president of Cornerstone University, Joe has stayed connected to today's young adults in a leadership role. A popular speaker and a former pastor, Joe has written a number of books over the years.

MARION STROUD (1940–2015) After a battle with cancer, Marion went to be with her Savior in August 2015. Marion began writing devotional articles for *Our Daily Bread* in 2014. Two of her popular books of prayers, *Dear God, It's Me and It's Urgent* and *It's Just You and Me, Lord*, were published by Discovery House.

HERB VANDER LUGT (1920–2006) For many years, Herb was senior research editor at Our Daily Bread Ministries, responsible for checking the biblical accuracy of the booklets published by the ministry. A World War II veteran, Herb spent several years as a pastor before his ODB tenure began. Herb went to be with his Lord and Savior in 2006.

PAUL VAN GORDER (1921–2009) A writer for *Our Daily Bread* in the 1980s and 1990s, Paul was a noted pastor and Bible teacher—both in the Atlanta area where he lived and through the *Day of Discovery* TV program.

MARVIN WILLIAMS Marvin's first foray into Our Daily Bread Ministries came as a writer for *Our Daily Journey.* In 2007, he penned his first *Our Daily Bread* article. Marvin is senior teaching pastor at a church in Lansing, Michigan.

KAREN WOLFE Karen was originally from Jamaica but now lives in Tennessee with her husband, Joey. She became a Christian as an adult, and she later received theological training at New Orleans Baptist Theological Seminary. Her debut article in *Our Daily Bread* appeared in August 2017.

JOANIE YODER (1934–2004) For ten years until her death, Joanie wrote for *Our Daily Bread*. In addition, she published the book *God Alone* with Discovery House.

SCRIPTURE INDEX

Help us get the word out!

Our Daily Bread Publishing exists to feed the soul with the Word of God.

If you appreciated this book, please let others know.

- Pick up another copy to give as a gift.
- Share a link to the book or mention it on social media.
- Write a review on your blog, on a bookseller's website, or at our own site (ourdailybreadpublishing.org).
- Recommend this book for your church, book club, or small group.

Connect with us:

⬛ @ourdailybread

⭕ @ourdailybread

🐦 @ourdailybread

Our Daily Bread Publishing
PO Box 3566
Grand Rapids, Michigan 49501 USA

✉ books@odb.org